The Professional Golfers' Association Tour

A History

by
Mike Gabriel

McFarland & Company, Inc., Publishers
Jefferson, North Carolina, and London

ISBN 0-7864-0844-8 (softcover : 50# alkaline paper) ∞

Library of Congress cataloguing data are available

British Library cataloguing data are available

On the cover: Chi Chi Rodriguez (*author's collection*)

Manufactured in the United States of America

*McFarland & Company, Inc., Publishers
Box 611, Jefferson, North Carolina 28640
www.mcfarlandpub.com*

Contents

Introduction

The marquee players of the Professional Golfers' Association (PGA) Tour are a perennial source of fascination for golf fans, and the history of the sport is appreciated best if seen through the eyes and memories of the professional stars whose individual personalities and characters have colored the sport. The lives and careers of golf superstars have supplied a lodestone of anecdote and legend. Decade by decade through the 20th century, one charismatic player after another strove to dominate the Tour — Walter Hagen and Bobby Jones through the 1920s and 1930s, Ben Hogan and Sam Snead in the 1940s and 50s, and Arnold Palmer propelling the sport to unprecedented popularity in the 1960s before being superseded by Jack Nicklaus.

Golf fans of the modern era benefit from a knowledge of past achievements in order to better appreciate players like Greg Norman, John Daly, and Tiger Woods, as with baseball where a knowledge of the past enhances informed comparisons of Babe Ruth, Roger Maris, and Hank Aaron. To know what each of those players achieved in different eras, under widely divergent circumstances, is critical to a fuller understanding of the attributes of superstardom. To know what Ben Hogan accomplished in his career will illuminate the magnitude of effort required of Tiger Woods if he is to equal or surpass the records set in previous decades. To know how the golf balls and clubs of the 1920s performed in the hands of men like Bobby Jones and Walter Hagen is to better understand the power of titanium in the hands of John Daly and Greg Norman. To watch Norman call a penalty on himself that disqualified him from winning a 1996 tournament is to recall a truism, that golf is a sport in which individual integrity is a paramount virtue, and to remember that Bobby Jones insisted upon calling a penalty when his ball moved through no fault of his own at the 1925 U.S. Open. He lost the championship by one stroke, which prevented him from becoming the only player in history to win five U.S. Open crowns.

Fans may argue at length about the relative merits of golf's premier players. Hagen, Jones, Byron Nelson, Snead, Hogan, Palmer, Nicklaus— these are the names that immediately come to mind when the best in the sport are chronicled. But from year-to-year there were many, many other fine touring professionals who helped contribute to the huge success of the PGA Tour. In the following chapters the careers of those golf pros are contrasted, with descriptions of the courses and equipment they played in each era, and the summation reveals who the very best players were irrespective of decade.

Early History

"My advisor tried to instill in me a reasonable pattern of economy, but I was completely immune to any such foolish suggestion. As long as I kept playing in competition and winning the championships, I saw no need to cut down in my mode of living. I needed to go first class!"

— Walter Hagen

Golf in the United States dates back to the Revolutionary War when Scottish officers transplanted their native sport to North America. During those years and the decades following, golf clubs were established at Savannah, Charleston, and White Sulphur Springs, but the tenure of those sites was brief. It was not until 1888 that the club with the longest continuous existence in America was formed, appropriately named St. Andrews Golf Club, in the New York City suburbs. The founder, Robert Lockhart, was a native of Scotland. One of the earliest members was another Scot, industrialist Andrew Carnegie, who never stayed at the course after the sun set, for contemporaries said he lived in dread of kidnapping.

All of the equipment at St. Andrews was brought back from Lockhart's many trips to the British Isles. Within a year a tournament was organized and a golf medal awarded to the winner of the club championship, Piet Meyers. Later, the rapid growth of New York City forced officials to look for open land to the north, and a new course was laid out with a substantial clubhouse, locker room, and other amenities. Soon after expansion the club hired Scottish pro Willie Park, Jr. to give exhibitions. Park, winner of the 1887 British Open, arrived in a red coat and blue collar, colors of his home course, and stitched onto the coat lapel was a motto he had appropriated from Scotland's St. Andrews, the ancient "Far and Sure." Park proceeded to honor his predecessors by easily breaking the existing course record.

Wealthy Americans of the era had become fond of golf at Pau, a French winter resort with a golf course dating from 1856. Americans who had played at Pau were instrumental in starting The Country Club at Brookline, Massachusetts, in 1893. Many of the earliest American courses were resorts like Pau. Three of the first five United States Golf Association (USGA) members were resort courses: Newport, Shinnecock Hills, and the Chicago Golf Club. St. Andrews did not enjoy the distinction of being the first to incorporate. That honor belonged to Shinnecock Hills, constructed in the Scottish links tradition on a strip of land between the Atlantic Ocean and Great Peconic Bay.

Shinnecock Hills, incorporated in 1891, was a 12-hole course with an impressive clubhouse. Designed by a very young Scot, Willie Dunn, the course was laid out on old Native American burial mounds which the architect converted to sand bunkers. Dunn had traveled to Shinnecock directly after finishing an 18-hole course at Biarritz, France, and was eager to return to Europe for additional lucrative contracts. He believed that France was in the early stages of a golf boom and would one day rival Scotland as a great golfing country. As for America, Dunn doubted her prospects because, as he was heard to theorize, the new country was much too far from the golf center of Europe.

By 1900, only a dozen years after the founding of St. Andrews in New York State, more than 1,000 golf clubs were in operation in the United States, a remarkable explosion of the sport which paralleled the enthusiasm of golfers in England during the same years. The boom gave employment to an entire generation of Scottish teaching pros, clubmakers, architects, and greenskeepers who were eagerly recruited for positions in Great Britain and America. Each American state boasted at least one course, with New York in the lead at 165, Massachusetts next with 157, Pennsylvania 75, New Jersey 63, and Connecticut 57. Illinois also had 57.

The new clubs began to stage tournaments, some national in scope, and it soon became apparent that a governing organization was necessary to oversee the sport just as the Royal and Ancient operated in Great Britain. The secretary of St. Andrews, Henry Tallmadge, took the initiative of inviting representatives of Shinnecock Hills, Brookline, Newport, and the Chicago Golf Club to an organizational meeting at which the millionaire New Yorker, Theodore Havermeyer, was elected the first president of the USGA. A constitution and bylaws were prepared, following the rules subscribed to by The Royal and Ancient, and strictly setting out definitions for amateur versus professional status. This attention to the fine points of law (as set down by the USGA), plus the aristocratic status of the USGA's earliest members, established the locus of the organization for many decades to come. If the founders were among American's wealthiest and most status-conscious men, and their clubs as elitist as anything to be found in Victorian London, then many of their decisions inevitably would come to be seen as regal edicts benefiting little but the self image of the organization's founders. Early American golf professionals, in particular, formed this opinion early.

Francis Ouimet, the first American to be lionized by golf fans, is a case in point. A member of the wealthy Whitney family had tried to bring the amateur status of Walter Travis and Arthur Lockwood into question as early as 1901 because it was alleged they had been ensconced free at Southern resorts in exchange for endorsements tendered to the hotels. Travis and Lockwood retained their amateur standing, but Ouimet was not so lucky. The national hero following his victory in the U.S. Open went into business with a sporting goods store in Boston in 1916. The governing board of the USGA viewed this as a transgression of the rules and stripped Ouimet of his amateur standing. The American press and public lined up behind Ouimet, and when the USGA persisted in enforcing its decision the outcry was so great many other golf organizations, including the new Western Golf Association, refused to follow the lead of the national body. Ouimet was encouraged to play in the Western Amateur Championship, among other slights to the USGA, and after the First World War when he came home a veteran all was forgiven and his amateur standing restored.

Inexplicably, however, the USGA refused to let well enough alone and proceeded to bar golf architects (by now a fair number in America) from playing in amateur tournaments. Although the decision was later reversed, unpopular actions of this type caused so much notoriety the USGA took on the appearance of a hidebound, caste-crazy oligarchy at odds with what was soon to become a popular sport open to anyone in America irrespective of class.

One of the chief contributing factors in golf's popularity with ordinary Americans was the arrival of Harry Vardon, a famous English pro, for an American tour in 1900. Vardon started in New Jersey, went on to Florida and then to the West. His favorite stratagem was to play against the best ball of two competitors, and many of the two man teams he played against were top flight golfers of the era. Nonetheless, he prevailed in virtually every match. The tour was very successful, Vardon's exploits captured favorable press and excited galleries, and he stayed longer than expected in order to enter the 1900 American Open at the Chicago Golf Club, which he won easily. His subsequent return to America in 1913 was the occasion of a milestone in the sport's history and genesis of Francis Ouimet's fame. Vardon and Ted Ray, the best British professional golfers of the day, journeyed to the States for another series of exhibitions, and, most importantly, to capture the American Open trophy at the conclusion of the tour.

The 1913 Open was held at Brookline, and at the final hole Vardon and Ray completed their rounds in a tie. The young Francis Ouimet, however, remained on the course with six holes to play. Ouimet, who was barely known outside New England, having won the Massachusetts Amateur Championship, would have to complete the last six holes in one under par to tie Vardon and Ray, and in a driving rainstorm at that. Ouimet parred the 13th and 14th holes, scrambled to a par on 15, and sank a nine-footer for par at 16. Ouimet was not a member at Brookline, but he knew the course well from having caddied there, and he put the knowledge to good use by making a difficult 15-footer for birdie on 17. Now he needed a par to tie, or a birdie to win the Open. He made a par for the tie. This set up a classic match, the object of every sportwriter's dream, a young amateur against two seasoned, foreign professionals. The amateur astonished everyone by trouncing Vardon and Ray, beating the former by five shots and the latter by half-a-dozen. The victory was front page news across America, and Francis Ouimet vaulted to the status of a national hero. From that day forward golf progressed rapidly to become one of the most popular mass participation sports in the United States.

During subsequent decades Vardon and fellow pros occasionally were beaten by amateurs like Francis Ouimet and Chick Evans, but these heroics would never be duplicated again by amateurs except by the likes of Bobby Jones. American professional players began to dominate tournament golf. The end of the age of Vardon and Ray was the beginning of the era of Walter Hagen, and the start of a decade-by-decade progression that saw one or two outstanding players, like Sarazen and Armour, Snead and Hogan, Palmer and Nicklaus, dominate their fellow competitors with a flair that attracted legions of new fans to the sport.

Walter Hagen was a blacksmith's son and gifted athlete. He gave up a promising major league baseball career after noting the luxurious lifestyle of some of the wealthiest men in America. While caddying at the Rochester County Club Hagen met the founder of Eastman Kodak, among other tycoons, At the end of the day he noted the dress and manners of club members arriving for lavish dinner dances. These lessons were preparation for a style that Hagen later made famous all over the world. He employed a press agent whose imagination overcame the few deficiencies with which the young, impetuous Hagen embarked on a golf career, one that saw him become a figure of envy not just for the relatively small legion of golfers of the day, but also for the growing army of sports fans throughout the country, just as the charismatic Arnold Palmer was idolized by the general public a half century later.

Hagen acquired silk shirts, jeweled cuff links, colorful knickers, chauffeured limousines, adoring companions, and an appreciation of expensive vintages. He used the fledgling advertising industry to burnish his image, endorsing whatever products came his way and barnstorming across the world to whatever audience could be persuaded to pay an average fee of a dollar per person at exhibitions and golf clinics. As his playboy reputation expanded, Hagen took great care to heighten the effect by always arriving late, looking as if he had cut a party short to give an exhibition. Climbing out of a limo, he would stagger to the first tee amidst the nudges and winks of his audience to let fly with an often wild first drive. Even simple recovery shots might be surveyed so nervously the gallery assumed each shot was tougher than the last as the unparalleled showman trekked from one obstacle to another.

Photographs of the day show Hagen on the tee, wide chin aggressively high, splay legged, with his loose baseball swing launching the ball off into

Walter Hagen (©Corbis).

one seemingly hopeless peril after another. After he became the first American-born golfer to win the British Open in 1922, his press agent quoted Hagen as saying: "I don't want to be a millionaire, I just want to live like one." He already had triumphed in the 1914 U.S. Open at Chicago's Midlothian C.C., where for the first time golf pros horned their way into the clubhouse. Hagen was given credit for marching into the locker room instead of changing shoes in the parking lot as pros were compelled to do in the past.

The year after he won the 1922 British Open, Hagen arrived at Troon only to find professionals banned from that clubhouse. So he brought along a gourmet picnic lunch in his hired Rolls Royce, spread the delicacies out on the club lawn, and let the members gawk. They neither appreciated the gesture nor relented on the restrictions. Hagen got his revenge later at St. Andrews when he accompanied his new friend, the Prince of Wales, future King Edward VIII, to the clubhouse door for a nightcap. Told by the gatekeeper that Hagen's menial status would deter him from the bar, the prince replied, "You may be the 'Royal and Ancient Golf Club' this evening, but tomorrow you will only be the 'Ancient Golf Club' if Mr. Hagen can not join me!"

The secret of Hagen's popularity with people throughout the world was best summed up by the perceptive views of friend Gene Sarazen: "Hagen was at home with all classes of society, far more than Dempsey or Ruth, the other great champions of the 1920s whom he resembled in the blackness of his hair, his amazing magnetism, his love of admiring crowds, and his rise from humble beginnings."

In 1918 Hagen was offered a lucrative job at the new Oakland Hills Club near Detroit. Hagen played the Florida tournament circuit in the winter, returning to Detroit for the summer golf season. After winning another Open at Boston, however, he was ready to try a new tack for pro golfers. Hagen gave up the security of his club job at Oakland Hills, one of the best to be had anywhere, and set off as an independent "businessman golfer" as he liked to describe the carnival-like enterprise of daily exhibitions and staged matches that drew fans for decades. At the same time he decided to tackle another challenge unusual for American golfers. Hagen decided to enter the British Open, and in his inimitable way arranged to go first class with an American sportswriter named Dickie Martin. The duo missed their ship in New York, but the next sailing was the famous *Mauritania* on which starlet Constance Talmadge was bound for London.

Since Hagen and Martin had neglected to make reservations, Talmadge offered free use of her suite at the Carlton Hotel. The day after checking in at the Carlton, Hagen telephoned newspaper magnate Lord Northcliffe who had played golf with the young pro at Rochester some years earlier. Northcliffe immediately invited the Americans to stay at his country estate, which boasted a private golf course. Northcliffe's newspapers ran front page stories about the brash, young American pro and his strategy for winning the Open. Although Hagen was foiled in his first battle with gale force winds and the links style course, finishing 53rd in a field of 54 entrants, he set the pattern for the rest of his long career on this trip — the happenstance attention to schedules, the immediate affinity with aristocrats, starlets, and all those who would beg to do a favor for Walter Hagen, the ceaseless fascination of the media with every aspect of his life — all combined to create a persona of royalty for Hagen, one he shamelessly gloried in for the remainder of his life.

Hagen, like a great many fellow Americans, constantly chased financial rainbows in the 1920s. First he set off for California where he was scheduled to star in a film with Mae West. The starlet suffered one of her frequent illnesses, and Hagen was delegated to lesser roles, none of which offered promise of a career in movies. Returning to New York he was talked into buying a seat on the New York Stock Exchange. He had money enough only to rent an office and hire a bookkeeper. While he tried to line up investors, the price of a seat on the exchange rose day by day through the $100,000 ceiling, which scared off the financial amateur's advisors. One who remained in Hagen's camp was the famous tycoon, Jesse Livermore, whom the press labeled "Wolf of the Street." Livermore was yet another of Hagen's golfing partners, and the tycoon gave the younger man a few words of instruction. "Buy when I buy, sell when I sell, and most important of all, never let a day end with one single share of stock unsold."

Hagen had a complete line of credit at Livermore's brokerage. When Jesse bought millions of shares in a specific company, Walter bought a few hundred. When he sold, Hagen followed suit. They sat together silently in the same palatial office from ten to three every day for two weeks. At the end of that time Hagen had enough money to finance his trip to the 1921 British Open in the style to which he had become accustomed.

"I traveled first class," Hagen recalled,

> and that included a suite at the Savoy at five pounds a day, the Chez Paris, Cocktail hour at the Ritz, the Daimler car with chauffeur and footman, fine silk shirts

custom tailored by A.J. Izod on Conduct Street just off the Strand. It also included planes chartered for hunting trips over the moors or fishing trips to the northern part of Scotland, and parties at the Savoy Hotel in London where the service was so wonderful. Before I returned home I'd somehow managed to spend around $10,000.

Free from financial strain due to the largess of Jesse Livermore, Hagen went on to win the next year's British Open and became the first American-born pro to accomplish that feat.

Not only were the 1920s good for the stock market, but the decade also was a speculator's bonanza for real estate, especially in Florida. Hagen remembered, "The Florida boom fitted in perfectly with my design for living ... sunshine, beautiful scenery, people with time on their hands for fun, and of course, money." One of the biggest developers enticed him to the Sunshine State with an offer of the highest salary ever paid to a golf pro up to that time. The course was called Pasadena on the Gulf, and Hagen's duties were to arrange tournaments and clinics for the months December through March, then represent the club at tournaments around the country. One of the most vital although unspecified duties of the Haig was to play frequent rounds of golf with prospects rounded up by the developer's legion of salesmen. For this Hagen was rewarded with choice lots in his own name. This was one of the most luxurious periods in Hagen's long life of splendor. He and his spouse resided in a grand Spanish villa surrounded by flowers and trees culled from the developer's private nursery. The couple was fond of hosting parties, especially for the many new property owners and those still looking for lots, and the arrangement was so mutually beneficial the pro's contract was extended for another three years on remarkably generous terms.

Since the New York Yankees and other teams held spring training nearby, Hagen soon was playing golf with Babe Ruth, Jimmy Foxx, and Rube Marquard. But his main talent was as an all-around booster for the real estate tycoons who controlled Florida's new golf courses and attached housing. This was a market for which the phrase "Speculative Hysteria" is inadequate, as millions of Americans bought Florida land indiscriminately, some without seeing as much as a photograph of the swamps they were purchasing.

When the bubble burst Hagen had enjoyed three years of regal living. At the stupendous salary for that time of $30,000 a year, he could have financed a larger real estate speculation and a margin account on Wall Street. However, all that he owned and subsequently lost were the lots awarded to him in compensation for exhibitions given at the Pasadena Club. When the crash came and bankruptcies among Florida real estate magnates rivaled the savings and loan debacle of the 1980s all Hagen squandered was his salary at Pasadena.

During those years Walter Hagen was winning golf tournaments all over the world — four British Open titles, four consecutive PGA Championships

(1924–1927), and frequent trophies at the Western Open. He also captured many lesser championships, defeating Bobby Jones, Gene Sarazen, Bill Mehlhorn, and other rivals. With his roving eye for fresh sources of income Hagen got the idea of starting his own golf equipment company. He built a manufacturing plant in Longwood, Florida, and began churning out clubs bearing his name. Unfortunately, Longwood was an inopportune locale to build hickory-shafted clubs. With excessive humidity hickory swelled slightly during production. The finished clubs often broke apart upon arrival in Arizona or California when the fittings shrank in drier air, and the iron heads frequently rattled right off the shafts. An added menace was the discovery that in dry climates the wood shafts often produced small slivers of hickory resembling porcupine quills when they penetrated golfer's fingers. Rapidly falling into debt Hagen approached several wealthy advisors who counseled him to sell.

L.A. Young of Detroit purchased the company and kept the Haig on retainer, paying him royalties on every set of clubs. Young continued to market the Hagen line successfully for many years, then in 1944 sold the company to Wilson Sporting Goods, which expanded the product line. But it was disappointing for Hagen, who had benefited from the advice and fatherly interest of the wealthy L.A. Young, himself a colorful rogue with interests in automobile manufacturing in Michigan and a movie studio in Hollywood. Long afterward Hagen remembered the influence of Young.

> I drew no salary in the years after L.A. took over. I never got my hand in the till because I wasn't looking for that level of small stuff. I preferred his signature on a check. There were sessions between us when he swore he would never sign another check for me, but he paid and paid and paid. He tried to instill in me a reasonable pattern of economy but I was completely immune to any such foolish suggestions. As long as I kept playing in competition and winning the championships, I saw no need to cut down in my mode of living. I needed to go first class. I was the front for the company and L.A. recognized that, although he was also convinced it could be accomplished without the enthusiastic exuberance I devoted to it. Our business association was one of the wildest financial merry-go-rounds in history. But it resulted in financial security for me, and a profit for L.A. Young.

Many of the most memorable golf events of the 1920s were the competitions between Walter Hagen and Bobby Jones. Hagen had won the U.S. Open twice, and also the British Open twice by 1926. Jones had won the U.S. Amateur twice, and had finished ahead of Hagen in five of the last six tournaments they entered. On the day of the first challenge match arranged between the two stars, Hagen was in bed with flu. He telephoned Jones's hotel and asked one of the people there to come over and verify the temperature of 102, with a doctor's recommendation to cancel the match. Jones suspected chicanery, replying: "If Hagen isn't on the first tee in an hour, there'll be no match between us. We'll go back home."

Hagen found a pith helmet similar to those worn by the British in India and lined it with leaves from a rubber plant. Jones soon saw that his opponent truly was ill, apologized, but played on anyway and won the first match. Two weeks later the contest was renewed. Playing on the amateur's home ground, Hagen decisively beat Jones, closing eight strokes ahead at the finish of 36 holes. The following week the two journeyed to Hagen's home course at Pasadena, and Hagen excelled again. He won the match 12 up with 11 to play, and won $7,600, the largest sum ever secured up to that time for a challenge match or a golf exhibition. The fame derived from this match, and the fact that Hagen won at least one major tournament every year for 12 consecutive years, meant that he could always draw a profitable gallery for exhibitions. He remembered those years with fondness:

> I'd endorse everything I could possibly use on the golf course, and then we'd hit the exhibition circuit. We had a regular caravan – three or four Cadillacs or Lincolns, my chauffeur leading the group in one, business manager Bob Harlow in the second, my caddie with my clothes and golf equipment in the third. I must have played at one time or another every golf course in the country. Guarantees didn't mean much to me. I'd play for the gate and pray that I'd acquired the type of personality and game to draw the crowds. After the matches we'd stuff the money in a suitcase and gun the motors to the next date. The cash I collected in those years went almost before I had a chance to check its color.

The stock market crash of 1929 stunned the nation, but Hagen retained his habitual optimism. "The fast spreading depression put golfing interests in the background," he recalled, "people were too busy vainly trying to recoup huge losses or jumping out windows. For once I was very thankful I had spent my money as it arrived rather than investing in the market to make a million."

Modern pros often lament the amount of travel they endure, uncomfortable air plane flights, unfamiliar hotels, and strange cuisine. All these things Hagen loved. It is doubtful if any modern players, including those who served apprenticeships on the Asian Tour, ever saw as much of the world as Walter Hagen or enjoyed as much of it as he did. From the time he first sailed to Great Britain for the British Open, Hagen ceaselessly looked forward to his next getaway. Constantly enlisting fellow pros to his plans, he never was more happy that when planning excursions to Fiji, Shanghai, Manila, Calcutta, Tokyo, and the Belgian Congo. Through decades of competition, Hagen gave hundreds of exhibitions and went first class every time. He especially was fond of visiting France, Belgium, and Switzerland where all the hoteliers and maitre d's met his high standards. Then off again to Rangoon, Zanzibar, Dar-es-Salaam, and Mombassa before finishing a series of exhibitions at Nairobi where the greenskeeper advised packing rifles in the golf bags because lions had been seen crossing the ninth fairway the night before.

Hagen placed a premium on high energy and fortitude in his companions. He said that the women who played and followed the game of golf helped his play immeasurably, and was quick to confess that his wardrobe was planned with them in mind, "to attract the glances of the feminine ticket purchasers." He remembered meeting "beautiful and charming women all over the world. In India it was the high caste girls of Calcutta, in Japan Geisha girls in silk kimonos, in Africa female caddies in dishabille." Contrasting with these were equally appealing British and Australian women with their "attractive fresh complexions, vibrant health, and joie de vivre." Arriving in Bali he was captivated by "dusky-toned beauties clad only in floor length sarongs, their silhouettes affording relaxed viewing for our putting-tired eyes." Yet, having seen the world, the Haig always returned to say that nothing could compare with the attractions of New Orleans and Minneapolis, where he was "host many times to the languorous beauties of New Orleans…. But in the 20's and 30's and I'm ready to state this for the record, those second and third generation [Minnesota] Norwegian, Swedish, and Danish girls were among the most beautiful and the healthiest I've ever met. Nicolet Avenue and the Flame Room of the Radisson Hotel glowed with their fresh blond beauty. Nothing gave me greater pleasure than catering to those healthy appetites." Still robust, Hagen was photographed with Miss Minnesota at the 1954 PGA Championship. The picture of the old fox and his beauty queen made the cover of *Golf World*, which rekindled fond memories of the Haig for generations of his fans.

Walter Hagen enjoyed his retirement years in his adopted state of Michigan, in the only house he ever owned during a long, prodigiously successful career. On a lake near Traverse City, now one of the premier golfing destinations in the world, he was surrounded by fine hunting and fishing attractions. He had enjoyed those pursuits in many exotic locales across the globe with the flair of royalty, which in a sense he was. His fans reveled in the Haig's exploits, in his liaisons with starlets and monarchy, and in his flamboyant arrivals at exhibitions. Many years after Hagen's retirement, his caddie-chauffeur revealed that much of the Haig's partying and many late arrivals were staged.

"Hagen was an early riser, despite the reputation he had for showing up late at the course. He seldom slept past 7 a.m., and usually was up and about by six, unless he had been out all night, which he seldom was in his championship years. But he liked to pretend he had been. After rising Hagen could dally around for hours." In the meantime the chauffeur would remove Hagen's tuxedo from the closet. If it had been pressed he would roll it in a ball and throw it against the wall.

> Dressed in that wrinkled tux and dancing pumps, his bow tie undone, Hagen never left the hotel until he was sure that a large paying crowd was on hand and that he would be at least thirty minutes late at the golf course. At the course Hagen would run to the tee, removing his coat in the process and act as though

he had been out all night. After the first hole Hagen would sit on a bench and remove his dancing pumps and exchange them with the chauffeur, who would be wearing Hagen's golf spikes, custom made at $500 a pair. In the clubhouse, Hagen would order drinks for everybody in sight, a double for himself. When nobody was looking he'd pour most of it out in a toilet.

Walter Hagen was the first pro to start his own golf equipment company. He also was the first to have sponsors for tournaments. He gave about 200 exhibition matches every year, and charged from $150 to $1,500 a show. He was the winner of the first big money purse in tournament history, the 1915 Panama-Pacific Open in San Francisco, where he won $1,000. Hagen was revered for his scrambling prowess. In match play he astounded even the best pros by hitting recovery shots out of seemingly impossible situations. Between 1916 and 1927 in the PGA Championship, then played in match, not medal (medal is total strokes per round play; match is hole-by-hole), Hagen won 32 out of 34 matches. His average victory margin was five shots.

The 1920s

Starring Walter Hagen, tournament golf in the 1920s was a traveling carnival composed of such wildly disparate personalities as Gene Sarazen, Wild Bill Mehlhorn, Tommy Armour, Jimmy Barnes, Bobby Cruickshank, Chick Evans, Horton Smith, Craig Wood, Francis Ouimet, Willie MacFarlane, and, of course, Robert T. Jones, Jr., who eventually surpassed Hagen's popularity with sports fans in America.

Bobby Jones was born in 1902 in Atlanta, Georgia. His family lived adjacent to the East Lake Golf Club, and by the age of six Jones was an habitual kibitzer at the course. The club pro, Scottish transplant Steward Maiden, made a shortened set of clubs for Jones. By the age of nine he began coming home with trophies from local tournaments, the first a victory in the Junior Championship at East Lake. By age 14 he was good enough to capture the 1916 Georgia State Championship held at Atlanta's Brookhaven Country Club. He shot a 70 on the last day, weathered a tornadic temper outburst that would be repeated often in subsequent years, and won the title on the last hole. Later in the year the U.S. Amateur Championship was held at Philadelphia's Merion, and the 5'4" 165-pound Jones departed Atlanta's slow Bermuda greens to play for the first time on Northern Bent grass putting surfaces that were like green glass compared to those at home. He carded the best qualifying round of the entire field, and at the start of the second round a large gallery arrived to watch the child prodigy.

Never before the subject of so much attention, Jones had an attack of stage fright that ballooned his score to 89. Following this embarrassment the gallery drifted off to follow other players, leaving Jones free to recover in the next two matches which he won easily. The next, however, was a quarter-final against top competition with restored galleries, and again Jones was faced with the pressure of playing before a large audience. He was beaten 5–3 by one of the top amateurs of the day, but held up better than in the previous round. Only 14 years old, Jones succumbed easily to the effects of stress. High strung and prone to magnify the high expectations of friends and family, Jones thereafter suffered anxiety on a scale that few golfers successfully withstood.

As a teenager Jones played frequent tournaments but came away with few victories. He also played against professionals in a series of golf exhibitions organized to benefit the American Red Cross during the First World War. Improving steadily, by 1920 Jones was in his sophomore year at Georgia Tech University and the star of its golf team. Early that year he won the Southern Amateur Championship, and buoyed by that performance he decided to go to Chicago to enter the Western Amateur and challenge perennial favorite Chick Evans. The favorite held true to form in this contest, but is was the last time Evans was able to defeat Jones in a major championship.

In 1922 Jones moved to Harvard University to study English literature. The rules of the college game at the time forbade him for playing for Harvard's golf team. Nonetheless he was awarded a Crimson H by the Athletic Council for his previous achievements in golf. Returning to Georgia in 1923, he joined the Adair Realty Company in Atlanta, which provided ample time for him to travel to tournaments around the country. That summer the U.S. Open was held at Long Island's Inwood Country Club. Jones won the championship by defeating Bobby Cruickshank in a playoff, and it was widely anticipated that Jones now would turn professional to share in the growing financial bonanza of tournament play. He surprised everyone by retaining amateur status, and went on to win both the 1924 and 1925 National Amateur Championships.

In those years Walter Hagen was ensconced at the plush Pasadena Golf Club in West Florida, while Jones was mining the rich prospects of a real estate boom in nearby Sarasota. Hagen owned the distinction of best match player and 1924–1925 Professional Golf Champion of the U.S., while Jones built a reputation as the leading medalist in golf. A contest between the two in the celebrity-driven years of the Roaring Twenties was sought by promoters who finally talked the men into a 72-hole match, the first 36 to be played at Jones's golf club, and the second at Hagen's Pasadena club. In match play Hagen crushed Jones 12–11, birdying the 25th hole to end the contest. Hagen played some of the best golf of his career in this match. His medal scores were 71–70–69, while the struggling Jones recorded 76–74–73. In the previous half dozen U.S. Opens, Jones posted better scores than Hagen in five of the six tournaments, but Hagen's match play record was incomparable. In the previous five years of the older man's career he lost only four set matches. This, combined with his trouncing of Jones in Florida, established Hagen as the preeminent match play golfer of his era.

Later in the year Jones sailed to Great Britain to play in the British Open at Royal Lytham and St. Anne's. He posted a low total early on the last day,

Bobby Jones (©Corbis).

then could do nothing but wait for his old nemesis Hagen, who was two under par at the 13th hole. If he totaled 71 in the last round, Hagen could have defeated Jones again, but he came to the last hole needing to chip in to win. He went for broke as usual, hit the shot far past the cup, and Jones was champion. The young Jones sailed home on the *Aquitania* to a ticker tape parade on Broadway. Immense crowds gathered in Manhattan as the golfer marched down Broadway flanked by policemen and Georgia dignitaries.

After a brief vacation, Jones departed for Scioto Country Club in Columbus, Ohio, to play in the U.S. Open. He shot a 70 the first day, ballooned to a 79 the second, and was six strokes behind the pros Wild Bill Mehlhorn and Joe Turnesa at the start of the last day. Mehlhorn fell away, but Turnesa posted a strong score on the final nine before faltering on the closing holes. Jones made up four shots on the last nine holes to pull ahead. Within the space of 17 remarkable days, Bobby Jones won both the British Open and the U.S. Open Championships.

In those years of unparalleled amateur success, Jones played competitive golf during the summer months only. By 1930 he had become the undisputed favorite in virtually every tournament he entered. At 28 years of age, he completed a law degree and lived at home with wife and two daughters in Atlanta. Nervous strain and difficult long distance travel were becoming burdensome, but he practiced more than usual for the 1930 season and went off to Scotland for the British Amateur Championship at St. Andrews, which he won. Following that victory he played in the British Open, and won again with a score that was ten shots better than the previous record set by Hagen in 1924. This was the climax of a long love affair between Jones and Scottish fans. He had played St. Andrews for the first time in 1921. Then only 19 years old, he played so poorly he quit after 11 holes. But in following years he grew to revere the course. The galleries reciprocated. When Jones won the Open at St. Andrews in 1930, the galleries were immense, and it was said that the town was so deserted the novelist Gerald Fairlie selected the afternoon as the time when a villain in one of his mysteries committed a murder and escaped unnoticed.

The awe which Jones inspired extended well past his retirement. In 1936 he was traveling through Scotland on his way to the Olympic Games in Berlin, and with a group of friends decided to play the Old Course. When his group approached the first tee after staying overnight in the hotel, Jones was stunned to see upwards of 2,000 people waiting to watch him play. As they proceeded around the links that day the gallery increased by several thousand to watch Jones shoot 72. On subsequent trips he often attempted to slip onto the Old Course unnoticed, but the Scots seemed to sense that he was in town.

Robert Woodruff, Chairman of Coca Cola, remembered what it was like when he and Jones visited St. Andrews:

"We had lunch at the club, got into golf togs and went to the first tee. The entire town was there waiting. Mrs. Jones and Mrs. Woodruff reported that when they went downtown to shop they found all the shops locked up and most hung with a sign, 'Closed for the Day — Bobby Jones is in Town.'"

Late in his life Jones received the Freedom of St. Andrews award at the University of Edinburgh, the first American to be so honored since Ben Franklin. Jones made a moving acceptance speech. He said of the Old Course, "She is a wise old lady, whimsically tolerant of my impatience, but ready to reveal the secrets of her complex being if only I would take the trouble to study and learn." At the end he summed up: "I could take out of my life everything except my experiences at St. Andrews and I would still have a rich full life." As Jones left the hall in his wheelchair, the audience rose and began to sing, "Will Ye No Come Back Again."

Following the Scottish victories of 1930, Jones traveled home with both of the Empire's golf championships. Then it was off to the U.S. Open at Minneapolis. Giving the lie to Minnesota's reputation for cold weather, Interlachen Golf Club's thermometer registered 101 degrees. Humidity also was extremely high, producing coke-oven playing conditions. Attired in a silk shirt and tie in the fashion of the day, Jones was so drenched in sweat at the conclusion of the day his necktie had to be severed with a scissors by friends when he came in from the course. He trailed pros Tommy Armour and Macdonald Smith, and also high on the leader board were Hagen, Horton Smith, Harry Cooper, Craig Wood, and other prominent rivals. On the last day under continuing oppressive conditions Jones shot a course record and won the Open by two strokes.

The final leg of the Grand Slam was scheduled for Merion. Jones already had won four U.S. Amateur Golf Championships, but this 1930 competition was the toughest. He told a friend:

It is the first tournament in which I have played that I could not sleep at night. There is something on my mind that I can not shake off. I go to sleep all right from fatigue, but about midnight or later I wake up and have to get up. I have always been able to sleep ... there is something bearing down on me in this tournament that was never there before.

His putting especially suffered from nerves during this week. Nonetheless, Jones defeated his opponents to win the final part of the Grand Slam, the only person in history to do so.

At the conclusion of this remarkable 1930 season, Jones announced his retirement from competitive golf.

"I don't enjoy competition anymore," Jones admitted:

> When I was younger it was different. Nothing much was expected of me and I had a lot of fun battling with the boys. If I didn't win, or if I didn't show well, it made no difference. Golf was just a game and I loved it and met many good fellows. Every tournament was a big show for me. But along in 1925, golf became a serious business. I was expected to win or to finish well up. It got worse and worse and the pressure became heavier and heavier, and at long last came the big year, 1930, and I decided I had had enough. I'll never give up golf. I love it too well, and it has meant too much in my life. But it will be an easier and far more gracious trail from now on.

Jones's good friend, the sportswriter O.B. Keeler, had been with the golfer on several occasions when Jones experienced severe stress during competition — stomach cramps, and worse. If adversaries noticed, they paid little attention. Jones seemed to be admired as much by competitors as he was by the galleries. His humility had much to do with this.

> He could drink with Ted Ray, or Tommy Armour or Walter Hagen, or be just as likable not drinking at all with Francis Ouimet. Yet there was nothing calculating or priggish about his behavior. He smoked to excess on the course, drank corn whiskey off it, swore magnificently in either place, and could listen to or tell an off color story in the locker room afterward. He was spontaneous, affectionate, and loyal to his friends.

Jones often called penalty strokes against himself for infractions no one else witnessed. In the 1925 U.S. Open he insisted on taking a penalty because his ball moved at address. Officials tried to shrug it off but Jones insisted on taking the penalty. He finished in a tie with Macfarlane, who won the playoff and prevented Jones from becoming the only man to win five Open crowns.

In the final nine years of his career, Jones played in 12 national open championships, nine in the U.S. and three in Great Britain. He finished either in first or second place in 11 of 12 appearances. He was the first man to win five U.S. Amateurs, he equaled the British and American record of winning both the Amateur and Open crowns in the same years, he was the only man to win the U.S. and British Amateurs in the same year (twice), and he played in the first Walker Cup matches in 1922 and in four subsequent years, never losing a singles match. Jones had triumphed in at least one of the national championships for eight consecutive years from 1923 to 1930. He was 28 years old.

Jones sent his retirement letter to the USGA on November 18, 1930, announcing that he also would surrender his amateur status. He intended to make films for money, write a newspaper column and magazine articles, and prepare an instructional series to be broadcast on radio. Jones had spent much time in California in 1929 while playing a number of exhibitions that attracted large galleries.

He also met people in the movie industry, and the directors and producers among them immediately recognized Jones's stage presence. Sound films were a novelty, and directors were searching for new ideas. Jones was a national hero, and a natural before the cameras. In 1930 Warner Brothers signed him to do a series of shorts. The structure of those films was to have the golfer give lessons to well known actors. Reigning stars of the day were cooperative, and Walter Huston, Doug Fairbanks, James Cagney, Joan Blondell, Joe E. Brown, Loretta Young, and W.C. Fields, among others appeared in the films. Jones received $600,000 in salary, an extraordinary sum at the opening of the Great Depression, and put the money into a trust fund for his family. Warner Brothers expected the films to make money, but executives were astonished at just how successful they were. The series appeared in 6,000 theaters and was seen by 25 million people, 20 percent of the country's total population at the time. The studio signed Jones to another deal for a new series that would use the latest camera techniques and innovations that seem fresh even today.

Jones had such a natural way in front of the camera, and such a remarkable affinity with the actors, that he was in no danger of being upstaged even by Loretta Young or Joan Blondell. His supple, almost magical skill with a golf club was made manifest as never before. Not only were his shots remarkably accurate, but they also were very, very long, longer in fact than virtually anyone then playing the pro game.

Many years later when Ely Callaway, head of Callaway Golf Company, began to look for still useful prints of the Jones movies, he discovered that Warner Brothers could not locate the originals. No copies were found at the Library of Congress or movie libraries in Hollywood. After much searching, Callaway discovered that the originals, still in fine condition, were stored in a Warner Brothers warehouse in New York City. Working with the Syber Vision Company, Callaway had videocassette prints made and offered them with a biography of Jones to the modern golfing public.

After his retirement Jones also contracted to design equipment for A.G. Spalding. As much of a taskmaster at club making as Ben Hogan was after his retirement, Jones painstakingly tested the Spalding prototypes until he was satisfied with each model. The new Jones line had revolutionary steel shafts, and the monogram "Robt. T. Jones, Jr." on each club. They were great sellers for Spalding over many decades. At the same time that he was deriving income from several golf-related endeavors, Jones was practicing law at home in Georgia.

He had started off by studying mechanical engineering at Georgia Tech where he finished an engineering degree in three years. Then he decided he was not interested in that field as a career, so he enrolled at Harvard and studied English literature completing another degree. Finally he enrolled in the Emory Law School in Atlanta. Halfway through his second year he took and passed the Georgia State Bar Exams. Now he was at work with his father's law firm, whose most famous client was the young Coca-Cola Company. Jones often played golf with the company chairman, Robert Woodruff, and in time began to invest in Coca-Cola bottling plants.

At approximately the same time Jones met Woodruff, he also befriended Clifford Roberts. Roberts was born in Iowa, moved to Palacios, Texas, and became a traveling salesman of men's clothing. At age 23 Roberts enlisted in the Army during the opening year of the First World War and was assigned to Camp Hancock in Augusta, Georgia for basic training. Posted to France, he drove ambulances for a year, and returned home without injury. Roberts's luck continued all through the 1920s, and for much of the remainder of his singular life. At the age of 27 he was a wealthy man from having bought and sold oil leases in Texas. With those profits he bought a partnership in a New York City brokerage firm.

One of Roberts's clients was the owner of Augusta's Bon Air Hotel, and on a vacation trip to Georgia Roberts was introduced to Bobby Jones. Roberts began spending more and more time in Augusta, the birthplace of Jones's wife. When the sprawling Fruitlands Nursery was offered for sale, Jones and Roberts secured the property and began to plan Augusta National. Jones selected the Scottish architect Alister Mackenzie as co-designer. Mackenzie had built and remodeled many courses in Great Britain and had published a book on golf architecture. He already had finished Cypress Point in Monterey by 1928, and boasted a remarkable background. His father was a doctor who loved the Scottish Highlands, and who took his children on extended vacations to the wild Northern reaches of Great Britain.

Mackenzie earned academic degrees in chemistry and natural science, and a M.D. as well. He served as a surgeon in the British Army in the Boer War and had a successful medical practice afterward. In middle age, he left medicine to attempt the risky field of golf course design, and at once began to put into practice his ideas that courses should be "less artificial in appearance, more nature-made and thus more pleasurable, and less costly to maintain." When the First World War started, Mackenzie reentered the army, but instead of continuing in the Royal Army Medical Corps he joined the Royal Engineers to head the first school for camouflage. He soon became the top expert in this new field of research.

Mackenzie eventually designed five courses in the U.S., including two at Ohio State University, Bayside on Long Island, Cypress Point, and Pasatiempo at Santa Cruz, California, which he finished in 1929. Bobby Jones played an exhibition at the dedication ceremony for that course. Mackenzie was a long-term member of St. Andrews, and he attempted to carry forth the ideals embedded in that design by using the best natural features of the available land. When it was time to begin work on Augusta National, Bobby Jones turned over control to Mackenzie as the architect while remaining at his side as advisor and consultant.

After winning the Grand Slam in 1930, Jones was a favorite of sports-writers, and when Augusta National opened it received enormous coverage in the national media. One characteristic that attracted special attention was the marked difference between Augusta and the typical American courses of the 1930s. Augusta opened with approximately 80 acres of fairways and very little rough. A typical course of that era had half that fairway acreage. Not only that, at Augusta each hole was unique, while other courses had very similar layouts from hole to hole. Greens usually were flat, small, and uniform. Augusta sported enormous greens, and each green had remarkable contour and outline.

One of the most prized features of the era was the sand trap. American courses took great pride in the number and size of their bunkers. Oakmont, for example, had more than 200 traps, but added still more to get ready for the 1925 U.S. Open. Jones and Mackenzie designed a grand total of 29 bunkers at Augusta National. Because of Jones's fame, Augusta attracted a prominent and influential membership which disseminated the lessons of the new course throughout the United States. Soon other clubs began subtracting bunkers. One famous course eliminated 200 sand traps, and was left with 200. Augusta National influenced other designers, who began to emphasize scenic beauty and to follow Mackenzie's principle of preserving and enhancing the best natural features of the land.

Among all the salient characteristics of Augusta National, however, one stands out above the rest. Jones and Mackenzie designed some of the most difficult-to-putt greens encountered anywhere in the world. The contour and speed of these greens demand great skill in placement of approach shots, otherwise the hapless golfer faces three or more strokes to finish what seemed at first to be a relatively straightforward and simple hole.

The beauty and difficulty of Augusta National made it a natural for a major tournament site, and Jones's presence was all that was needed to make it a success. He played in a dozen tournaments but never finished higher than 13th place. His last Masters was 1948, by which time his health was failing rapidly.

The best years for Bobby Jones occurred in a span of only eight seasons. Over a lifetime no one ever beat him twice at match play. From 1923 through 1930 he captured 13 of the 21 majors he participated in. He won five of eight U.S. Amateur contests, and was runner-up in one. He established a long string of records. He won one of the two British Amateur Tournaments he played in. His best performances seemed to be reserved for the U.S. Open and British Open. In 11 of the last 12 Open Championships he played, Jones finished no worse than second, capturing seven of them. He was the first man to win the Open in both countries, in 1926, and the best professionals like Walter Hagen and Gene Sarazen rarely could win when Jones was competing. By modern standards Jones played little golf. Apart from the majors, he entered only seven non-championship tournaments from 1923 to 1930, winning four of the seven, and using them as tune-ups for the Opens. He played in an era when hickory shafts were the rule, and with a ball that was at least 30 yards shorter than today's balls, and on courses that were in far worse shape than tournament players enjoy in modern golf. In the 1920s it was illegal even to clean a ball before putting.

Jones was a man of unique character and talent whose last years and fading health were a sad memory for those who had known him in his prime. The films made by Warner Brothers reveal Jones in his most softspoken, patient role instructing duffers in the finer points of the golf swing. Yet like so many other great athletes who became champions in their sports, Jones had another side to his personality. His determination to win yielded nothing to the likes of future superstars Ben Hogan, Arnold Palmer, and Jack Nicklaus. The accumulated stress of that competitive fire had much to do with his early departure from tournament golf. Jones, a national hero most of his life, and arguably the most talented man ever to play the game, died in 1971.

The 1930s

"When Bob Jones was playing down a parallel fairway we all stopped what we were doing. You just could not play golf when you had the chance to watch him. He was like no one we had ever seen. What was the best part of his game? All of it. Damn, he was long! He was the greatest putter who ever lived. Nobody could do with irons what he did with them. And he's the only man I ever saw who could back up a 3-wood on a green!"

— Orv White

Bobby Jones and Chick Evans were the most prominent amateurs in the 1920s and 1930s, and they often defeated the growing corps of professional golfers in the United States, especially in major tournaments like the U.S. Open which Jones won five times. The leading professionals— Walter Hagen, Gene Sarazen, Johnny Farrell, Bill Mehlhorn, James Barnes, and Tommy Armour — began to attract sizable galleries, and by the mid–1920s a prosperous golf tour existed. At first it was a winter excursion starting in Los Angeles and then moving across the Southern U.S. in a pattern somewhat similar to that of the PGA Tour today. In 1927, for example, Bobby Cruickshank won the L.A. Open, the Texas Open, and a tournament in Hot Springs, Arkansas, before moving on to Florida. Over a three month period he won $11,000 on a tour that was paying a total of $77,000 in prize money.

At the time there was no Commissioner of the Tour as there is today. A sportswriter named Hal Sharkey served as unofficial PGA Tour manager in the late 1920s, and he was successful in gaining income tax deductions for players and in generating publicity for the tour. Despite Sharkey's success, he kept the position only until 1929 before resigning because of inadequate pay. When he quit, Walter Hagen recommended his business manager, Bob Harlow, for the job. Harlow had many friends in the sport and had managed the 1929 U.S. Ryder cup team. After he accepted, Harlow continued to represent Hagen and a few other players. Later these arrangements produced much trouble, causing him to be fired and rehired twice by the PGA for conflict of interest. But in the beginning everyone seemed to accept Harlow's credentials, and he was adept at organizing and promoting local tournaments. Prior to this date pros determined their own tee times and whom they would play with during tournaments. Harlow established committees to set guidelines for these and other procedures. During his first year on the job total purse money rose from $77,000 to $130,000.

Harlow's talents were tested in the opening years of the Great Depression. Many sponsors struggled just to maintain the tournament schedule. By 1932 conditions really grew difficult for the tour, and Bob Harlow's contract was not renewed. Many of his clients wanted to play all-year around, and Hagen, Ky Laffoon, Clayton Heafner and others were prepared to break away from the parent PGA organization to organize an expanded tour. Their threats spurred immediate results. Harlow was rehired to manage the tour, and the players stayed on board. Some of the personalities Harlow was forced to deal with were as temperamental as any to be found in the modern game. Clayton Heafner was a good example. It was said of Heafner that he enjoyed a very stable disposition — he always was angry. At one tournament the starter mispronounced: "And now on the tee, Clayton Heafner." Heafner put his driver back in the bag and walked off the course.

To meld all these flamboyant personalities into a manageable organization required considerable talent, and Harlow achieved it. By 1935 he had organized an additional 14 tournaments to be held in the summer months, finally realizing the pros' ambition to create a year-round schedule. Purses remained modest, but additional sources of income were emerging. Equipment manufacturers were signing up players for endorsements, and resorts were beginning to hire pros to represent them. Sam Snead was hired to be the playing pro for White Sulphur Springs, Jimmy Demaret for Kiamesha Lake, Ben Hogan for Hershey Country Club, and so on. The players economized by traveling together to one tournament site after another, and by bunking together in the most reasonably priced hotels available. Many of them commented afterward that a fond comradeship grew on the tour as players struggled to win enough to keep them in expense money. Those who could afford to do so loaned small sums to one another, as Henry Picard offered to do for Ben Hogan during one of his many rough stretches. Players drifted in and out of the tournament schedule as circumstances dictated, and Harlow worked hard to keep their names in the press.

However, in 1936, Bob Harlow ran afoul of the Professional Golf Association's (the organization was composed primarily of club pros as distinguished from tournament players) top man, tough George Jacobus, and he was let go for the final time. His replacement was legendary Fred Corcoran. When Corcoran took over, Walter Hagen was 44 years old, and Gene Sarazen had seen the last of his tournament victories. No new stars seemed to have their flair. Prize money remained modest, and sponsors had trouble meeting commitments. The first-place check for winning the U.S. Open was only $500, and no one could afford to travel to England to play in the British Open as Hagen and Jones had done in the 1920s.

In stepped Corcoran. He had served as executive secretary of the Massachusetts Golf Association to good reviews, and the players liked him on first meeting. More importantly, sportswriters enjoyed Corcoran's company, so much so they invited him into the press tent to set up permanent quarters, and there he stayed to their mutual benefit for the rest of his days. Corcoran knew the history of golf, and he could denote player idiosyncrasies without making enemies. He was also a nonpareil storyteller. Reporters knew they could always obtain excellent copy from Corcoran. The publicity he generated was so good for the tour, purses rose consistently all through his tenure, so that by 1947 — the last year of his reign — total prize money was over half a million, up from $140,000 when Corcoran took over in 1936. He also recognized the potential in corporate sponsorship of golf, and was instrumental in bringing firms like General Motors, Texaco, Time, and American Express to tournament golf. The players trusted him to handle their affairs, to the extent that stars like Sam Snead contracted with Corcoran to handle their personal finances.

One of golf's most popular stars of this era, and a close friend of Bobby Jones and Walter Hagen, was Gene Sarazen. Sarazen was born in 1902 in Harrison, New York. At age eight he began caddying at the Larchmont Country Club. His carpenter father insisted that Gene follow in his footsteps, but a serious illness prompted a doctor's recommendation to find an outdoor job. That was the excuse he needed to concentrate on golf. He advanced so rapidly that within two months he could beat everybody at the local municipal course where he played. His first golf job turned out to be that of the most menial assistant to pro George Sparling at the Brooklawn Country Club. Sparling kept him locked away in the shop constructing clubs for members, but little by little Sarazen was allowed out on the course and he began to defeat the head pro. Before long Sparling was backing Sarazen in any money match that could be made at Brooklawn, and Sarazen won consistently.

In 1919 Sarazen decided to move to Florida where he played well in several local tournaments. He entered the 1920 U.S. Open at Inverness, but did poorly as he watched friend Leo Diegel fritter away the championship on the closing holes. Sarazen played the winter tour for the first time in 1922 and quickly picked up a second place finish at Shreveport. The following week he won at New Orleans. He won $1,000 for first place, but kept only $200 because prior to the tournament he had agreed to divide the prize among four of his best friends in a purse-splitting agreement, a common practice in that era. That year the U.S. Open was held at Skokie Country Club and Walter Hagen, Bobby Jones, Jim Barnes, Francis Ouimet, Chick Evans and all the best players of the day competed. Sarazen at age 20 amazed everyone by winning the championship with a 288, beating Hagen by three shots and Jones by one.

Five weeks after taking the Open he won the PGA Championship at Oakmont. For the remainder of the decade, Sarazen compiled a record only Jones and Hagen could fail to envy. He won the Miami Open three times, won several PGA events in the New York City environs where he served as club pro at Flushing, won the Western Open, and recorded two second place finishes in the Canadian Open, won the 1928 British Open, and played on the Ryder cup team in 1927 and 1929.

Sarazen is remarkable for his many achievements on tour, but he is remembered almost equally as well for his invention of an indispensable golf club — the sand wedge. In the early days of the sport players who hit into sand traps would rely on a club with the loft of a modern 9-iron, and try to pick the ball cleanly off the sand. Walter Hagen was one of the most accomplished masters of this difficult trick. During the early years of his career Sarazen approached bunker play with as much dread as the greenest amateur. Then one day he observed how airplanes were able to take off by using drag from tail flaps. He began to tinker with a niblick, adding lead to the sole of the club until it acquired a wide covering flange. Then he took it to the course and made additional adjustments, hitting thousands of explosion shots until the sand iron was perfected. So confident was Gene with the new invention, he said he was "willing to bet anyone any amount that I could get down in two from any lie in any trap. I lost very few of those bets."

In 1932 Sarazen followed up his British Open win by setting a new record in the U.S. Open at New York's Fresh Meadow Golf Course. His 286 total, with a 66 in the final round, was three strokes better than runner-up Bobby Cruickshank. The following year Sarazen won the PGA Championship at Blue Mound in Milwaukee. After his great successes in 1932 and 1933 he departed for an exhibition trip with Joe Kirkwood. They visited Australia and South America, and gave a series of lucrative clinics of the variety for which Walter Hagen was famous. Ten years younger than Hagen, Gene Sarazen had many more years of competitive golf to play. And in all that long career few feats equaled Sarazen's double eagle at the 1935 Masters Tournament. In the last round he was paired with old crony Hagen. As the two men came to the 15th hole, Sarazen asked his caddie what he needed to tie the leader. The answer, to Hagen's amusement, was four threes. The 15th hole was a par-five of 485 yards. Sarazen hit a drive of 250, then took a four-wood and played one of the most famous shots in golf history. He hit the shot as hard as possible to carry the pond in front of the green. The ball cleared the pond on a low trajectory, hit the green, and hopped straight into the cup. As soon as the score was posted on the clubhouse board at Augusta, 5,000 fans rushed out to the 16th to watch as Sarazen played to par on 16, 17, and 18 to tie Craig Wood for the championship. The playoff was 36 holes. Sarazen beat Wood by five shots.

As it was for Byron Nelson and Sam Snead, owning a farm was a lifelong dream for the Sarazens. In 1933 they purchased their first 125 acres for $31,000 near Danbury, Connecticut. Ten years later they sold the farm to Gabriel Heatter and purchased another in Germantown, New York, where they lived thereafter.

Gene Sarazen may have been golf's all-time good will ambassador. He turned professional in 1920, and was still appearing in his prized green jacket at the Masters in the late 1990s. Host of an extremely popular television show, Sarazen was introduced to millions of young fans just as his competitive skills no longer made it possible for him to play well on tour. In all, however, he won 37 times, captured 30 second-place finishes, won two U.S. Opens, a Masters and British Open, and three PGA Championships. Bobby Jones gave Sarazen a glowing tribute:

> Sarazen has ever been the headlong, impatient player who went for everything in the hope of feeling the timely touch of inspiration. When the wand touches him he is likely to win in a great finish or a parade.... When he is in the right mood he is probably the greatest scorer in the game, possibly that the world has ever seen.

Another wonderful entertainer of the day was Tommy Armour. Born in Edinburgh, Scotland, Armour did not become a golf pro until age 29 after attending the University of Edinburgh and serving in the British Army during World War I. Armour compiled an unusual biography in the Tank Corps. He rose to the rank of major, and was decorated by King George V for heroism. Armour definitely possessed command presence. He wore ascots and silk handkerchiefs with expensively tailored suits. A muscular six feet, he had a full head of black hair which gradually turned gray, hence the nickname "The Silver Scot." Sardonic, temperamental, and dour in the best Scots' tradition, Armour could see out of one eye (the other was sightless following a gas attack on the Western Front) well enough to play for years on the PGA Tour. He played the violin, read the classics, dealt bridge at the Masters level, and imbibed prodigious draughts of malt whiskey at the various country clubs that hired him to be their professional representative.

Tommy Armour's first position was at Congressional Country Club in Washington, D.C., after he captured the 1927 U.S. Open at Oakmont, the 1930 PGA Championship, and the 1931 British Open. Later tempted away to Chicago's Medinah Country Club, he derived steadily increasing revenues from equipment bearing his name. Golfers from all over the world journeyed to see Armour in order to have their swings analyzed at $100 an hour, a fantastic sum for those days. He also profited when Simon and Schuster persuaded him to write a book of instruction. Assisted by the newspaperman Herb Graffis, one of the most knowledgeable men ever to write about golf, Armour's *How to Play Your Best Golf All the Time* amazingly made the *New York Times* best seller list and earned royalties for many years afterward.

Armour was the first golfer to win all the major championships, U.S.,

British, and Canadian Opens, and the PGA. When teaching he liked to sit under an umbrella sipping a drink while the pupil, often a millionaire or a fellow pro, toiled in the sun. He taught only in the a.m., never for more than an hour at a time, and charged much more than his contemporaries. Though well educated and a wonderful after-dinner speaker, he could fall into the language of a drill sergeant with little prompting. When he gave lessons to Frank Stranahan, the young and wealthy pro, Armour recalled that it took two weeks to get Stranahan into the proper mood to accept instruction. Armour started off by criticizing Stranahan's clothes, manners, and life style, until Stranahan had developed the necessary "humility required to learn."

One of the many fond stories told by members about Armour when he was still at Medinah Country Club concerned the old soldier's penchant for shooting squirrels with a .22 caliber rifle when he grew bored on the practice range. His last club affiliation was at famed Winged Foot Golf Club, where he was able to retire with ease on the royalties from his book and golf club endorsements.

Another of the wonderful characters in the 1930s was Jimmy Demaret, who left home in Houston in 1928 to drive to his first tour event, the L.A. Open. With $35 in his pocket he stopped in El Paso to shoot some pool and engage in a few hours of leisurely gambling. He lost the money and his car and rode a freight train back to Houston. After raising a new stake he entered the Sacramento Open, finished third, and won $380. The next stop, at Agua Caliente, produced $700 in winnings, and Jimmy was on his way. In all he won 31 tournaments, including three Masters. The early years, however, may have been the best despite hard economic times. He recalled how four pros would rent a hotel room for $3 and flip a coin to see who got the bed. There was a café always handy to provide breakfast, two eggs, bacon, potatoes, toast, juice and coffee, for 15 cents. Dinner in a good restaurant never cost more than a dollar.

"All of us were club pros then," Demaret recalled.

> We had to make a living. The best thing about winning a tournament was not the paycheck, it was the job offers that came in from the better clubs. Endorsements too, although nothing like today. Hagen and Armour made terrific deals with club manufacturers. Chesterfield cigarettes offered me $500 just to pose for a picture smoking their brand. That was a world of money to me then, but I didn't smoke and sent them to Hogan. We also played in a lot of exhibitions and put on clinics. We'd get $300 or maybe even $500, helluva payday, but I understand Tom Watson and Nicklaus could get $30,000. One thing stays the same though. I met a lot of important people on the golf course, I'm talking about the Fords and Mellons, brokers and oilmen, and I got some good tips. I got into some real estate. In short I made a lot more money outside golf than I ever made in tournaments. Maybe it was because we didn't have it and we weren't going to get it playing golf, but money wasn't that important to us. It was the competition that we loved. We were never happy with anything but first place....

We didn't have scoreboards back then and it didn't matter. We weren't playing for position. We were playing to win.... I might as well state up front that I've seen Jack Nicklaus and Craig Stadler miss more shots in one tournament than Hogan and Snead missed in a lifetime. In my book those were the two best ever. Most players today can't fade or draw the ball under tournament pressure. We could. We were better shotmakers. For one thing we had fewer clubs so we had to learn to hit four or five shots with each one. Something else: Judging distance was an important part of our game. It burns me up to see these guys checking their notebooks before every shot. Their caddies check the pins for them every morning and some of the caddies even read putts. If the caddie can putt as well as the player, the caddie should be the pro. If you ever saw Ben Hogan memorize a golf course during practice you would know why he would never use a notebook to tell him what club to hit. We used to work the kinks out among ourselves and help each other. There was a lot more comradery then. We had more fun. The new players are shooting for so much money their eyes are pinched in like BBs. The numbers are eating them up.

Demaret had one of the longest career spans of any professional golfer. He almost won the Palm Springs Classic in 1964 at the age of 53. Scheduled to work on the NBC broadcast of the tournament, he decided instead to enter the field. When he made the cut he asked Arnold Palmer (who had missed the cut) to fill in for him. With only two holes left to play Demaret was ahead by a stroke. But he bogeyed 17, and missed a birdie on 18 to tie Tommy Jacobs. On the first playoff hole Demaret missed a two-foot putt, then bogeyed the next to lose. When the trophy was presented to young Jacobs, Demaret told the spectators: "I don't feel so bad. This is a break for Tommy. He's so old he's about through, and I've got many years left."

Demaret's friend Jackie Burke also commented on the close friendships that developed on tour:

We had a whole different outlook on tour in those days. We didn't try to win so much for the prize money as to get a good club job. Nearly everyone was associated with a club, Nelson at Inverness, Hogan in Hershey, Worsham at Oakmont, Harmon at Winged Foot. Until TV came along you really couldn't depend on Tour winnings for a good living. You had to have a club affiliation. We were always trying to hook on with a more prestigious club, and the best was to win a tournament or two.

Demaret and Burke founded the Champions Golf Club in Houston. Demaret played well all through the 1930s, 40s, and 50s, winning for the last time in 1957. Always noted for a colorful wardrobe, Demaret was picked along with Gene Sarazen to host *Shell's Wonderful World of Golf* starting in 1961. He was befriended by many celebrities, especially Bob Hope and Bing Crosby. Crosby started the tournament that bore his name in 1937, intending it to be a weekend party for friends. Snead won the first tournament, and Crosby claimed even afterward that when the winner's check of $500 was presented, Snead asked: "If you don't mind Mr. Crosby, I'd rather have cash." Crosby moved the tournament from Rancho Santa Fe to Monterey in 1947 where three courses were played, Pebble Beach, Cypress Point, and the Monterey Peninsula Country Club. Prize money totaled $10,000, all from Crosby's pocket. When the event was first televised in 1958 its popularity zoomed, often rating as the most heavily watched of any tournament on television. Crosby loved golf so much he frequently played at 5:30 in the morning, finishing nine, then driving to the studio for a full day's work, then back to the club for another nine at the end of shooting. He was a five-handicap, and won his club championship several times. During the Second World War he and Bob Hope barnstormed the country, giving golf exhibitions to sell war bonds. These shows were surprisingly successful, selling as much as $5 million in bonds in cities like Dallas and New Orleans. At one exhibition in 1945 held at the Tam O'Shanter Club in Chicago, a gallery of 28,000 followed Crosby and Hope around the course.

In addition to the celebrities who participated in many pro-am events, there were many other colorful personalities on hand to entertain the galleries. Among the most idiosyncratic was Ky Laffoon, born in Zinc, Arkansas in 1908. He became a teenage club pro, tried to catch on with a Hollywood studio for an acting career, then became a touring professional golfer in 1931. At one tournament an Eastern sportswriter thought that Ky's high cheekbones and ruddy color signified Native American heritage, and other players began calling him "Chief." Laffoon played along, even embellishing the story with tales about his fictitious Cherokee family.

What was true about Ky Laffoon, however, was his reputation for maniacal temper. After missing a short putt on the final hole of one tournament the seemingly deranged pro raced to his car, threw open the trunk, and withdrew a pistol which he fired at the balky putter. On one trip to a tournament site Laffoon's friend, Ben Hogan, was sleeping in the back seat of Laffoon's car. Hogan was startled when he awoke and saw no one at the wheel while sparks were flying up at the side of the speeding car. Hogan was relieved when he peered over the front seat to see Laffoon leaning out the open door and holding onto the steering wheel with one hand while he dragged a sand wedge along the pavement to grind down the flange. Other players told of seeing Laffoon roaring down the highway with a recalcitrant putter tied by a rope to the rear bumper.

Laffoon was married, and like so many of his contemporaries he and his wife had no children. "That was planned parenthood," Ky explained. "Kids were a lot of trouble for all the traveling we did. A lot of us didn't have any kids, including Hogan and Nelson." Laffoon was an accomplished gambler. "I could tear a new deck of cards in half," he bragged. "Tommy Armour used to make money on it. He'd be playing bridge and drinking in the clubhouse and see me coming. He'd bet whoever was with him $50 that the next man to enter the room could tear up the deck. I'd do it, but he never shared his winnings with me."

Laffoon won 12 Tour events in his career but no majors. His best years were in the heart of the Depression, just before Hogan and Snead came into their own. When newspaperman Al Barkow interviewed Laffoon at age 71, the old trouper was using his car as a spare apartment just as he and his peers had done for so many years in the past. Laffoon had a rod stretched across the ceiling of his Cadillac on which a wardrobe of pants, coats, and shirts stretched from end to end. In the trunk Barkow found four sets of golf clubs, two golf bags, an assortment of shoes, socks, two handguns, a shotgun with extra shells, two bottles of whiskey, a vibrator, heating pads, a spotlight, a case of chewing tobacco, sardines, peanut butter, and much else besides.

In the mid–1980s Ky Laffoon was told by his doctor that he had inoperable cancer. He went to the trunk one last time for the shotgun.

Rivaling Laffoon for flamboyance in the 1930s was William "Wild Bill" Mehlhorn, who was said by Hagen to be one of the best tee to green players he had ever seen. He won 23 tournaments during a career that lasted intermittently to 1940. At the 1929 El Paso Open Mehlhorn shot 271 on a course that had greens composed of milled cottonseed hulls, a fact that contemporary golfers find hard to believe but with which players of that era were all too familiar. The 271 stood as a PGA Tour record for 14 years.

Mehlhorn spent most of his hours off the course at the bridge table where he was good enough to make living expenses. "Wearing his distinctive broad brimmed hat," Paul Runyan recalled,

> Mehlhorn always was a distinctive figure on the course. Short and broad shouldered he had a walk like a charging bull elephant and a gruff voice that carried three fairways over.... A stickler for the rules, Bill was quick to call any violation, on himself or anyone else, a trait which didn't exactly endear him to fellow competitors. He was outspoken and ill tempered with people whose etiquette was questionable, and he would be very curt with a slow player. He had the sharpest finger you've ever seen. When he was making a point with you, he'd move in with his chin right up against yours and poke that finger right through your chest.

When he was interviewed late in life, Mehlhorn was not too shy to talk about his accomplishments. "I'd almost bet anything in the world that I wouldn't be off the fairway more than once in 72 holes," Mehlhorn said of his accuracy.

> And I was long enough too. We had some long hitters in those days. But one fellow had a standing bet — he'd take me against anybody on fifty tee shots and spot the other guy 500 yards. But the balls had to be on the fairway. Otherwise they counted nothing. And no one would take the bet. When I played if you missed the fairway, you were in rough at least a foot tall, sometimes two feet. In 1926 at the U.S. Open in Scioto the rough was up to my shoulders. I couldn't see Bobby Cruickshank when he got in it. I hollered, "Crooky, where are you?" And he held his club up above the rough so I could see him. They never had a

rake for a bunker, and the only time they raked them was in the mornings. Also the fairways and greens are so much better now than they used to be. And they've taken all the undulations out of the greens. I can remember undulations in the greens as high as my waist — as high as my shoulders in a couple of places. Now the greens are all dished in like a punch ball. They let you clean the ball and repair ball marks on the putting green and they never did back then. Twice in my time I had to play balls that were embedded in the green. They wouldn't let me move them, so I had to play them out with a nine-iron and tear up the green.

Bill Mehlhorn was born in Glencoe, Illinois, near Chicago. He played on the caddie team at Skokie Country Club. By the age of 13 he was shooting par at that tough course, site of the 1922 U.S. Open, and he turned pro at age 15. He had a remarkably smooth swing with extraordinary balance. His swing was so fluid and slow that he often played in bedroom slippers. Wild Bill gained a selection to play on the 1927 Ryder Cup team, and in the following year's British Open he engaged in a fierce set-to with the Sandwich Golf Club's secretary. In 1929 he married a Ziegfeld Follies starlet, Virginia Raye, and gave up the Tour for teaching and jobs at various country clubs. He had finished among the top ten money winners on Tour for ten straight years, but never made more than $9,000 a year.

Mehlhorn and Laffoon were lifelong gamblers, but their exploits paled in comparison to contemporary John Montague. Born LaVerne Moore in Syracuse, New York, Montague earned the nickname "Mysterious Montague" in Hollywood by befriending celebrities before fleecing them. With the magnetism of a movie star and the talent of Tommy Armour, Montague should have been a very successful touring pro. However, he avoided any event where photographers were present, and if one turned up Montague was known to smash a camera or two. He disdained any outing where a large gallery was likely to appear. Capable of holding his own with legendary drinkers like W.C. Fields and Oliver Hardy, Montague played for high stakes with Johnny Weismuller, Al Jolson, and Bing Cosby, among others. Weismuller, like Montague, was an extremely long hitter, but too often his shots went off in the wrong direction. When he connected solidly he would let go with a Tarzan yell that could be heard in the farthest corners of the golf course. But Montague was as strong as Weismuller, and witnesses alleged he could lift the rotund Oliver Hardy off the ground with one hand.

Montague's lifestyle propelled his weight to nearly 300 pounds without diminishing his talent for defeating opponents. He won a bet from excellent amateur Bing Crosby by playing with a rake and shovel but no golf clubs, and he set the course record at Palm Springs Golf club with a 61. He lived lavishly, partied incessantly, bought expensive clothes and automobiles, all without revealing his source of wealth. Finally, in 1937, a photograph of Montague ran in *Time* magazine and police in New York State recognized him as the man who had assaulted and robbed a hotel owner. He was arrested and returned to New York for trial, where Hardy and Crosby supplied character references. Conflicting testimony freed Montague, whereupon he returned to Hollywood and wed a rich Beverly Hills socialite. Unafraid of photographers now, Montague began to play in tournaments and qualified for the 1940 U.S. Open, only to shoot 80 in the first round and then withdraw. He lived until 1973.

No professional golfer saw more of the century's best players than Gene Sarazen, and he was seldom reticent in discussing their careers. He said the greatest putter he ever saw was Walter Hagen, whose style was to keep the putter square to the ball all the way back. And his backswing was very short.

"When you look at the great putters who lasted a long time," Sarazen asserted,

> they all had short backswings. Bobby Jones was a brilliant putter but he had a style that couldn't have held up over the years. He used the type of stoke that is only good between twenty and thirty when you have that fearless feeling. The thing about Jones that I never would want to copy was his backswing. You know he took the club way back and it was way off the ground. It was sort of a swing at the ball. It was beautiful. But as a player gets a little older and the nerves tighten a little he tends to lose a little of the feel necessary for the effectiveness of that long backswing.... Francis Ouimet was a beautiful putter, very rhythmic. He used to point that left elbow out, but he didn't look stiff. With that elbow out there was very little chance of the right hand dominating because the left elbow and left hand blocked the right as he came into the ball.... Great players seldom become great because of the long shots, they become great because of their putting—chipping and putting. You know if you can't get down in two from off the green four out of five times, you're going to be trailing the field.

The 1940s

*"I know that I have had greater satisfaction than anyone who ever
lived out of the hitting of golf balls!"*

— Ben Hogan

The entry of the United States into the Second World War had much the
same impact on golf as on baseball, football, and other major sports. Cancel-
lation of schedules, the enlistment of stars, and rationing of gasoline making
unessential travel impossible were imposing hurdles for the PGA Tour. Lloyd
Mangrum, Clayton Heafner, Horton Smith, and other leading Tour players
went overseas with various military units, while Ben Hogan, Sam Snead,
Jimmy Demaret, Lewis Worsham, and Porky Oliver all served in one service
capacity or another in the States. In 1941 Ben Hogan was the leading money
winner, but after Pearl Harbor the Tour dwindled away to a handful of events.
The U.S. Open was canceled from 1942 through 1945, and most of the leading players concentrated on exhibitions for the Red Cross and for war bonds.
Byron Nelson was a hemophiliac and 4F. He dominated tournaments and set
records in 1945 that appear unapproachable in the modern age. Nelson was
scorned by many veterans for defeating weak fields during the war years. Over
the span of half a century, however, Nelson's record speaks for itself. By 1945
many golfers in uniform were returning to competition. By the last year of
the war Snead, Oliver, Henry Picard, Hogan, and other stars were back playing the PGA Tour.

Ben Hogan was born in 1912, the same year as Byron Nelson, in Dublin,
Texas to a blacksmith father and fiercely independent mother. When Hogan
was nine his father, disillusioned by failed businesses and declining health,
shot himself, leaving a widow and three children with no means of support.
Clara Hogan moved to another less expensive house in Fort Worth. Royal
Hogan, Ben's older brother, became the breadwinner at age 13. Hogan started
selling newspapers at the Fort Worth railway station. He walked the trains as
they arrived, often through the night.

After two years of this grind, Hogan learned that he could earn more by caddying at a local country club. Although only 11, Hogan was soon carrying bags larger than himself. And the typical hazing of new and smaller boys ceased abruptly when Hogan challenged two of the biggest caddies and whipped each of them in turn. His regimen during these years was to be out of the house by dawn on a seven mile walk to the course where an 18-hole assignment netted 65 cents plus tip, usually another dime. His free time was given over to caddie inventions, one of which called for every boy to hit a ball as far as he could down range. The boy whose ball traveled the shortest distance inherited the chore of retrieving every shot. Hogan lost consistently at first, but constant practice soon saw him keeping up and then surpassing larger boys.

Byron Nelson caddied with Hogan at the Glen Garden Club. Years later Byron looked back to those early days and attributed Hogan's unusual power and shot-making to those contests at the caddie grounds, contests that Hogan strove to win as fiercely as any subsequent major championship. When someone asked Hogan how he had started in golf, his answer was that he could make more money caddying than he could selling newspapers, and that the only way for a new kid to break in was to win a fight with one of the older boys. This he proceeded to do. In the early mornings caddies hit balls at the practice field until members arrived. Hogan began to wait for the club's best golfer so he could caddie for him despite the fact that he was not the best tipper. Hogan tried to imitate this man's swing, establishing a pattern that would continue through his early golf career as he closely watched other golfers and adopted what seemed best for his own needs. Later, at the height of success, he was asked how often he tried to hit a ball dead straight. He replied:

Never! It's virtually impossible — at least it's an accident. Besides you give yourself much more margin for error by maneuvering your shots one way or the other. Much more control.... To me there's not enough daylight in a day to practice all the shots you ought to be practicing every day. It's a question of running through the complete routine every day as much as you can, working on every conceivable shot. I'm talking about practicing chip shots, sand shots, all kinds of shots. I'd start with the wedge up against the green and I'd hit I don't know how many balls—I'd almost hit a bag with each club — until I was shooting at that green with a driver.... If you find something that's not working you've got to go out and work about three days harder on that one thing. I used to go to a tournament and play a practice round by myself and hit several balls on each hole: Tee shot, second shot, not just the drive. In order to be very sharp you have to familiarize yourself with the course and have a feel of it. When I say a feel, you have to try to place your tee shots and then get a feel of the distance for that second shot, because you have to familiarize yourself with the course and have a feel of it. When I say a feel, you have to try to place your tee shots and then get a feel of the distance for that second shot, because you have to be inside twenty feet to make any birdies. You can't be thirty feet long or thirty feet short. I didn't know the yardages. I didn't want to know them. There are too many variables—the wind, air density, how you're playing that day. I would

Ben Hogan, at Hershey Country Club (©Corbis).

remember if I had been beside a certain tree or trap or something like that and what I hit and how I played that shot, but I don't think I could play by yardage. Maybe I could. I've never done it.

The Hogan family struggled after the death of Hogan's father. Hogan's mother was critical of the time the younger brother was spending at Glen Garden, and she constantly encouraged him to emulate his older brother. But Hogan had discovered a passion for golf. At age 15 he had progressed to the stage where local tournaments for caddies seemed to be his only interest. And there was only one obstacle to his triumphing in those events, a boy of the same age named Byron Nelson. When the membership at Glen Garden decided to bestow a junior membership on the most deserving caddie, the caddie master was called on to nominate one boy, and he said: "Byron Nelson is the only caddie who doesn't drink, smoke, or curse. I think he should have it."

Nelson went on to win several of the club tournaments while an embittered Hogan was relegated to caddie competitions. Nor was Hogan permitted to practice at Glen Garden. The rebuff rankled, and it would take a long, long time before Hogan returned to visit the course after his success.

His mother again began counseling Hogan, telling him that in her opinion a future in golf seemed very remote. She advised giving up the game entirely to devote attention to working with Royal. When she described this conversation to acquaintances decades later, Clara Hogan said Hogan listened to her with suppressed fury, then politely bit off the words: "Mother, someday I'm going to be the greatest golfer in the world!"

In a happy fable, Ben Hogan would have gone on to immediate riches and acclaim; however, with the exception of Tiger Woods, Arnold Palmer, Jack Nicklaus, and a few others it is rare in golf to find immediate rewards of the magnitude enjoyed by basketball and football stars as they graduate from amateur to professional status. For Hogan, the 1930s were years of self-doubt and meager returns. He entered many tournaments, the first in 1932 at Los Angeles where he garnered $8.50 in prize money. He played in a few others that year until, too broke to afford entrance fees, he drifted back to Fort Worth to try working in the oil fields, then as a mechanic, then in a bank, and even as a hotel clerk. He also filled in occasionally as golf pro at small Texas country clubs. One of his responsibilities included teaching, but Hogan rarely had much patience for instruction. His mood was variable, even in the press tent following a tournament. He expected intelligent questions from reporters. Instead of an answer, more than one writer received chilled glares and Hogan's retort, "That's a stupid question!"

Modern day pros marvel at how hard Tom Kite worked on the practice tee, but Hogan was even more diligent. According to Dave Marr, Hogan would leave Fort Worth in the early spring and travel to the Seminole Golf Club where Claude Harmon was pro. Hogan arrived at the practice range at exactly 10:00 every day and would hit shot after shot, for hours, then play 18 holes in the afternoon with Harmon, Marr, or other friends. After about six weeks of this regimen, Hogan could hit hundreds of practice shots, each a carbon copy of the last, with exactly the same trajectory and distance and unbelievable accuracy. By this point he felt ready for the Masters Tournament in early April.

Another contemporary pro, Paul Runyan, said: "Hogan had to strike three practice balls for every one that Nicklaus hit. That's how hard he worked at the game." His swing in the early years was very loose and wild, almost the antithesis of what it eventually became. Sam Snead observed:

> Hogan swung the club back so far around on the backswing that the shaft pointed to the ground. He could whack the ball out of sight with a big hook, but he didn't know where it was going. Most people don't realize he started on tour in the early thirties and didn't win a tournament until 1940. But in that time he worked longer and harder than anybody else trying to find a swing that would repeat. Then all of a sudden he started putting red gravy on the scoreboards.

One of the few people at this time who believed Ben had a future in golf was Valerie Hogan. Married in 1935, she saved every dollar to finance Hogan on Tour, and in 1936 he began to play well enough to qualify for the U.S. Open at Baltusrol. He and Valerie traveled from one end of the country to another staying in the cheapest hotels they could find and eating nothing but oranges for days on end, eking out so little in winnings they barely covered the price of gas for their second-hand Buick. But for the next two years he played more and more consistently, finishing 1938 as the 15th leading money winner.

Hogan's breakthrough year was 1940. Early in the year he entered the winner's circle with a tournament record score at the North-South Open. He leapfrogged Sam Snead by three shots, and Byron Nelson by nine. Finally, after nine grueling years as a pro, Hogan achieved victory. During the next scheduled events at Greensboro and Asheville, he blew away the competition by winning more money than he had ever seen in his life. In the space of little more than two weeks he won three tournaments, played in 34 strokes under par. The fast start enabled Hogan to finish the 1940 season as the Tour's leading money winner with $10,655. By the standard of today's prizes this may not seem impressive. But in 1940 spare ribs were selling for seven cents a pound, salmon 20 cents a pound, dress shirts went for 69 cents, and fine leather jackets could be purchased for $3. Valerie and he finally could cease worrying about their next meal.

It was about this time that Hogan began to be as demanding about his food preparation as he was about the trajectory of his four-irons. More than one hotel chef took instruction personally from Hogan on cooking his scrambled eggs in cream, not milk. And more than one room service or restaurant waiter carried Hogan's meal back to the kitchen with exact instructions on how to remedy the damage. In any case, winning now became the expected norm in whatever event he entered. In 1941 he increased his prize money to $18,000 and no one came close to his scoring average.

The World War put an end to consecutive annual records, however. Much of the next season was canceled, and Hogan was called up for the draft. Enlisting in the Army as a private, he soon went off to Officers Candidate School and was commissioned a second lieutenant in November. As with so many professional athletes, Hogan's principal contribution during the following years was to promote the sale of war bonds. He teamed up with Bob Hope and Bing Crosby on one junket that attracted galleries as large as 4,000, and raised $1.5 million in bonds. Joe Kirkwood, Jug McSpaden, and Louise Suggs also went along on these exhibition tours, traveling to New Orleans, Atlanta, Chicago, and other major cities.

After Hogan's discharge in August 1945, he renewed the battle with Byron Nelson. Between August of 1945 and August 1946, Hogan won 18 tournaments, Nelson ten. Hogan finished second in the Masters, and also was a runner up in the U.S. Open. Finally he won the PGA in Portland, his first major championship. The years of ceaseless practice had paid off.

He discovered a revolutionary improvement for his swing that resulted in an exclusive *Life* magazine article. Hogan changed two things. First, he altered his grip so his left thumb rested directly on top of the shaft, and two, he cupped the left hand up and in forming a V at the top of the backswing. He asserted that the changes made his swing hook-proof. By 1948 his career was at its zenith. He won the U.S. Open, the PGA Championship, the Western and L.A. Opens, and seven other events that year. He captained the Vardon Trophy for lowest average strokes per round, and came out on top in prize money at $32,000. He started off the 1949 season in the same style, winning two of the first four tournaments. After finishing play at Phoenix the Hogans started the trip home after 14 years of marriage.

On February 2, 1949, Hogan pointed his Cadillac onto Route 80 to complete the last leg of their trip. That day an early morning fog covered the Pecos

River Valley. This reduced the Cadillac's speed to what Hogan later described as "practically nothing." Coming in the opposite direction were a large truck and an overdue Greyhound bus. The impatient bus driver pulled out to pass on the two-land road. He picked up speed going down a hill, but before the bus could safely slide back into its own lane the headlights of Hogan's Cadillac appeared in the fog only a few feet away. Hogan wrenched the steering wheel to the right but a concrete abutment ran along the side of the highway preventing an escape. At the last possible second he vaulted to the passenger side of the front seat to shield Valerie. The 20,000 pound bus pulverized the front of the Cadillac. The steering wheel shot back through the front seat breaking Ben's collarbone. The engine also was catapulted backwards, pounding Hogan's left leg and lower body.

When the bus rolled to a stop the numb but unhurt passengers stumbled out to look for the cause of the crash. When they discovered the mangled car, Hogan was wedged between the dashboard and Valerie, who was cut and bruised but in far better condition than her barely conscious husband. It took an hour to safely remove the couple and to secure an ambulance for the drive to El Paso. Lucky to have survived the impact, Hogan's slight body suffered horrendous damage. The doctors discovered a broken rib, broken ankle, extensive bladder injury, a fractured pelvis, broken collarbone, and a deep gash next to his left eye.

Weighing 138 pounds at the time of the accident, Hogan nonetheless had been in excellent physical condition as would be expected given his achievements on the Tour. The lower half of his body was placed in a cast and a number of specialists were flown in to examine the patient, who after only a few days was pressing hospital administrators to sign his release. Two weeks after the accident Hogan's condition suddenly grew worse. A blood clot formed in his left leg and moved through the pulmonary artery into a lung. Doctors handled that one successfully, but they grew worried over the possibility that a larger clot might form and close the artery. Called a pulmonary embolism, this could easily prove fatal. Another surgeon was flown into El Paso to perform an emergency operation tying off one of the major blood vessels so that no clots would pass through to Hogan's heart or lungs. The procedure saved his life.

Recovery required not only a two-month stay in the hospital, but also subsequent long days of physical therapy at home in Fort Worth. Hogan started off by walking five laps around the living room each morning, and gradually worked up to long walks around his neighborhood. Cramps often cut short these walks and kept him immobile until Valerie went out to search for him with her new car. He began speculating about whether he could ever play golf again, whether the shattered left leg would heal enough to allow the effort required to hit full shots. Then he began pondering whether he could play tournament golf again. Soon he was examining tour calendars. Relentlessly, he pushed his body to respond much, much faster than any specialist had predicted.

By the spring of 1949 Hogan was convinced that tournament play was a possibility, and he mailed in his entry to the USGA to play in the U.S. Open. When the Open started the following month Hogan remained at home, nowhere near ready to walk 18 holes, much less compete in a major championship. His lawsuit against the Greyhound Bus Company was settled out-of-court. The dollar sum was to be kept confidential, but one newspaper account claimed that Greyhound would pay all of the medical expenses plus $150,000 in cash. Another story alleged that Hogan was to receive $25,000 each year, tax free, for life. Hogan characteristically would not comment on either story. The court also ruled that the driver of the bus had been negligent as charged, but his sentence was the lightest permitted by law, $127 in fines and court costs.

In the summer of 1949 Hogan captained (non-playing) the U.S. Ryder cup team to victory in Great Britain. Returning home he started to play full rounds at the Colonial Country Club, and played so well acquaintances pressed him to try competition again. Walking 18 holes was agony, however. After a round he often was so weak he needed to stay off his feet for a full day afterwards. But when the date for the 1950 L.A. Open approached, on the Riviera Country Club course where he had won three times before, he decided to take the train west and find out whether it was possible to play tournament golf.

In his first practice round at Riviera, one of only four rounds he had played since his accident, he recorded a two-under 69. Afterward he rested in a bathtub filled with Epsom salts, then wrapped his legs in elastic bandages. Only after successfully completing four practice rounds did Hogan finally commit to playing in the tournament. A record gallery of 9,000 showed up to see him tee off. By the end of the first nine he was limping badly. He shot a remarkable 34 on the front but rapidly tired and skied to a 39 on the back nine. The next day he carded another 34, followed up with a 35, and tied for third place after 36 holes. Then he shot two additional 69s to finish the tournament at a remarkable 280 total. There was only one golfer left on the course who could threaten. Sam Snead was three under par at 14, needing birdies on two of the last four holes to tie. He sank a 15-foot putt on 18 to tie Hogan. Hard rains postponed the playoff for several days. When Snead and Hogan returned for the match neither player excelled, but Snead recorded a 1-over 72 to Hogan's 76. What amazed the sportswriters and thousands of fans who watched was not so much the accomplishment of tying for the lead as Hogan had done, but the fact that he was able to compete at all and to walk the extremely demanding 18 holes of Riviera. His shotmaking skills seemed undiminished, but his stamina was far below that required for the grind of tournament golf.

In the three months before the Masters Hogan had time to work on conditioning and to slowly build back his strength. The slopes of Augusta, however, took their toll. He tied for fourth, only five strokes off the leader. The following month he played the Greenbrier Invitational and whipped the field with 64-66-65-66 for a 259 that tied Byron Nelson's record for low score in the tournament.

Now confident that his comeback was assured Hogan looked forward to the 1950 U.S. Open to be held at Merion. He played well in the first two rounds; a 72 and 69 left him two shots behind Dutch Harrison prior to the start of the final day's 36 holes, setting up what many believed to be the most memorable of all Hogan's achievements. By the time he approached the 12th hole of the final round at Merion, the leaders were in and it was clear that Hogan would win if he could play in at one over par or better. He parred the 13th and 14th, but missed a par putt of two and one-half feet at 15. He parred 16, then bogeyed 17. Now he needed a par just to tie Lloyd Mangrum and George Fazio.

The 18th hole at Merion is an extremely tough uphill par-four, and Hogan hit an excellent drive. This set up one of the most famous golf shots of all time, immortalized by a photographer who snapped Hogan's picture just as he completed the follow through on a one-iron that soared up and onto the green about forty feet to the left of the cup. Hogan sent his lag putt to within three feet and sank the last to tie. In the 18-hole playoff, Hogan went on to beat Mangrum by four shots and Fazio by six to win the Open and to cap what many sportswriters considered the most memorable comeback in the history of sport.

At the end of the 1950 season Sam Snead had recorded eight wins, while Mangrum had five. Neither man won a major in 1950. Jimmy Demaret took three tournaments, including the Masters. Hogan's comeback figured heavily in the voting for PGA Player of the Year. Hogan had tied for the top spot at L.A. in the first tournament after his accident. Then he won at Greenbrier, and the U.S. Open. The award was given to Hogan.

The following year's Open was scheduled at Oakland Hills. The previous time the Open was held there was in 1924, 27 years earlier, and new equipment made the course vulnerable to men like Snead, Mangrum, Demaret, and Hogan. So the membership called in Robert Trent Jones, who lengthened half the holes, narrowed many fairways, and built 40 new sand traps. When the pros arrived they were livid about the changes Jones had incorporated in the old course. It now played close to 7,000 yards, and a 280, par for 72 holes at Oakland Hills, seemed impossible.

Jones enjoyed an enviable career in golf architecture. His courses are popular all over the world, and his two sons have built similarly impressive reputations. But over the years Jones was criticized publicly by many touring pros who disparaged some of his work, for example, at Hazeltine. The animosity may have had its origin at Oakland Hills in 1951, when the pros arrived to find the classic course transformed into a much longer and tougher test of golf.

After the first two rounds of the 1951 Open, Bobby Locke led with 144 strokes. Hogan, Snead, and Mangrum were well back in the field at 149. The event in those years still required a 36-hole conclusion on the final day of play. At the end of 54 holes Hogan's 71 placed his total at 220. Julius Boros and Paul Runyan were at 219, with Bobby Locke and Demaret at 218. On the final 18 holes Hogan played miraculous golf, coming in with a 67, three under par on a course that probably was the toughest of any Open course up to that time. Only one other player had been able to crack par, Clayton Heafner, with a 69. Boros, Locke, Demaret, and the others fell away as Hogan finished his brilliant round. The 72 hole total for the victory was 287. Heafner finished strongly to take second with 289.

The Open at Oakland Hills, on a track that many of the pros publicly claimed was so difficult as to be "unplayable," became Hogan's third consecutive U.S. Open Championship. He had won in 1948, then missed the 1949 event after the accident. Returning in 1950 he won at Merion, then followed up in 1951 by conquering Oakland Hills.

Hogan almost won the Open again in 1955 at San Francisco's Olympic Club, but lost in a playoff to Jack Fleck. In 1960 at Cherry Hills, playing with rookie pro Jack Nicklaus, Hogan was tied for the lead with only three holes to play. Age and a failing putter conspired against him. He closed with bogey and triple-bogey to see Arnold Palmer vault ahead of the field and win. Hogan's achievements in the Open surpassed even Bobby Jones's remarkable record. Between 1940 and 1960 Hogan played in 15 Open championships. He won four times, and finished second twice. He recorded the most sub-par rounds of any player in the 15 Opens; he scored 72 or lower in 38 of 60 rounds; he had the most rounds under 70; and he set the Open record at 276 in L.A. in 1948, later broken at Baltusrol in 1967 by Nicklaus.

In 1953, Hogan decided to enter the British Open for the first time. Valerie and he arrived at Carnoustie well in advance of the tournament to allow time for practice. However, the smaller English ball and unusual typography bedeviled Hogan. Playing regular practice rounds provided little improvement. The fairways were hard and divot-strewn, the greens slow and ragged. He never seemed to find a level lie, and there were very few trees or other landmarks to aid in targeting many of the blind shots to difficult greens. He played from the back tees for several days before discovering that championship tees, referred to by the Scots as "Tiger Tees," were hidden far back in the heather and stretched the course to 7200 yards.

Frustrated by his failure to judge distances on the unfamiliar course, Hogan took to walking Carnoustie at night. The locals who often played until dark — 11:00 in summer — watched Hogan walk the course in reverse trying to memorize bunkers and other hazards, as well as slopes on the greens, and they gave him the inimitable description "Wee Ice Mon."

Before embarking the Hogans had considered shipping enough frozen steaks and vegetables to Scotland to last during a three-week stay, but canceled because of the criticism of the 1949 American Ryder Cup Team which had done the same thing. During his stay at Carnoustie, Hogan lost weight steadily on the hotel's menu of mutton and the same three vegetables every day for three weeks. After sitting down to this repast each day, he set off for the course to continue his memorization. Each day he inquired about registering for the tournament, but no one seemed to know the correct procedure, or the Hogans failed to decipher the thick brogue, and it was not until the day before the championship started that a guest ticket for Valerie and a credential for Hogan to play arrived in the mail.

The first day of play dawned cold and extremely windy, with occasional hail showers. Hogan shot a respectable 73, then followed it with a 71, one shot behind Roberto DeVicenzo after 36 holes. Hogan required a shot of penicillin to ward off bronchitis before the third round. Some 20,000 Scots arrived at Carnoustie to see the finale, and hundreds of thousands more followed the action at home on their radios.

At the conclusion of the third round Hogan was tied for the lead with DeVicenzo, only one stroke ahead of a strong complement of British players. On the final 18 Hogan played without making a serious error on any of the holes that he had so painstakingly studied during the weeks before the event. He finished with a course record 68, and his 72-hole total of 282 also was a new record, beating by eight shots the previous best total for Carnoustie. The press and Scottish people who at first had given Hogan a lukewarm welcome, now could not find enough superlatives to describe his exploits. Hogan reciprocated with compliments of his own. Although he never found much good to say about the national cuisine, the people he encountered in Scotland and their love of golf impressed him very much.

Hogan returned a hero to the United States. For the first time since Bobby Jones returned victorious from England in 1930, New York City gave an athlete a ticker-tape parade and the keys to the city. Still exhausted despite a leisurely crossing on the liner *United States*, Hogan came alive during his 20-mile ride around New York. A mob estimated at 150,000 souls packed Broadway alone as the Hogans passed. At the press conference Hogan's admiration of the Scots came forth again:

"Rain doesn't bother them," he remarked:

> They just put on rain suits and keep playing or watching. And when a strong wind and rain comes across the course, they squat down under their umbrellas like rabbits or chickens, you know, until the rain and wind quits, then they'd get up and go on — darndest sight you ever saw.... Kids and dogs, they let everybody and anything on the course; more dogs than you ever saw. The people would come from everywhere to watch. Ladies with a small child on each arm would drag them the full eighteen holes. They'd bring babies in buggies and push them the full eighteen. They'd bring their lunches and stay all day.

Hogan enjoyed the people in Scotland:

> They're wonderful people. They don't have very much, but they do with what they have and they're very enthusiastic. The caddies drop the bag on the greens when you get ready to putt, and when the hole is finished the people just walk right across the greens. It's a public course, and they let everybody and anything on the course. I almost hit a dog teeing off one time. They'd work all day, come home at six, and have their dinner and go over and play eighteen holes. Just everybody played golf. The first day I was to qualify, the course is right along the railroad tracks and a train pulled up and the engineer gave me a wave and a toot, tooted on his whistle when I was on the tee.

Hogan was temperamental, aloof, stubborn, and a continual source of fascination for the golfing public and for his fellow touring pros. Jimmy Demaret, who was thought to be closer to Ben than anyone excepting Valerie, once told Sam Snead: "I can't really say I know the man." Snead always claimed that he and Hogan were friendly despite their deep rivalry and prickly dispositions. Snead recalled: "Ben never talked on the golf course and didn't have much to say off it either. He's been consistent there." Hogan's concentration, which was legendary, often was misconstrued as disdain. At one of the Masters tournaments, Hogan was paired with Claude Harmon. On the 12th hole Harmon made a hole-in-one. A huge cheer went up from the gallery. The two golfers marched up to the green, where Hogan sank his long putt for a birdie. When they walked to the 13th tee Hogan asked: "What'd you have back there, Claude?"

"I had a one, Ben." Harmon watched for a reaction. But Hogan already was staring at the fairway, absorbed in the next shot.

"Ben wouldn't recognize his own wife on the course," said Snead. "He concentrated so hard he just didn't see anybody or anything and didn't want anyone to talk with him or break his concentration."

Jackie Burke, Jr., recalled a Masters in which Hogan and he were paired, and criticisms were lodged against Hogan's leisurely pace. "Of course there was gamesmanship out there that you had to deal with," Burke said.

> But they were very natural about it. You take a look at who starts out walking real fast. Well, you know, good players like Lloyd Mangrum, they're not going to change their timing. He'll slow down the fast walker, he'll walk twice as slow as he usually does. You see, a slow player is not only using his time, he's using your time. So you've got to go over and talk to him a little bit. Except maybe if it's Hogan. I remember we were a couple of holes behind. An official asked me to go over and talk to Ben, and I said, "You go over. Hell, Ben Hogan's wife doesn't talk to him too much!" But I did tell him, "Ben, they're going to put two strokes on you." He said, "Let 'em come out here and do it then!" He wasn't going to change his timing for any group of officials or anybody else!

Hogan once had a run-in with Clifford Roberts, emperor of the Masters Tournament in the early years. Roberts ordered Hogan to speed up. Hogan told Roberts to stick it, give or take a couple of hard bitten words. It was Roberts's style to intimidate everyone with whom he came into contact. Those attempts failed with Hogan. He focused on each shot as if it were his last one on earth. He told Claude Harmon that if he wanted to win golf tournaments he needed to look at the grass all the time. If he made eye contact with anybody, he might begin to say a few words, and the concentration would evaporate. "You don't talk to anybody," Ben said, "because if someone wants to talk with you, you know they're not your friend. Friends know not to speak to you on the golf course."

When he was 75 years of age Hogan was asked if he was still discovering things about the golf swing. "Yes," he answered, "I think I am, although these days I get very few surprises."

When Ben Hogan started his equipment business his mania for perfection confounded associates and terrorized workers. One day Hogan walked into the plant and told everyone to leave, they had made enough mistakes for one day. But over time the Hogan clubs came to represent the same standard for performance that Hogan had set for himself. And the Hogan ball was so dependable a majority of players on Tour began playing it.

Hogan is one of the few whose will and athletic ability carried him to a different plateau, one that lesser mortals struggle to climb but rarely succeed. In Hogan's case any number of contemporaries tried to put their finger on what set him apart, what it was that made him a superstar. "It took Hogan a lot longer to reach the top than Nicklaus," asserted Sam Snead. "And it all stems from the fact that he never had somebody to tutor him right in the beginning."

Bob Toski believed: "Hogan's attitude reflects all the adversity he suffered to succeed. He's known for not being very helpful to players when they ask advice, probably because he figures nobody helped him along the way."

"Nicklaus never had to stop like Hogan and go into the service," argued Cary Middlecoff:

> From the time he was sixteen years old until he went on tour at twenty-two, nothing ever stopped Jack. The prize money jumped dramatically about that time too. I've always thought how nice it would've been to have my own private airplane on tour, because that's what Jack had. Hogan drove a car 50,000 miles a year on tour.

Tom Watson's struggle to succeed took longer than Nicklaus, but it was much, much shorter than Hogan's. Watson arrived on tour in 1971, won his first tournament in 1974, collected his first major in 1975, and was top money winner in 1977 for the first time. Like Nicklaus, Watson had a college education and a supportive family. "If there is one attribute that made Hogan, Nicklaus, and Watson elevated above their peers," asserted Byron Nelson, who closely observed all three golfers over many years, "it is a great, great determination to excel." Nelson continued:

All three have an uncompromising willingness to do anything, work as hard as necessary to attain their goals. Along with this they have a self confidence that makes no achievement seem impossible. They are positive thinkers of the first order. I've seen perhaps better swingers over the years never reach Ben's or Jack's or Tom's level because they couldn't keep negative thoughts out of their minds. I've never heard Jack say that he was hitting it poorly and didn't know what was wrong. When he's in a slump he always knows what's wrong and how to correct it. At least he thinks he does, and that's the key. If you ever hear Jack say, "I'm not playing well," you can be sure he'll add, "But it's starting to come around." The same was true for Ben in his later years and to a lesser extent is true for Tom. Tom may not be as good at this as the other two, because he's a bit younger and still learning.

Hogan was the most determined golfer I ever saw. He even was more determined than Nicklaus especially in everyday play. If Hogan were playing today he'd probably concentrate on the majors as Jack does because a player's record in the majors now has evolved into his measure of greatness. In the days when Ben and I played we had to participate in all the tournaments if we wanted to make a living.... Hogan told me he never made more than five good swings in a round; naturally this was by Ben's standards. The less than good swings did not bother him because he thought in terms of a whole round or a whole 72-hole tournament. When Ben played a course in practice before a tournament he would try to get a feel for what he had to shoot to win, and he would come very close to that score regardless of what anybody else shot. He set scoring goals, and achieved them better than anybody, I think.

When the Senior Tour started there were many active players who had been contemporaries of Hogan and who wondered how he would play, now in his 70s, if he came back on the Tour. One of them, Tony Penna, recounted how uncompromising Hogan could be.

"One time in Minneapolis we were walking off the first tee as partners in a four-ball match, and Ben told me, 'You're the captain.' Meaning I'd decide on conceding any putts. At the fourth hole I knocked away a short putt that Willie Goggin had. Coming off the green Ben glared at me. 'You're not the captain anymore,' he said. 'You can't give anybody a putt that long!'"

Another player remembered watching Ben as he looked over a shipment of new balls at the U.S. Open one year. "He opened up the carton, then he took out a magnifying glass and looked through it at each ball, one by one. Every so often he tossed a new ball in his shag bag. I couldn't believe it, brand new balls. I finally asked him why? 'Some of the dimples have too much paint in them,' he said." Herman Kaiser, who played the PGA Tour for many years with varying success, recalled: "I once told Ben, 'GREAT SHOT' and he turned to me and said, 'I wish you wouldn't say that, I'm the only one who knows how I wanted to hit that shot.'"

The 1950s

"I was raised in a steel town, in a coal mining area in the 1940's. I played golf, but very few people in the town knew anything about it. There was one golf course. It was the Country Club. A man who worked in the steel mill thought there was only one thing for his son to do, play football or basketball. Today there are more golf courses than you can count in that area. That same man who had a one-sided opinion about sports is playing golf himself and encouraging his sons to take up the sport. That's where television has had a tremendous impact on the game. It has taken golf into the coal mines, the steel mills, into every business and walk of life."

— Arnold Palmer

After the Second World War strong economic conditions in the United States contributed to the rapid growth of professional sports. In the 1950s, golf received a terrific boost from President Eisenhower, who missed no opportunity to play at one of the Washington, D.C., clubs or to arrange a long weekend at Augusta National where he was the club's most prestigious member. President Eisenhower lent an air of stability and prestige to the game, enhanced by generous media attention.

Ike became president at precisely the time television was beginning to dominate professional sports, and the camera was as kind to Ike as it was to Arnold Palmer. The president often traveled to Palm Springs for winter vacations where he would appear in the galleries at many tournaments. He became a loyal member of Arnie's Army, and a close friend of the golfer. Ike was a good player in his own right, as buttressed by the president's financial advisor, Clifford Roberts, who said the president was a better player than many people realized although he suffered a congenital slice and was a poor judge of contour on the greens. He could break 80 even at Augusta National. He was an impatient player, one who charged ahead of his partners and often played his shots as if the others were too slow in playing theirs.

Arnold Palmer's rise to fame coincided with the prosperous tenure of Eisenhower's presidency. Both men came from humble origins. Palmer's father

Arnold Palmer (©PGA Tour).

was a club pro in an era when class differences were more noticeable in American life, and the senior Palmer was closer to a hired hand than the more prosperous touring and teaching professionals of today. Palmer socialized with the caddies, not the club members' offspring, and he undertook virtually every job possible at a country club. His least successful endeavor was caddying. By the age of 11 he knew the course at least as well as any of the members, and was strongly opinionated in any discussion of club selection.

Deacon, the elder Palmer, had cut down an old set of clubs and rewrapped the grips, and from the age of three Arnold Palmer had been in every nook and cranny of the course. His access to the first tee was strictly rationed as it was for the other caddies, but the rough near his house always was available. The Country Club at Latrobe, Pennsylvania at the time lacked sand traps, and throughout Palmer's career many of his contemporaries were far superior with a sand wedge, but out of the rough Palmer seemingly could get it up and down from anywhere. As a boy he had practiced hitting balls off pine needles, twigs, leaves, using the club blade turned backward, hitting off first the left foot, then the right.

Because the greens and fairways usually were verboten, he became adept at hitting shots from all points of the compass. And since he usually was alone he created imaginary competition in which he was facing down Bobby Jones at Augusta, or Byron Nelson at Oakmont. "Always hit it hard," Deacon taught, and the young Palmer complied. There was little time for lessons. Deacon gave him the fundamentals — an overlapping grip and a compact, square-to-square swing, but Palmer was left to work everything else out during practice. His high school golf team coach said, "I was his coach, but I didn't teach him anything. He knew more about golf as a freshman than anyone in school. He taught the team, I managed it."

Palmer followed his father's advice and ignored other sports to concentrate on golf. There was still time for billiards, however, and Palmer was said by friends to be the best pool player in town. He also loved poker. Later when bridge was a popular pastime among tour players Palmer became the favorite partner of President Eisenhower.

Palmer had excelled on the school golf team, played in tournaments at the country club, and entered amateur events throughout Pennsylvania. He met Buddy Worsham at an amateur tournament and the two became close friends. When Worsham accepted an athletic scholarship from Wake Forest, he talked Palmer into one as well. They worked and lived together for three years, and Palmer went through much of that time without ever losing a college match. This was the golden era of college stars. Ken Venturi was playing for San Jose State, Gene Littler at San Diego State, Don January at North Texas State, Mike Souchak at Duke, Dow Finsterwald at Ohio University. Art Wall, Billy Maxwell, and other soon-to-be-famous players also were opponents of Arnold during those years. Then, in the autumn of 1950 Buddy Worsham drove to a dance at Duke University, which Palmer ordinarily would have attended but for another commitment. On the drive home Worsham was killed in an accident.

Devastated by the death of his closest friend, Palmer impulsively volunteered for the U.S. Coast Guard. After three years of service he returned to Wake Forest briefly, then went to work with a friend who offered a job in Cleveland calling on painting contractors in the morning, leaving afternoons and weekends free for golf. The year was 1954 and the U.S. Amateur Championship was scheduled for Michigan. Palmer won. He immediately thought of the PGA Tour. First he had to find backing. Several sponsors offered inducements, but the terms were very tough. In return for $10,000 in seed money, Palmer would have to turn over 50 percent of his earnings over the first five years of his career. Finally he got an offer from a sporting goods company for just enough money to go on Tour, and in November 1954 he turned professional.

During the Fred Waring tournament at Shawnee on the Delaware that year, Palmer met his future wife. The match was an attraction of opposites. He was a domineering, aggressive extrovert. Winnie was a passive introvert. He was a hunter and fisherman, she a symphony and theater fan. Palmer read balance sheets and the sports page. She loved books and loathed sports. She was a classmate of Fred Waring's daughter at the Pembroke School, to which she matriculated after the Moravian Seminary for Young Ladies. After meeting Winnie for the first time Palmer departed for the Miami Open. He missed the cut, and his father said, "What's wrong with you? Are you too lovesick to play?" Palmer said he was, and drove back to Pennsylvania to collect Winnie. He had to borrow $2,000 for the wedding.

With small loans from deacon and his father-in-law, Arnold and Winnie Palmer set off in a house trailer. Winnie recalled that the first year on Tour they joined up with Gene and Shirley Littler, Bill and Shirley Casper, Doug and Marilyn Ford, Dow and Linda Finsterwald, and traveled from one event to another cross-country in small RVs. That was the least expensive way to travel, so the couples settled into the same trailer camps sharing barbecues and the few possessions they enjoyed at the time.

After six weeks Palmer had won nothing and a shoulder injury seemed likely to drive him off the Tour. Hitting down sharply into the sun baked tees and fairways of Texas and Arizona had badly damaged the muscles in his right shoulder. A doctor diagnosed the problem and administered cortisone shots that eliminated the pain. In January 1955 Palmer won $700 in the first pro-am he entered, won another at Greenbrier, finished second in the Pan American Open for $900, took $700 at the Masters, $1,300 for a third place finish at the St. Paul Open, and, finally, a first place finish in the Canadian Open worth $2,400. By the end of that year Palmer had pocketed $8,200 and had paid off all his debts.

For the remainder of the decade Palmer went from one triumph to another. Perhaps his greatest achievement took place at the 1960 U.S. Open. At the start of the final round at Cherry Hills Palmer trailed Mike Souchak by seven shorts. Palmer had attempted to drive the first hole without success during previous rounds. On the final day he tried again, reached the green, just missed an eagle, and started a string of birdies that carried him to a total of 30 shots on the front nine. With a closing 35, he won going away, beating the second place finisher by two shots. No golfer in history had ever shot such a low round on the last day to win an Open, nor had anyone come from so far behind. The television cameras recorded it for posterity. Palmer's exuberant, slashing play was the antithesis of Hogan's methodical, patient strategy. The galleries responded wildly. Even more remarkable was the reaction of television audiences. A producer claimed that the watershed event occurred the year before with the 1959 Masters Championship when Palmer, the defending champion, strode over the brow of a hill into camera range on the 15th hole, hitched up his pants, flipped away a cigarette, and went for broke. He lost, but a director said his "losing was better TV than anybody else winning. He lost to Art Wall, whom we privately nicknamed the 'ribbon clerk' because he looked like he was a clerk in a five and dime store. The cameras capture the essence of a person. They either love you or hate you, and they loved Arnold."

Many of Palmer's contemporaries hated television. Palmer made speeches about how important it was to the Tour. When the skins games became popular, director Don Ohlmeyer said: "Arnold is welcome at the skins as long as he can lift a club. When he won most of the money one year three photographs of the event appeared on the front page of the L.A. Times. Arnold turns the public on."

Television was good for Arnold Palmer, and for golf. Tournaments with Palmer became high drama, where he staged famous last minute charges. "The guys used to kid me, and the galleries too," Palmer said of himself. "'Arnie always waits till the cameras come on to start making the putts!'… In a lot of cases that's what happened. I just happened to make putts on the few remaining holes to win tournaments. And that captured the imagination of the audiences."

Palmer's enormous popularity transformed him into a marketing phenomenon. International Management Group's founder, Mark McCormack, started with Palmer as sole client and very soon he was a millionaire as well. Palmer was so much in demand, he was besieged not only by advertisers, charities, and autograph hounds, but also by politicians who wanted him to run for public office first in Pennsylvania and then nationally. The golfer turned down all offers. When at home in Latrobe Palmer usually could be found at a workshop he had built where he could relax and tinker with golf club designs. What began as an unwanted job repairing broken clubs at his father's pro shop during the Second World War evolved into Palmer's chief hobby later in life, as he endlessly tinkered with shaft weights, grips, and lofts. His shop was crammed with drills, grinders, power saws, and other machinery.

In subsequent years he shuttled back and forth between Florida and Pennsylvania, constantly in the limelight and winning consistently. He won the Masters again in 1962 and 1964, won the British Open in 1962, and was the Vardon Trophy winner in those years. No one could attract the crowds the way he did. His appearance in any event was enough to guarantee the sponsors a profit, and his face in a commercial was enough to sell virtually any product. He liked to emphasize the competitive, individualistic aspect of pro golf. "My attitude was that I wasn't just trying to win money. I wanted to win the golf tournament," he said. When Palmer turned 50 and was playing the fledgling Seniors Tour at a reduced level of skill, he still was quick to challenge anyone who looked as if he were going through the motions merely to pick up a paycheck.

> The Senior Tour is a wonderful thing for active guys. The seniors we are looking at now, the just over fifty group, are the first guys who came out of what I consider the modern era — the playing pros; the professional golfers, not the golf professionals. A lot of them haven't gone into club jobs, so the Senior Tour is a break for them. It gives them added life. Yet, a lot of them aren't accepting it as well as they should. They aren't contributing as well as they should. Some of their attitudes are exactly the same as they were twenty-five years ago — that is, just let me play and leave me alone. That's bad because the Senior Tour needs players who are gracious and who enjoy the game and let the people supporting senior golf know they are enjoying it.

Palmer had reached a pinnacle far above other golf pros. He had achieved a fame that transcended the sport, and he saw no reason others could not achieve the same results with good intentions and hard work. He occasionally criticized the influence of the media, and he went out of his way to defend younger players who were often mocked for blandness. Producers were quick to respond, however. NBC's Larry Cirillo said, "God knows we try. If there were more Fuzzy Zoellers, Lee Trevinos, and Chi Chi's golf would be the most watched sport on television."

Arnold Palmer's contributions to golf are incalculable. His peers acknowledged their debt to him without reservation. The success of the Senior Tour was attributed almost wholly to Palmer, despite the many other colorful pros who played from week to week, and his name on a program announcement for a skins game translated into high TV ratings even in the late 1990s.

Arnold Palmer may have occupied center stage on the Tour in the 1950s and beyond, but there were many other charismatic stars continuing successful careers from preceding decades. Snead, for example, continued to play strongly, as did Hogan. Cary Middlecopf was one of the most admired players on tour, and Tommy Bolt was among the most colorful and idiosyncratic of all professional golfers, although he never achieved the success his contemporaries anticipated. Ben Hogan said that "If Bolt had a head on his shoulders he would have been the best golfer who ever lived!"

Tommy Bolt's father was a carpenter in Shreveport, Louisiana. When Tom was 12 he started caddying at a local course for 50 cents a bag, 18 holes. Tom liked the caddie life. "A kid could go a long way on fifty cents," he remembered.

> We bought food, went to the movies, bought cigarettes. We'd buy cigarettes at five for a nickel. They'd bust open a package and sell 'em individually. I liked caddying. That caddie pen was wild. We'd fight over anything that came along. We played cards, shot dice, bet dimes and quarters on everything. They were pretty good days. I learned a lot about the way of the world.... On Saturdays we had to give the caddiemaster four golf balls to play nine holes. We had to go out on the golf course and find balls and give them to him. He wasn't supposed to charge us like that, but he was a big guy and nobody threatened him. We started at five a.m. and played until noon. Oh I just ate it up. I loved it from the start! My first set of clubs cost $15.00. I knew I wanted to be a professional golf player early on, from the time I was twelve. I had to work at other trades to get there, but I knew what I wanted to be.

When Tommy was asked to talk about the tournaments he remembered from his days on the road, he immediately began to talk about Augusta National.

> I guess I always was envious of people who had a lot of money but didn't earn it. That's what the people there were about mainly. The first time Lee Trevino went there Clifford Roberts treated him like a caddie. I know because I was there. Trevino wouldn't eat in the clubhouse where they had free steaks and all that. He ate sandwiches with the caddies in the caddie pen. That's what Clifford Roberts made him feel like, and that's why Trevino dislikes Augusta. Also they always ruled in Arnold Palmer's favor. Oh Yeah! One time Arnold put his ball in the bunker on the second hole, tried to hit it out but left it in there, then slammed his club into the sand. Yes, Arnold Palmer had a temper. So Jack Tuthill said, "That's two shots. You grounded your club, Arnold. Add two shots to your score." Arnold was in danger of missing the cut but by the time he finished the Masters Committee took the penalty away so he could qualify for the last thirty-six holes. They did that so he would be there over the weekend. This kind of thing happened a lot back then.

Bolt quickly acquired a reputation for volatility, which seemed to grow over the years. But he asserted that throwing clubs for him was merely a routine designed to entertain fans. "The writers had me to write about. You know that!" Bolt insisted.

> I got a lot more than I deserved, but people recognized who I was. That reputation made me a lot of money. Once at the Colonial in Forst Worth Porky Oliver and I weren't playing very well so we made up this little game. I pretended to be about to throw my club after missing a putt on eighteen and Porky ran over, took it from me, and just tossed it in the bag gently.... Everyone knows Bobby Jones threw clubs. Arnold Palmer when he was young threw clubs with the best of them, that was before Mark McCormack changed him. And Bob Rosburg! I played behind him once and he shattered eighteen tee markers in a row with his club. One on every tee. And there never was a guy like Lefty Stackhouse. He'd plunge his hand into a thornbush, telling it, "Take that!" because the hand misbehaved during the shot. Sam Snead broke a lot of putters. I saw Chi Chi throw a fit in Las Vegas a few years ago, kicking his bag with both feet and cussing in Spanish because he wasn't playing well and nobody was following him. We're all human.

Bolt's walk, a defiant swagger, epitomized the man. He marched with his head thrown back, weight on his heels, expecting trouble and often finding it. Sometimes he would take his young son along when giving an exhibition. "Get up and show the folks what I taught you," Tommy would command his son. Whereupon the boy would hurl a nine-iron 50 yards in the air.

Bolt called Ben Hogan the only teacher he ever had. As a caddie he had watched other pros and modeled his game after theirs. As with so many other players from those decades his game was almost entirely self-designed, but the compliment to Hogan was genuine. Bolt won the 1958 U.S. Open, but that was his only major victory. Looking back to that triumph Tommy said,

> One thing I'll always remember about the Open I won at Southern Hills was my caddie. He was a little Indian kid and had never caddied before. That was fine with me. A caddie can make mistakes you know, and I always preferred to make my own mistakes. He just cleaned my ball and clubs, held the pin. Anyway, after I won I gave that little guy $500.00, and you've never seen such a happy kid in your life. Years later somebody told me about him. He went on to college, graduated and came back to Tulsa. He did well ... I thought, I don't need to do anything else now. I'm the U.S. Open champion. And I didn't. I only won two tournaments after that. I won some lesser known tournaments, but no more majors. I did a lot of endorsements. They weren't worth as much as they would be today, but I had a contract with Eastman Kodak and a club contract with Ram Golf. I won $8,000 in the Open. Today, they get what, $800,000? But that's all right, I'm happy with the way things are.

When Hogan was asked for a list of the finest players he had ever seen, he said: "Snead, Nelson, Nicklaus,..." He paused, glanced over his shoulder at Bolt strutting down the fairway and pronounced: "You see that fellow over there? If we could have screwed another head on his shoulders he would have been the greatest golfer who ever lived!" And Tom Weiskopf, who spent so much time with Bolt, had nothing but fond memories of his mentor. "Those four and one-half hours you spend on the golf course are no measure of a human being. Sure, Tommy's walked off a number of times but he's such a gentle guy and unbelievably patient when it doesn't concern his game."

When Tommy Bolt was asked if he had any regrets about his uncontrollable temper, or if he wished he had done things differently, he replied:

"No. It was better than being a caddie!"

Another colorful contemporary, the exact opposite of Tommy Bolt, was Cary Middlecopf. He rivaled Hogan and Snead for being one of the most consistent winners on tour. Two times U.S. Open champion, plus one Masters, Middlecopf played fewer than 20 tournaments a year, choosing to spend most of his time as pro at the Diplomat Club in North Hollywood, Florida. He had left a dentistry career to play golf, won more than 40 tournaments, then passed into semi-retirement at age 40. Cary was typical of the many great players who suffered severely with bad discs or other back aliments. He went to the Mayo Clinic in 1963 after enduring pain and muscle spasms for six or seven years. X-rays were unable to pinpoint the problem, but surgery revealed that he had a completely fragmented disc in his spine. Surgery was successful in Middlecopf's case, but the enormous strain created by the acceleration and torque of a golf swing meant that tournament golf and constant practice for Middlecopf were no longer feasible.

When told that he had a reputation as an extremely slow player, Middlecopf responded:

> I don't guess I was as slow as they said. Seems like I remember some national open two or three years ago where they took five hours and something a round. I read that the U.S. Open compared to ten years ago averaged about a full hour longer per round. There are a lot of fast players and a lot of slow players, and a lot of medium players. I don't think anyone who gets a tag for being a slow or fast player, whatever it is, ever loses it. Jack Nicklaus has speeded up his pace of play quite a bit, but he doesn't get any credit for it. I was very slow at times, but I got most of my reputation because I used to have tremendous trouble with hay fever. I'd get it in Jacksonville, and each week as we'd go north, we'd catch a new spring coming in. I'd have three months of it.... I was a very deliberate player, but I didn't get much sympathy for the cause of it.

Between 1945 and 1961, Middlecopf compiled 39 PGA Tour victories. Statistically one of the most impressive golfers of any generation, he played against the best competition ever assembled, then faded quietly away to let younger men contend. "I think the players obviously are getting better," he said in 1968. "I don't think the two or three super players that you have in each generation are better. But there are more of the next step of players—the guys who can win a tournament."

It's hard to find a better rags to riches story in golf than Orville Moody's.

Born and raised in rural Oklahoma, Moody was the state amateur champ in 1952 but dropped out of college to enlist in the Army. Most of his duty assignments had more than a little to do with golf. He won the All-Army title in 1958, in which he shot the best round of his life, a 63. He hit out of bounds on the first hole before birdying 11 straight. In 1959 he represented the Army in a tournament against the Marines, who were represented by Lee Trevino. Orville won that tournament by 18 strokes.

Moody decided not to reenlist but to try his fortune on the PGA Tour. Playing poorly and without financial resources to fall back on, he again looked to the Army. This time he stayed for four years. Upon returning to the States he entered the PGA Qualifying School and became a full-time player the following season. In 1969 he stunned the golf world by winning the U.S. Open.

When Moody won the Open, columnist Jim Murray wrote: "It was like unhitching a horse from a plow and winning the Kentucky Derby, or a guy stepping out of the audience, removing his coat and knocking out the heavyweight champion of the world." President Nixon got the shell shocked Moody on a telephone connection in the clubhouse immediately following his victory for one of the strangest conversations between two golfers in memory. Then Lee Trevino's agent signed Moody for a wide-ranging array of opportunities. One was with the U.S. Army Post Exchange system to sell red, white, and blue golf clothing worldwide.

Then a series of misfortunes occurred. Moody divorced his second wife and remarried. The house he signed over to his former bride burned and Moody and his new spouse were inexplicably found responsible for the damages. Some of his modest winnings were garnisheed to pay the suit. Then he loaned $30,000 to his sister and her spouse to start a restaurant. The couple soon unloaded the restaurant and Moody lost all the money. He entered into a contract to lease the Lake Arbor Golf Club in Denver. The project drained $200,000 from Moody's pockets before he gave up and considered bankruptcy. In addition to all his other woes he required a special exemption to continue playing the Tour because he had failed to enter the minimum number of events. When he resumed regular play, his putting was inconsistent. He played the Japanese Tour without notable success. His putting yips had grown progressively worse, so that he was averaging only $25,000 a year in winnings. Many pros thought him the best ball striker on tour, but Bob Toski described his putting best: "How bad is he on the short ones? For someone at the level he plays on, he's as bad as I've ever seen. Anytime he gets within four or five feet, you literally want to go over and help the guy." Toski recalled one round he played with Moody when he four-putted from ten feet, and tried hard on all of them.

> I was the kind that always got nervous, and I tried everything to cure the problem. I putted with my eyes closed. I putted looking at the hole. I putted watching the

putter go back. I putted cross-handed. I putted split-handed. I even putted sidesaddle. I tried almost everything.... I had problems putting even in my army days, when I was playing my best golf. When I was at home and had the confidence I played great. Conventional grip and everything. But I'd go into the army tournaments and I'd always have to switch to cross-handed because I couldn't make the three and four-footers.

Moody never won again on the regular Tour after his U.S. Open victory. But when he turned 50, his life was transformed. In his first year on the Senior Tour, 1984, he captured three tournaments and $200,000. He was now putting cross-handed with a toeshafted putter. When he hit the ball, Moody allowed his upper body to move forward. On short putts he seemed to slide the ball at the hole with his whole body. "I have to steer it," he explained. "I couldn't release it if I didn't move. If I got the putter back and tried to hit the ball without moving my head I'd give it a flip, a jerk."

Early in 1984 he won at Daytona Beach, then finished first again at the Tournament of Champions. He was fifth on the money list, posting $184,000, but then the yips reemerged worse than ever. "Holding that putter was like trying to hold a rattlesnake," Moody complained. "I didn't have any confidence at all. I'd get over a three-footer and just hope I didn't fan it." Other players blanched when they tried to watch him stroke putts. One day at the Seiko-Tucson Match Play event, TV commentator Bruce Devlin said: "If you had to pick one man you would not want putting for your life it would be Moody!"

One day on the practice green Moody noticed Charlie Owens with a long-shafted putter. Overnight the 50-inch putter improved his scoring dramatically, and he posted a dozen top ten finishes in the months following, won four events and $400,000 to push his career earnings over the $1 million mark. For the 1989 Senior Open he traveled to Arnold Palmer's Laurel Valley course and defeated Frank Beard on the final day to win the championship. Moody's daughter Michelle caddied for her father and helped read putts. Aided by that and by the new longer putter, he shot a Senior Open record 64. The new shaft cured what had been a "terrible jerk" in his stroke, and carried him to a victory over Beard, Don Bies, and Al Geiberger. The tournament was worth $80,000 to Moody. He gave all the credit to the long putter and his caddie. Other players who earlier could not bear to watch Orville stand over putts now took up the beanpole shaft. Gay Brewer, Harold Henning, and Jim Ferree followed his lead.

Another immensely talented star of Palmer's opening years, one who may have rivaled Walter Hagen for flamboyance and popularity if only he had enjoyed more time, was the uniquely hedonistic Tony Lema.

Lema grew up in a tough section of Oakland California. His father died when Tony was three. He began caddying at a very early age and played golf as much as circumstances allowed. After high school he joined the Marine Corps and served in Korea as a forward artillery observer. At home after the war he played for the Marine golf team in various inter-service events, then took his discharge and headed back to Oakland. On his first day at home he was stopped for driving 70 in a 50-MPH zone, and the highway patrolman turned out to be a former golfing buddy who tore up the ticket and passed along the news of an opening at the San Francisco Golf Club. Lema drove to the club and got the job of assistant pro. He progressed rapidly, qualified for the 1956 U.S. Open in Rochester, and made the cut but finished in next-to-last place.

Following Lema's Open performance, he landed a position as head pro at a nine-hole course in Elko, Nevada. The job at a small course in a dusty gambling town gave Lema sufficient opportunities for practice, and he soon won the Idaho and Montana Opens. There he attracted a sponsor who put up $200 a week in exchange for one-third of any winnings.

The first tournament he played was the 1957 Imperial Valley Open, whose total purse was $5000, yet many of the leading pros of the day were there. Lema played well, and in the last round he sank a long birdie putt on the 17th green, then drained a 60-footer on the 18th to record a 65. In a sudden death playoff, he won the tournament.

Next it was off to the PGA Tour for the 1958 season and contests with Palmer, Mike Souchak, Art Wall, Don January, Julius Boros, Tommy Bolt, and other leading players. He soon made close friends of Johnny Pott, Jim Ferree, Gary Player, and Tommy Jacobs. He finished in the top 40 money winners that year, taking home about $10,000. He eagerly looked forward to the 1959 season, tinkering with his swing to produce a more accurate left to right rotation and a high trajectory. The sponsor enhanced the terms of their contract in a way that Lema thought at the time was mutually beneficial.

At the opener in Los Angeles he finished 17th and watched Ken Venturi edge out Art Wall, then hurt a disc in his back at the Bing Crosby Clambake before recovering to enter the San Diego tournament. After two rounds he was in fifth place only two shots behind Mike Souchak, then collapsed.

A large part of the fault was Lema's libertine style. Later and later hours and unceasing conviviality were not conducive to consistent golf. A quick temper and erratic schedules did not help. He withdrew from tournaments often after shooting high scores, and it wasn't until 1961 that his behavior moderated. A friend from that time recalled: "I don't think he had much money, but you never would have guessed it. We'd be staying at the same hotel and I'd always see him in the barbershop getting a manicure, or having his shoes shined in the lobby. He traveled first class."

Always keenly observant, Lema took from successful friends lessons that eventually helped change his life. He won three tournaments in 1962 and finished second in two others. This was the year he acquired the nickname "Champagne Tony." Leading in the third round of the Orange County Open, Lema told the reporters in the press room that if he won, the next day there would be champagne for all. He took the playoff against Bob Rosburg, and the champagne arrived as announced.

The following year Lema married Betty Cline, and his new spouse provided much-needed stability. He was fourth on the Tour money list that year, and received an invitation to play in his first Masters. Staying with the Venturis and Byron Nelsons, Lema played several practice rounds with Venturi, who had lost the tournament in 1960 by one shot to Palmer.

Lema played strongly during the first three rounds of the tournaments. On the final day he was in fourth place only three shots back of Jack Nicklaus. Sam Snead and Gary Player also were in contention but faltered on the closing holes. Lema birdied the difficult 18th hole to pull within one stroke of Nicklaus, who was in the last group of the day. On 18 Nicklaus hit his approach shot 40 feet above the hole and suddenly Lema — sharing drinks with Bobby Jones, Clifford Roberts, and Arnold Palmer in the clubhouse — saw he had a chance to tie if Nicklaus three-putted. The first putt rolled four feet below the cup. Then Nicklaus rammed it home to win.

Despite the loss, Lema's second-place finish and long television exposure brought him more attention than he had gained up to that time. Freddy Corcoran signed on as his business manager, and endorsement offers poured in. The following season, Lema won four tournaments including the British Open.

Tony Lema died in a plane crash following the 1966 PGA Championship. The Lemas had chartered a small plane to take them from Akron to Chicago for a pro-am. During the flight both engines stalled and the pilot glided down to attempt a landing on the Lansing Sportsman's Golf Course. Just before touchdown the pilot swerved to avoid some people who were in the flight path. The aircraft bounced heavily, veered into the edge of a pond, and burst into flames. No one survived.

One of the few men who could challenge Tony Lema's popularity with the galleries was Doug Sanders, the Cedartown, Georgia native nicknamed the "Peacock of the Fairway." Sanders lived next to Cedartown's golf course and began caddying there at age ten. By the age of 17 he was working as an assistant to the pro. Offered a scholarship at the University of Florida, Doug stayed for three years before leaving to sell insurance and to play amateur tournaments nationwide. In 1956 he was the first amateur to win the Canadian Open, and the following year he turned pro.

Every decade of American golf presented an unofficial fashion model, Hagen in the '20s, Gene Sarazen in the '30s, Jimmy Demaret in the '40s, and probably the most flamboyant of them all, Doug Sanders in the '50s and '60s and on into the '80s and '90s on the Senior Tour.

"I spent thousands of dollars every year for clothes," Sanders said in 1969.

Palmer enjoys planes. Nicklaus loves planes and boats. Well I enjoy jewelry and clothes. However, I don't want people to think I'm just a fashion plate. I want them also to go back and check my golf record. I think it can stand by itself. It just makes me so comfortable knowing that regardless of how many great players there are, what they are shooting, how long their drives are or how good they're putting, I am as well dressed as if not better than anyone on the golf course. It makes me feel refreshed to be able to look down and know that my shoes are clean and my shirt if the best quality money can buy. I'm very fortunate, and knock on wood, that I have the type figure or build that allows me to wear different styles and look fairly decent in them. The average male does not seem to have the ability to coordinate colors well. All too often I see golfers who look as if they dressed in the dark. They've got on green and yellow and red and blue and pink, and everything combined, and they think they look very clever because it's all good quality merchandise. I've even had people come to me and say, "You know, the only reason I bought color TV is to see what you wear." This is fashion consciousness. I have even worn white and white — an entirely white outfit. They call me the White Knight.

Between 1956 and 1975 Sanders won 20 PGA Tour events and finished second 21 times, a very, very impressive record that is often overlooked when fans think of Doug Sanders.

The antithesis of Doug Sanders in the 1950s was Billy Casper. His first Tour victory was the 1956 Labatt Open, and he won a total of ten events in the 1950s. He went on to become only the third golfer in history (after Palmer and Nicklaus) to win a million dollars in prize money. The big lift for Casper came when physicians began to successfully treat his allergies. Like Cary Middlecopf, Casper suffered severely from hay fever. In addition to that he also was found to be allergic to many natural substances in foods. When put on a strict diet his weight dropped from 230 pounds to 185. His penchant for buffalo meat earned him a lot of press during those years, as did his active attempts to be friendlier toward the galleries and press. When asked for a description of Casper, Gene Sarazen offered the following:

> When Casper came onto the tournament scene he was a jolly fat man with a taste for beer. He was one of the boys, well liked all round. His game was correspondingly flamboyant, a foot-dragging, shut faced style unique unto himself that had him knocking the ball all over the lot, from where he would make spectacular recoveries that led to many one-putt greens. In only a few years though, Casper's personality seemed to change. He asked that the Billy be reduced to the more staid Bill. He became a cold fish loner and less popular among some of the tour players. Bill agrees with this somewhat harsh appraisal. As he explains it, when he became a winner and a public figure, he felt a larger degree of responsibility toward those who now looked up to him as a hero, and to himself to maintain his newly acquired stature.... He withdrew more and more within himself, and the surface picture became one of a stern, precise, nononsense professional. On another level, Casper, son of a broken home, raised in the pastel shaded, whimsical environment of southern California, began to seek a more solid, disciplined foundation on which to build his life. He has become very much a solid family man, with three natural children and four more by way of adoption. And, he has come to religion and the Mormon Church.

Billy Casper (©PGA Tour).

When golf fans learned of Casper's conversion to Mormonism and his food allergies they began to send very unusual letters. One fan wrote:

Dear Mr. Casper:
    I have read that you are a Mormon and that you don't smoke or drink. Statistics show that the average American male smokes thirty-seven and one-half cartons of cigarettes a year and drinks forty-two gallons of liquor. I would appreciate your sending me your unused cartons of cigarettes and gallons of liquor because I do smoke and drink.

Another fan was even more specific.

Dear Billy:
    I read in the papers where you will make over $100,000 this year. I'm sure you don't need that much money and I do. I don't know much about business or taxes but I think you could claim me as a dependent if I didn't work no more and you could send me money and have me as a dependent. Do you have a dependent? I sure would be proud to be your dependent?

Despite the odd requests, Casper's business manager said that Billy answered every letter he received. And some of his contemporaries sympathized with his situation. Despite an enviable record and solid all-around talent, Casper was overshadowed throughout his career by more charismatic players. Dave Hill claimed that

> For years I considered Casper the most underrated player on tour. When Palmer and Player and Nicklaus were getting headlines as the Big Three, a label trumped up by their business manager with little justification, Casper was playing better golf. He never got the ink because he didn't have Mark McCormack managing him and he didn't have as much personality as a glass of water.

Billy Casper won 51 PGA tournaments and finished second 36 times. He won a U.S. Open and a Masters, and won the Vardon Trophy five times. On the Senior Tour he continued to play well. His weight had climbed back to well over 230, and his plus-fours and unusual putting style drew many quizzical spectators. Sarazen thought it was the most unusual putting technique to be seen anywhere. "I wouldn't recommend his style to anybody because it suits him and nobody else," Gene commented. "He hits that ball so hard it would give you a heart attack to see it go toward the hole. How many people could putt that way?"

Frank Beard was a man who compiled impressive statistics on the PGA Tour, but like Casper he never achieved the recognition of more charismatic players. Beard wrote books about his life on the Tour and he had his share of trouble with critics, at home and on the circuit. In his columns for magazines he took gentle digs at his fellow competitors, especially the superstars who attracted the galleries and major endorsements. Despite finishing on top in the money standings, Beard never attracted a large following, and he was accused more than once of being a Scrooge. He disparaged the close affinity some players had with caddies, and poked fun at the reliance of those who depended on caddies to line up putts. And he had fixed views on compensation:

> I work on a weekly basis. Some caddies and players who do this have an agreement before the week starts, but I won't do that. The only time a caddie came to me with an agreement beforehand I told him to go find another deal. I won't be worked on like that. I'll pay the caddie what I feel like paying him. Through the years I've been accused of being a cheapskate. But I feel like paying for what I get. I've never gotten much free in my life, I don't think very many people have. But some of these caddies expect it. I had a local caddie at Westchester in 1969, and he was supposed to be one of the best. On the first two holes I checked him on the yardage, and he was ten to twenty yards off, so I just never consulted him again. All he did was carry my bag and keep the clubs clean. Well I won the tournament and the $50,000 first prize. I was going to give him $500 but Dick Schaap, the magazine editor who helped me write my book, talked me into giving him $750 to keep the press off my back. When I gave the boy the check he just exploded.... Called me every name in the book right there in front of the clubhouse. I told him if he could tell me why he really deserved any more than $100 for all he contributed, I'd be glad to pay it. He said that everybody did it, that it was part of the deal. Not for me it wasn't!

Beard was considered to be one of the more cerebral men playing the Tour, but some contemporaries regarded him as humorless and preoccupied with business. He played briefly but well on the Senior Tour, then signed on as a television commentator.

In marked contrast to the rotund Casper and dapper Sanders was a foreign player whose shot-making attracted many new fans. Gary Player came to the United States from South Africa in 1959 when he was 19. The Hogan Company offered $2,800 if Gary endorsed Ben's golf equipment, but First Flight came up with a $9,000 counter-offer. Player went on to win a Masters and a PGA Championship and in subsequent decades he was a force on the PGA Tour. When he turned 50 he hit the Senior Tour with similar effect. Player's near obsession with winning at all costs was not leavened with the grace of Nicklaus or Palmer, and there was much humorous talk concerning his intellect among reporters who were subjected to repeated platitudes and clichés on subjects not necessarily connected to golf. He worked long hours on his game.

"I wanted the practice ground to be mine," Gary said on one occasion. "I resented anyone else being there. I never went away until the rest had gone. I made myself be the last to leave." He was fond of introducing changes to his diet and lifestyle and announcing them with fanfare, first that bananas improved fitness, then raisins helped concentration, peanuts provided strength, and black shirts and pants absorbed the sun's beneficial heat.

Gary Player (©PGA Tour).

Whether his pronouncements were sound or not was unimportant since Gary believed them so implicitly they seemed to work for him if for no one else. With much talk about one-dimensional golfers by television commentators, Gary Player stood out always. Was he the man who tried to one-up every opponent in a single-minded obsession to win at any cost? Or was he the God fearing, simple-minded humanitarian he liked to portray fro the press? One moment he could be engaged in bitter tirades with galleries or foes, for example arguing with Tom Watson about rule infractions, and the next he could be heard uttering platitudes for the sportswriters. Nevertheless, he won 21 PGA Tour events and finished second 33 times. He is one of only four players to win all four of the major championships in golf, joining Gene Sarazen, Ben Hogan, and Jack Nicklaus.

The 1960s

"*Jack Nicklaus and I have been friends for a long time, and he is always a gentleman. He always compliments you when you're playing well, and he's a great champion. The thing is ... it seems he's always one stroke better than me!*"

— Tom Weiskoff

When John F. Kennedy was elected president in 1960, he pursued golf with almost as much ardor as his predecessor. Kennedy was said by companions to consistently score in the high 70s or low 80s, despite omnipresent back trouble and other health ailments.

As with the national government, the decade of the 1960s saw a younger generation take over the PGA Tour. In those years golfers could apply to the PGA for tournament player status. If approved, a player was able to enter tournaments for five years before becoming a full PGA member. All the PGA demanded was a background check and letters of recommendation from club pros before approving an application.

A screening committee comprising five full-time PGA staff and four touring players made the final decision. A typical tournament of the era might have 150 places, but three-quarters of those could be filled by exemptions, those who had been among the top 50 money winners or who had made the cut in the previous week's event. Anyone else was compelled to play an 18-hole qualifying round on the Monday preceding a tournament, and the highest finishers made the entrance field on Thursday. In a popular event there might be only 20 slots available to the qualifiers, who came to be known as rabbits.

In 1965 touring players became dissatisfied with the management of the PGA. Thomas Crane had served as the organization's executive director for more than 20 years. He and the PGA president ran the association with methods the touring pros considered too conservative. It was an association controlled by several thousand club pros, and the touring pros continued to seek more influence. The incident that brought both sides to incipient warfare was the PGA's decision to deny Frank Sinatra a rich tournament in Palm Springs because it would encroach on the Bob Hope Tournament. The loss of this prize money angered many touring pros and they began to think about starting a separate tour.

Dave Marr was chairman of the tournament committee in 1964, but his and other pros' efforts to strike a truce did not succeed. There were many complaints about scheduling conflicts that pitted the Western Open against dates for the British Open, and the rich World Series of Golf against dates for the Denver Open. Another source of conflict was the top-heavy bureaucracy of the PGA, whose executive committee contained only one touring pro. The committee had ultimate authority for scheduling, as well as myriad other vital matters.

The most important item on the touring pros' agenda was to create a managing director for the tour, a man who would report directly to the players instead of to the PGA. Some players wanted a very strong personality for the job and recommended Ben Hogan. "Not that strong!" countered others. In addition, touring players sought to have fields reduced from about 150 entrants for a typical tournament to 100, with automatic exemptions for all but a small number of players to be admitted from the newly established Tour qualifying school.

Relations between the touring pros and the PGA deteriorated further when Gardner Dickinson, Doug Ford, Frank Beard, Jack Nicklaus, and others decided to form a rival organization called the Association of Professional Golfers. A commissioner was named, and sponsors of tournaments were organized. By 1968 most of the touring pros were ready to join the rival organization. The PGA contacted its tournament sponsors, but only two supported the traditional organization against the touring pros. The rest were not interested in hosting tournaments that lacked the sport's major stars.

Then the PGA tried to enlist long term supporters in opposition to the new group. Only Sam Snead showed up. Arnold Palmer, trying to act the role of peacemaker, offered a compromise plan, but the PGA rejected it, whereupon Palmer joined the rival group. Late in 1968 Gardner Dickinson announced that 28 events had been scheduled by the new tour with purses totaling $3.5 million.

At that point the PGA caved in. A new president of the PGA, Leo Fraser, fashioned a compromise. He agreed to form a Tournament Players Division within the PGA that would have a ten-man policy board. Joe Dey, Jr., was named commissioner of the new organization. Dey was a former head of the USGA and widely known and respected in golf. The possibility of a permanent fracturing of the PGA was avoided. Players' incomes immediately rose. Prize money on the Tour had risen by about $150,000 between 1958 and 1961, and by $300,000 between 1961 and 1967. The following year, with redistribution of television rights and other adjustments, total prize money jumped by more than $1 million.

In 1960 the U.S. Open was held at Cherry Hills. The event was momentous for several reasons. Although spectators could not know it at the time, the 1960 Open marked the zenith of Ben Hogan's career. Never again would he come as close to winning a championship. He almost did win, falling back only on the final holes after a disastrous miscalculation in strategy that was wholly uncharacteristic. Cherry Hills also marked the emergence of amateur Jack Nicklaus, who played with Hogan and almost won as well.

Tommy Bolt put on one of his best performances. After hitting a shot into the pond on number 12, he began to argue with an official about the proper place to take a drop. Continuing a slow boil, Bolt three-putted the next green, bogeyed the next, then proceeded to hit two drives into another pond. With all his strength he flung the driver far out into the water and turned away just as a boy dove into the lake and swam to the spot where the club had disappeared. In a moment he was back on the surface and swimming toward shore. The gallery began to cheer as Bolt approached the shore to retrieve his club. But instead of returning the driver to Bolt, the boy took off for the fences with the driver gripped in his fist.

To cap this extraordinary championship, Arnold Palmer shot a 65 on the final day to win the tournament. There would be other momentous days for Palmer, but few fans at the time could have imagined that this tournament was the highlight of his career. Afterwards he would gradually concede his throne to a new challenger — the much younger and vastly talented Jack Nicklaus.

The rivalry of Jack Nicklaus and Arnold Palmer, which began in 1960 and continued into the 1990s, constituted one of the most entertaining matchups in American sports. In the 1990s the two superstars still exulted at beating one another in skins games or in senior events where Palmer frequently was a surprise winner in spite of his age. Palmer was still adored by the galleries to an extent unrivaled since Bobby Jones.

"The one person Arnold always wants to beat," Mrs. Winnie Palmer confessed, "is Jack Nicklaus. They are not chums. There's a ten year age gap and Arnold is inclined to treat Jack as a youngster, which Jack probably resents. And I'm sure he doesn't appreciate Arnold's advice with which Arnold is apt to be fairly free."

Jack Nicklaus's background was very different from Arnold Palmer's. His father had been an all-around athlete in high school and college. Charles Nicklaus began to play golf in his teens, graduated from Ohio State with a degree in pharmacy in 1935, and joined the Scioto Country Club in Columbus, site of Bobby Jones's 1926 U.S. Open victory. When son Jack was ten, a famous teaching pro moved to Scioto. Jack Grout grew up on the Glen Garden Club in Fort Worth with Ben Hogan and Byron Nelson, and from there he joined Henry Picard as assistant pro at the Hershey Country Club, eventually landing a job of his own at Scioto. He had won two PGA Tour events, but his true metier seemed to be teaching.

Jack Nicklaus (©PGA Tour).

In 1950 young Nicklaus started taking weekly lessons from Grout. The first nine holes he played, Jack scored a 51. Before the summer ended he posted a 95 for 18 holes. After two years of additional lessons and frequent play, Jack was able to card an 81 at Scioto. The summer he was 12, Jack shot eight straight 80s. Ready to give up trying to vault that barrier he surprised everyone by breaking through with a 74, then the following summer broke 70 for the first time.

Charlie Nicklaus and Jack Grout believed that Jack should be entered in as many tournaments as possible, and at age 13 he began to play in local amateur events. By age 16, he had captured the Ohio State Open. Charlie traveled with Jack to tournaments and reveled in his son's success. But when Grout and Charlie thought the young man was developing an oversized ego, they were quick to point out how Bobby Jones had won his club's junior championship at age nine, the Georgia State Amateur title at 14, and the Southern Amateur Championship at 15.

Matriculated at Ohio State University, Nicklaus continued to play in many amateur tournaments and for the Walker Cup team. In 1959 he won the amateur championship at the Broadmoor Golf Club in Colorado Springs. In 1960 he made the cut at the Masters for the first time, and tied for low amateur with Billy Joe Patton. Later in the year he finished second to Arnold Palmer in the U.S. Open. In July of 1960 he and Barbara were married.

The ensuing honeymoon destination was New York City. The route from Columbus to New York took them past Hershey, about which Grout had reminisced. Stopping at the country club, Jack obtained permission to play and shot a 71 while Barbara spent the day sightseeing. Arriving in New York, they attended a musical on Broadway. Feeling restless the next morning, Nicklaus called Claude Harmon at nearby Winged Foot, telling the famous pro that it would be criminal to have come this far without playing the venerable club.

Harmon arranged everything. Unfortunately it rained the entire day, but Nicklaus played a full 18 with Barbara walking beside him. Back in New York that night they saw another musical. The following morning Nicklaus suggested taking a side trip toward Pine Valley. One of the members took Nicklaus in tow, and he played a complete round at the course that is routinely rated as the best in America. Unfortunately Pine Valley had a men-only rule. Barbara was able to watch her husband hit one or two tee shots from her vantage point on roads bordering the course. In the years to come Mrs. Nicklaus continued to travel with her husband, and in time theirs was considered to be the most stable and prosperous partnership in professional golf.

By 1961 Jack Nicklaus was earning $6,000 a year selling insurance while continuing to collect credits toward a degree at OSU. In November he called a press conference — well attended owing to his stature as the best amateur golfer since Bobby Jones— and announced that he was giving up amateur status to play the pro tour. Mark McCormack became his agent, and he arranged $100,000 in immediate endorsements.

Jack's first tournament as a pro was the 1962 L.A. Open held at Rancho Park, where he won $33.30 for last place. The next stop was San Diego. Here he did much better, finishing in 15th place and winning $550. From there he went on to events in Florida and Texas without rating headlines until the U.S. Open at Oakmont, where he shot four excellent rounds for a 72 hole total of 283 and tied Palmer, who up until that tournament had dominated the 1962 Tour. At Oakmont Palmer was playing in front of a hometown gallery, and during the subsequent playoff the fans clearly were favoring him. Nonetheless, Nicklaus shot a 71 to win the Open Championship.

Nicklaus's first major victory in his first year as a pro put an end to the indifferent confidence he had exhibited in the early part of that year. He went on to win the World Series of Golf, then took the Seattle World's Fair Open, and the Portland Open. His winnings for the year totaled $62,933.

In 1963 Nicklaus won his first Masters. His distance off the tee became a distinct advantage over the competition. At a driving contest during the PGA Championship of that year, Nicklaus won with a smash of 341 yards, and went on to win the tournament at the Dallas Athletic Club. Those two remarkable years of 1962 and 1963 may never be duplicated by any other golfer except Tiger Woods. When he beat Palmer in the playoff in 1962, he became the youngest man to win the U.S. Open. Named "Rookie of the Year" with no disclaimers, Nicklaus won back-to-back Tour stops at Seattle and Portland, won the World Series of Golf and $50,000, finished second in three other tournaments, and in third place on four occasions. He took home a check from all 26 of the events he entered in that inaugural year.

The following season Nicklaus became the youngest-ever winner of the Masters by beating Tony Lema by one stroke. He also won the PGA Championship, and finished in third place in the British Open after bogeying the final two holes. He repeated his victory in the World Series of Golf, pocketed another $50,000, and also won Tour events at the Tournament of Champions, Sahara Invitational, and Palm Springs classic. He finished second in two tournaments, and in third place on three occasions to push his 1963 winnings over $100,000.

In 1964 Nicklaus won four tournaments, and in 1965 five more including the Masters. He was to money winner two years in a row. In 1966 he again wore the green coat at Augusta, then won the British Open to become the youngest golfer in history to win the four major championships. Completing his fifth season as a pro Nicklaus compiled a staggering record for never having finished lower than third in the money standings, and had made the cut in a remarkable 110 of the 114 tour events he entered during 1962–1966. His incomparable play continued through the remainder of the decade.

Nicklaus's first ten years as a pro may be a measure of excellence for as long as golf is played. In 1971, his tenth year on the PGA Tour, Nicklaus's victory in the PGA made him the first golfer to post two victories in each of the four major championships. That year he almost won the U.S. Open and the Masters a third time, failing in a playoff with Lee Trevino at the Open and winding up second in the Masters, only two shots behind the winner. Again he was the year's leading money winner, pushing his total career prize money to $1.5 million.

Nicklaus became concerned about his endurance and physical conditioning at age 30. His weight at about 210 pounds had served him well, no doubt contributing to the power game that so awed his contemporaries. Now he began to lack endurance and remembered a family doctor who many years before had cautioned that he might have to lose weight if he began to tire easily. He read over the major diet plans and selected Weight Watchers. A friend gave all the instructions to Nicklaus, and he avoided the sign-ups and will power meetings other dieters followed. Nicklaus played golf every day, jogged between each shot, and followed the diet plan religiously. In two weeks he lost 20 pounds, dropped eight inches of fat from around his hips and two inches from his thighs, but only one inch from waist and chest. This, of course, called for a new wardrobe.

A radically new Jack Nicklaus appeared at Tour stops. The diet brought him down to 190 pounds. Only 30 years old, he seemed to undergo a metamorphosis. His spirits lightened as he spent long hours in press tents joking with reporters. He continued to lose weight and eventually dropped all the way to 175 pounds. He came to prefer a range from 180–185, which seemed to be the best balance for health and power. Like Arnold Palmer, Nicklaus smoked heavily for several years, but he went from two packs a day to zero on will power alone. At the same time he gave up red meat, and began to spend time each morning on calisthenics and stretching exercises.

Moving to Palm Beach, Nicklaus bought a 37-foot sports fishing boat. He started playing practice rounds at the Lost Tree Golf Club, and spent more time than ever before on the practice range.

"If you play you only hit thirty odd full shots during a four-hour round," he said.

> I can practice for an hour, hit all my clubs, and spend the other three hours fishing. Golf without competition to me just isn't fun. I have always thrived on

competition. The reason I took up golf in the first place was because it was one game you could play by yourself. You against the course. You didn't have to go dragging around the neighborhood hunting for guys to get up a game of football or baseball.... I was a reasonably good quarterback, but the only thing I could do in football by myself was to learn how to kick, and I was a good kicker, a good placekicker, and a good punter. Basketball is the same way. You need other fellows to play with for the game to be really good. I was never a good defensive player and not that good a team player. I was good at shooting because that's the one thing I could practice and do by myself. Baseball was the same. Golf was the only sport at which I could try to become a complete athlete by myself. When I got the golf bug I went overboard. It was nothing for me to go out in the morning in the summertime, hit golf balls for an hour or two, go play eighteen holes, come in, have lunch, hit more golf balls, go out and play eighteen more holes, come back in and hit more balls until dark. Truly, that was nothing — that was a very normal routine for me during my early teens. In the summertime, I doubt if I would miss three days of doing that. We never took vacations, I never went to camp as a kid. I played golf. That's what I wanted to do. I'd occasionally play as many as fifty-four holes a day carrying my own clubs. Once I played sixty-three holes in a day. Sometimes I'd play only thirty-six, but maybe hit 500, 600 balls. Hit em, pick em up, hit em, pick em up.... I was chosen for the Walker Cup team at nineteen, and I won the U.S. Amateur that year. When I turned pro I had one deal with the Ohio State Life Insurance Company and I was just about making my minimum, which was a draw of about $6,000 a year. And I had a $12,000 a year deal doing some traveling and selling insurance for Parker company. And I had another deal, a slacks deal which involved promotions in the cities I traveled to for golf or the insurance business. So I was making over $20,000 a year at age twenty and playing amateur golf. The future looked bright from the dollars standpoint. $20,000 in 1960 was a lot of money. But it really wasn't working out. I had the freedom to play a lot of golf, but the truth was I couldn't afford on that salary to play all the amateur golf I needed to play to become a Bobby Jones.... I couldn't become the greatest that way.... I lost only four matches in three years of amateur golf, and now suddenly I'm a pro, and I'm surprised to win here too. I do not like to get beat. It's as simple as that. Pride is probably my greatest motivation, because I just refuse to get beat. I do not want to get beat, I can't stand to get beat, and I hate to have somebody come along and beat me!

In the late 1960s and early '70s, Nicklaus's power with the driver and finesse at putting placed him at a level that Byron Nelson had enjoyed in his halcyon years. Cary Middlecoff said of Nicklaus during these years:

> He is probably the best player who ever lived, but only time will tell that.... He does everything so well. He's very long. He hasn't driven too well the last couple of years—for him. When Jack is good, he is real good. When he has it going he is overpowering with his distance. He's a tremendous long iron player, and he's improved his short game a lot. And of course, when he was seventeen he had a great mental maturity that most people don't have. He doesn't panic, and he doesn't do too many stupid things on the golf course. That's a tremendous edge. He's a good putter, an excellent putter. He's an inconsistent putter, a little the way I used to be. But when he putts well he is real good. Jack has just

about every thing, including the perfect mental attitude. He's not gonna pressure himself into a upsetting state of mind that could cost him more shots just because he made a few bad ones.

In the late 1960s Nicklaus decided to build a course similar to Augusta National near his hometown of Columbus, Ohio. He commissioned a friend to search for appropriate acreage. A spot was found near Dublin, and the course was finished in 1973. Nicklaus named it Muirfield because his first British Open victory occurred at Muirfield in Scotland. He inaugurated the Memorial Tournament in 1976 at Muirfield, an event that honored golfers who played the game with "conspicuous honor." Deane Beman (PGA Tour Commissioner) cooperated by allocating the Memorial Holiday dates to Nicklaus for his tournament, and a very strong field entered the first event. One exception was Dave Hill, who returned his invitation with the comment that a new tournament did not deserve such favorable treatment.

Nicklaus's persistent attention to detail was nowhere more evident than at the Memorial Tournament. He was fond of relocating portable toilts to inconspicuous locales, of turning ponds into streams, of replacing gallery ropes with new fibers, in short, of doing whatever was necessary to create incomparable conditions at his course. He organized a committee composed of Gerald Ford, Bob Hope, Byron Nelson, Gene Sarazen, and Joe Dey to select the golfer to be honored annually, and from the beginning a distinguished roster was selected that encompassed all the great names in the history of the game excepting Hogan, who was reluctant to travel to Ohio for the induction ceremony.

The design and construction of Muirfield mushroomed into a thriving golf architecture business. Nicklaus first dabbled with architecture when he served as a consultant to Pete Dye at Hilton Head's Harbour Town course. He went on from there to design scores of popular courses, including standouts Glen Abbey, Shoal Creek, Castle Pines, and Desert Highlands. Some tour players alleged that many of those designs favored Nicklaus's own golf game: Long holes, fairly open driving areas, no run-up shots, and demanding iron shots to greens that more often than not slanted left to right (favoring his soft fade). His par-fives were criticized most of all, primarily for a tendency to force players to lay up well back in the fairways. As one critic alleged, "There are no twenty to eighty yard wedge shots at Muirfield. Jack always had trouble with that shot!"

Nicklaus's ego carried him into a maze of business ventures far afield from the tour and architecture. He came to believe that dominating the professional golf universe and successfully managing and personally supervising myriad businesses was not only possible but also practical. A series of denouements in the mid–1980s challenged those assumptions. After his departure from McCormack's IMG in 1969, Nicklaus undertook several entrepreneurial ventures. Under the rubric of Golden Bear Enterprises, Nicklaus's company expanded to include everything from a shrimp farm to a travel agency. Most did well, rolling along as healthily as the Bear's tour record.

In mid-decade two massive real estate developments put his overall finances in jeopardy. Nicklaus had signed on to redesign St. Andrews in New York State and to sell condominiums adjacent to the layout. He also was developing Bear Creek, a community featuring a new Nicklaus-designed course north of San Diego. Imperfect planning almost torpedoed the first development, while sales started slowly at the costly new venture in California. Golden Bear lost millions on those two deals alone, yet other parts of the company also were in trouble and losses mounted at Nicklaus's other real estate developments. Rumors circulated at the time that Golden Bear might be forced into bankruptcy court. At that point Nicklaus retired close friend and CEO Charles Perry, who had directed Golden Bear for the previous six years, and replaced him with Richard Bellinger and a new executive committee.

Then Nicklaus's fortunes were transformed by a near miracle. At age 46 he amazed the golf world by winning the 1986 Masters Tournament. This was followed by a marketing bonanza for any product with the Nicklaus name on it. By 1992 Golden Bear Company was very prosperous again. Nicklaus left MacGregor to team up with Nelson Doubleday and a new line of golf clubs, and his architectural business was booming. Nicklaus was charging as much as $2 million to design courses in Japan, and he was approaching his 100th layout as an architect. Intended as a legacy for his children, Nicklaus's firm had more than 100 employees in offices at New York, Palm Beach, Los Angeles, and Tokyo.

The Masters win not only rekindled business for Golden Bear, it also stirred some of the old competitive fires in Nicklaus himself. Conscious always of his station in the game and never hesitant to speak his mind, Nicklaus watched his Ryder Cup team fall to the Europeans in 1987 at his beloved Muirfield Village.

"I had twelve great players on my team," Nicklaus said following the defeat. "I couldn't have asked for better players, but winning breeds winning and these fellows don't win enough. I know those guys from thirtieth to two hundred on the money list will say: 'There goes Nicklaus again,' but I'm going to keep preaching. Without stars you don't have a tour. The tour is based on stars."

Suddenly reminded of Payne Stewart, Jack was prompted to continue: "How old is he? Thirty? He's won only three PGA tour events in his career. A player as good as he is should have won fifteen by now. You have to taste victory to learn how to win."

The defeated members of Nicklaus's team reacted badly to the headmaster's lecture. The younger players like Stewart and Fred Couples, widely perceived as easy-going underachievers, resented the comments and were in no mood to forgive them. Matters were not improved when Nicklaus's good friend Greg Norman went out of his way to tell reporters why the European players were better shotmakers than the younger American pros. Nicklaus had many complaints about the all-exempt tour and the tendency for younger players to focus on making cuts and paychecks. He and Palmer had nothing but scorn for that approach, and Nicklaus was much freer with his opinions than anyone else. When asked to rank the best competitors in the sport, Nicklaus claimed:

"Gene Sarazen did not bother to hide his competitiveness, but let it work for him as a psychological weapon." He considered that the golfer closest to Sarazen in this respect was Hale Irwin, who

> cannot help showing his intense competitiveness, his will to win, in his facial expressions and general mannerisms, and sometimes when the fires burn particularly strong, even in his conversation.... Bobby Jones seemed to combine strength and suppleness in an ideal blend. So, probably more than any other great golfer, does Sam Snead. Both were naturally blessed with great mind/muscle or hand/eye coordination, which was probably the source of their great tempo and rhythm. The one quality above all others that makes a champion, at golf or anything else, that one indispensable quality is desire. Desire to excel is the motivator, the ultimate thriving force. Ben Hogan is famous for having practiced probably more than any other great golfer, and that reflects huge amounts of dedication and self discipline. The same is true of Henry Cotton and Gary Player. Both of them, not being inherently powerful, disciplined themselves with vigorous physical conditioning programs and generally spartan life styles on top of their back breaking golfing regiments. You can miss an awful lot in life when you dedicate yourself totally to one activity, but for many who want to be champions it is the only way to get there. If I had to pick one mental characteristic above all others that has produced champions I think it probably would be will power: The will to achieve, to excel, to be the best, to win. And the fellow I'd choose to exemplify this quality is my old sparring partner Arnold Palmer.

Nicklaus's 1986 Masters triumph seemed a fitting last hurrah. He had set standards for future generations of tour stars to shoot at, created a business empire, raised a thriving family, prospered in architecture, and enjoyed hobbies as diverse as tennis and fishing. Fans wanted to know what he thought of the booming Senior Tour. What were his plans? Did he intend to continue playing both the regular circuit and the Seniors? He answered them in the inimitable Nicklaus style:

> The problem for me is that the guys who are competing are the same guys that I have beaten for thirty years. Now, most of the guys who are playing well, with a few exceptions, are the guys who were marginal players when they played on tour. Because they were marginal players, they now have the desire to keep playing. The guys who are dominating, I suppose, are Bob Charles and Orville Moody. They were good players, but marginal. They weren't exceptional.

Reaction was swift and predictable. An enraged Dave Hill claimed that he never again would speak to Jack Nicklaus, although he was quick to qualify that his enmity did not extend to Barbara Nicklaus, whom he admired and planned to continue to greet socially. When Nicklaus ignored the first few senior events for which he was eligible, either out of contempt or apprehension about his welcome, it presented an opportunity for Lee Trevino, who went on a spree winning three of the first four tournaments of the year. Trevino told the sportswriters that he was sending a dozen roses to Barbara for every week that she kept Jack at home. Later in the season reporters asked Trevino if he was continuing to send the roses. "Yes," Lee confirmed, "but I'm waiting until Thursday because he might show up. He's just liable to do that, get the flowers and then come to the tournament!"

Nicklaus could not stay away forever. He was invited to the Senior Skins Game in Hawaii after his 50th birthday. There he joined Arnold Palmer, Lee Trevino, and Gary Player. The four contestants had compiled a record of 180 Tour wins, 43 major championships, 14 PGA money titles, and 9 Vardon Trophies. The event was won by the oldest and most venerable of the four, Arnold Palmer.

Later, Nicklaus traveled to the major senior tournaments. He captured three tournaments in 1991, all on difficult courses—Desert Mountain, PGA National, and Oakland Hills—backing up the braggadocio that no one then playing the Senior Tour was likely to defeat him. When he won the 1993 U.S. Senior Open at Cherry Hills, Nicklaus defeated Tom Weiskopf, who was in his rookie senior season and appearing as a guest commentator in the television booth after finishing an early afternoon round that put him in the tournament lead at five under par. Tom was forced to watch as Nicklaus stormed in on the final holes and sank a very difficult putt on the final green to win the championship. In a resigned voice Weiskopf said:

"There will never be another Jack Nicklaus. Nobody can play like that guy can. Nobody! Who can tell me when he has ever three-putted to lose a major championship? He's the greatest pressure putter of all time!"

With his typical assurance Nicklaus told his fans why he excelled. "In my peak years I prided myself on being among the tour's longest, straightest drivers, a fine long and mid-iron player, and an excellent mid and short-range pressure putter. Although they were all great assets, none was my strongest competitive weapon. That was and still is my mind—what and how I think about the game."

His rivals probably disliked the way Nicklaus expressed this opinion, but they undoubtedly agreed with the substance. Frank Beard for one stressed that:

> Nicklaus, although he strikes the ball exceedingly well, doesn't hit it that much better than another one hundred or one hundred and fifty players. The reason he is better than all the rest of us is that he never, never makes a mental mistake on the golf course. When he misses a shot, it is purely mechanical ... he just mishit it, that's all. Every player in the tournament this week will hit and

mishit the same number of shots on a relative basis. But the fellows who finish second, third, fourth, or down the slit also will choose the wrong club a few times, will gamble when they shouldn't, will try to make a twenty-footer when they should be trying to lag it ... some type of mental error or some dumb mistake. Nicklaus never makes those mistakes. Lee Trevino makes very few of them. Any big winner eliminates his mental errors, and I think this is the difference. So the man — and Nicklaus is the epitome — who is able to control himself, to marshal his mental processes and make them perform the way they do on the practice tee is the man who becomes successful. Mechanical execution is a thing of the past. We can all do that. It's the man in command of himself mentally who will be the winner.

Even during Nicklaus's best years, Beard never ranked him among the best ball strikers. Beard considered Al Geiberger best with the driver, Ray Floyd with fairway woods, and Tom Weiskopf with long irons. Nicklaus appeared nowhere on the list except at the end where he was ranked tops at mental preparation. Nicklaus always could hit his irons higher than almost anybody else, a tremendous advantage with long and medium iron shots. He also was one of the strongest, if not the best, at playing from deep rough. In addition to his outstanding power, Nicklaus was blessed with extraordinary hand-eye coordination. Above all, he seemed to be impervious to pressure! Proof of that is his reputation as one of the all-time greats at clutch putting.

Jack Nicklaus turned pro in 1962. After eight years and 170 tournaments, he passed the $1 million mark in winnings, reaching that plateau at the Crosby event of 1970. His second million came much faster, within only four years and 76 tournaments, a fair representation of how he dominated the sport in those years. No one in golf approached the records that Jack Nicklaus compiled in his four decades of superlative golf.

The 1970s

"Learning how to play in competition is an evolutionary process. That's why it is so important to get juniors involved in the game at an early age, to get them playing in competition. That way they learn at an early age what it really means to choke, to be really nervous and not be able to perform. Everybody goes through that. I remember when I was thirteen in the Kansas City men's amateur medal play tournament. I played two good rounds to qualify for the last 36 holes and then I shot 81. During the last round I was crying out there. Literally crying."

— Tom Watson

Arnold Palmer was born ten years before Jack Nicklaus, who gradually superseded the older man in number of tournaments won and in total winnings as the 1960s progressed. Golf fans anticipated that another major superstar would emerge in the 1970s to challenge Nicklaus. For a time it appeared that several men might ascend the heights achieved by Hagen, Jones, Hogan, Snead, Nelson, Palmer and Nicklaus. Lee Trevino, Johnny Miller, Raymond Floyd, Tom Weiskopf, Tom Watson — all seemed to have the necessary talent to gain superstardom, and among the contenders Watson seemed to have the most promise.

Despite his imposing talents Tom Watson never matched Palmer's and Nicklaus's enormous popularity with the galleries. Lacking the easy charm of Palmer and the imposing physical presence of Nicklaus on camera or in person, Watson nonetheless possessed a facile intelligence that more often emerged in one-on-one print interviews. Palmer and Nicklaus enjoyed a natural affinity with the camera. They had an instinctive, unconscious ease of command and knowledge of their place in history, and this was readily communicated to audiences. Theirs was a charisma possessed by few in the history of American sport, and it is unjust to fault Watson because he failed to attain their rank. Golf perhaps was poorer for his faults, for the years after Nicklaus's best performances provided no one to command the allegiance of American golf fans the way Palmer and Nicklaus had done.

Tom Watson, the son of a Kansas City insurance broker and scratch golfer, attended a distinguished private high school before moving to Stanford University where he majored in psychology. His girlfriend Linda Rubin attended Mills College near Stanford, and they were married before Watson started on the Tour in 1971. He won his first event, the Western Open at Butler National, in 1974. In 1977 he came into his own winning the Masters and British Open in head-to-head donnybrooks with Jack Nicklaus. Until then Watson's performance under pressure was suspect in major tournaments. But long hours of practice week after week built a repeating swing that catapulted him to stardom.

Watson had acquired an excellent education as had his relatives, including in-laws, who were predominately professionals — brokers, lawyers, accountants, etc.— and Tom soon became known among fellow pros not only as "Karnak" (after the Johnny Carson character) for his quick displays of knowledge (one pro called Nicklaus "Karnak I" and Watson "Karnak II" because he said they knew the answers before the questions were asked), but also as possibly the only liberal Democrat on the Tour. When the pro ranks were polled during the 1972 presidential election it was discovered that Watson was the only man to favor George McGovern.

Tom Watson (author's collection).

Among Watson's many distinctive traits was a fiery competitiveness nowhere better illustrated than during the 1977 Masters. At 27 years of age, he overawed the world's reigning superstar, the 37-year-old Nicklaus. The highlight of the Masters occurred on the 13th hole. Watson and Nicklaus were battling for the lead when Nicklaus hit his second shot onto the par-five 13th green and two-putted for a birdie. When the crowd applauded, Nicklaus turned and waved in acknowledgment. Watson was waiting to hit his second shot to the same green and saw Nicklaus turn in his direction as he waved. Watson, infuriated, believed that Nicklaus was waving to him in a gesture of dismissal rather than to the gallery.

When Watson caught up to Nicklaus he heatedly confronted the older man, who was stunned. "Come on, Tom" he said. "I wouldn't do anything like that. I was just waving to the gallery." Watson realized his error immediately and apologized. But observers who knew Watson well believed that it was this flash of anger that spurred him to victory, and not only in that Masters but also in the British Open of the same year. Watson had made a mistake with Nicklaus, but the mistake was born of a fanatical desire to win and led to brilliant play down the homestretch both at Augusta and during the remainder of the season in which he compiled the best scores to win the Vardon Trophy and to be named PGA Player of the Year.

Watson's crowning achievement came in the British Open at Turnberry. He shot 68-70-65-65 and broke the Open record by eight shots. Nicklaus shot 68-70-65-66 for a 269, faltering on the last hole. Watson made four birdies on the last six holes to win.

In 1979 Watson continued to play extremely well. Then, at the Tournament Players Championship, he was ahead by two strokes with nine to play, only to balloon to a 77 and lose by four shots. One week later he was leading the Heritage Classic by four shots with the last round to finish. He shot a 74 and was beaten by one stroke. This was a reminder of 1975 when Watson was leading the U.S. Open after three rounds, then shot a 79 to lose.

"Everybody chokes," Tom explained:

> I choke, everybody chokes. But when I'm swinging well, I don't tend to choke as much as when I'm swinging badly.... I'm a jumpy person. Everything I do is fast. I walk fat, I waggle fast. I have to slow myself down. But when I won the Crosby, my tempo was very good. Much slower. I'm also a private person. I have to get away from golf every so often. That's one of the things that will let Nicklaus play for a long time. He can get away. But I can't. I've got obligations. I've got to establish myself. Another thing, I'm not as good with people and with crowds as some golfers are. I'm getting better, but I've got a long way to go.... There have been players who have had great swings but they've never broken an egg because they never had the desire. You have to develop the desire. I started when I was a youngster, learning from my father. I played competitive sports all the way through school — kickball, softball, baseball, football, basketball, track. I was competitive in everything I did. Sports, schoolwork, everything. You have to be a competitor. You can't be soft. You have to want to be the best.

Watson's educational credentials and success may have been envied by some pros. But he commanded respect with an absolute lack of fear in challenging anybody, at any time, when he perceived that a protocol or rule of golf had been broken. At the first televised Skins Game, Jack Nicklaus, Arnold Palmer, Tom Watson, and Gary Player were invited to compete. In the middle of the event the gallery and a huge television audience watched with astonishment as Watson angrily confronted Player about a rules infraction. Watson alleged that Player repositioned a blade of crabgrass just behind his ball before playing a chip shot on the 16th hole. If true it would have violated the rule which prohibits golfers from improving a lie by "moving, bending, or breaking anything fixed or growing." Player chipped the ball close to the pin on 16, sank the putt to tie Watson, then won the 17th hole and a $150,000 carryover.

A visibly infuriated Watson approached official Joe Dey to argue the infraction, then he talked to Nicklaus before turning to Player. "I'm accusing you Gary," Watson said, arguing that the South African had moved the grass to improve his lie. Player refused to concede to Watson, and insisted that no rule had been broken. Later, Player explained to a reporter that Watson had been mistaken when he thought a leaf was removed from behind the ball. The incident was never resolved to either man's satisfaction, and it served to illustrate how deep personal rivalries could continue in a sport that many believed was genteel and seemingly without controversy.

When asked about Watson, longtime tour player Howard Twitty remarked:

> Superstars don't have friends out here. They have a lot of acquaintances. They're too busy, and in a way, if they let their guard down they can look vincible to the other players. When Watson was approached to do a TV special on his chip-in at Pebble Beach and try the shot over again, he declined. He wanted to leave the impression he could make a magical shot like that whenever he really needed to. I've heard those stories about Hogan concentrating so intently he went to the next tee unaware you had just made a great birdie. Are you kidding me? Hogan, who never missed the tiniest detail, doesn't know his partner made birdie?... I kiddingly called Tom "Karnak" because he has so many answers. But he has no enemies out here. The players thought he got burned by the press and public on the Gary Player rules incident. Tom was just being honest.

In 1990 Watson dropped his life-long membership in the Kansas City Country Club in disgust when Henry Block was rejected for membership apparently because of his religion. When the controversy about discrimination at golf clubs flared into the open at the PGA Championship at Shoal Creek, Watson had been among the most outspoken Tour pros urging caution. He reminded critics that private clubs had the right to choose their own members. But when Block, founder of H&R Block, Inc., was blackballed in Watson's hometown, the PGA Tour star immediately resigned from the club.

Watson was equally candid when asked about general conditions on the Tour. He was an advocate of the star system in sports, an environment where the top players rake in the most benefits. He wanted to see the PGA enhance such an environment by creating what he called a Super Tour, in which the top 20 or so players would compete for top money in special TV events. There would be a qualifier for the Super, and players would have to go up against the best in the sport and perform at the absolute peak in order to win. He believed the format would give the Tour far more exposure and success. Watson was one of a very few top players to keep a full schedule throughout his career on the PGA Tour. He played week in and week out, and even in his late 40s he could contend for first place at important tournaments. He accumulated one of the finest records in golf by winning 37 tournaments, two Masters, one U.S. Open, five British Opens, and six Player of the Year awards. At the age of 44 when top-ten finishes were no longer a matter of rote, Watson tried to explain what happened to his game.

"I miss a lot of short putts now," Tom ruled:

> I used to make 20, 30, 40, 50-footers. I remember playing with Doug Sanders in the Hawaiian Open, I made two 30-footers and a 40-footer on the last four holes. That didn't surprise me too much. I mean I had the line, I hit the ball where I was looking, and the ball went in the hole. But that doesn't occur now. I have a hard time seeing the line now. I started losing it when I was about twenty-two, twenty-three. Up until that time I was amazing. I aimed the putter and I knew the ball was going right along that line. By instinct you know it is the line of the putt. You know how much it breaks, you know exactly how to hit it.... When I was playing well I would take two practice strokes and look at the hole twice –then immediately hit the putt. I had a routine I used on every putt. Now I look at the hole two or three times then look at the ball, then back to the hole, then look at the ball so my actual routine is not as sure, not the same every time. That comes from lack of confidence. I have spasms. Sometimes it just goes off. Off line real badly. Those are nerves playing with your hand muscles.

When Watson captained the 1993 U.S. Ryder Cup team at age 43, his contemporaries Tom Kite, Ray Floyd, and Lanny Wadkins were still winning an occasional golf tournament. Watson was hitting the ball ten to 15 yards longer at age 43 than he had at 23, and his iron play was still startingly accurate. His putting was terrible. But in 1996 Watson concluded a long drought. At the Memorial Tournament at Jack Nicklaus's Muirfield Village Golf Club, Watson won for the first time in nine years. He was 46 years old, and could savor PGA tournament play again knowing he could win against younger talent and still have the Senior Tour to look forward to after only four more years.

Another remarkable talent of the 1970s whose potential seemed to have no limits was Johnny Miller. When Miller was five his father set up a canvas screen at a golf practice range in the family's basement. Lessons with notable teacher John Geertson followed. When Johnny was a teenager a lucky break occurred. The Olympic Club in San Francisco started a program for junior golfers that permitted Miller to play the course nearly every day. In 1964 his ability advanced so rapidly he was able to whip the field in the National Junior Amateur. In 1966, when the U.S. Open was staged at the Olympic Club, Miller qualified and shot an opening-day 70. He finished in eighth place overall in the championship.

After turning pro in 1969, Miller made a slow start. However in the 1970 Phoenix Open he shot a remarkable 61. The following year he won the Southern Open Invitational. At the Masters Tournament that year he could have won but bogeyed the final two holes to fall out of the lead. He had nine top-ten finishes that year. In 1972 he won the Sea Pines Heritage Classic. In 1973 came the event that marked him as a star — the U.S. Open at Oakmont. Starting the

Johnny Miller (©PGA Tour).

final round Miller was six shots behind the leaders. He began by birdying the first hole, then the second, the third, the fourth, and finished four under after nine to trail the leaders by three strokes. He birdied the 11th and 12th and 13th and 15th.

Miller shot a 63, the lowest round ever recorded in the U.S. Open Championship. He hit every green in regulation (beginning a reputation for phenomenal accuracy that would stay with him throughout his career), missed only one fairway, hit five iron shots to within six feet of the hole, two more within ten feet, and three others within 15 feet. He birdied nine holes and made only one bogey. The victory started a streak that was bettered only by Byron Nelson throughout the history of golf.

Miller won eight tournaments in 1974 and a record $350,000 in prize money. Beginning the annual Tour he won the first three events at the Crosby, Phoenix, and Tucson, and shot par or lower in his first 23 rounds of competitive golf.

After the fantastic 1974 season Miller bought a ranch in the Napa Valley and began working outdoors with a chain saw and wheelbarrow. He said he put muscle on muscle, and built up from 176 to 196 pounds. What he hoped would add strength and distance to his game only hampered his once flawless feel and flag-covering approach shots, so he shelved the conditioning regimen and went back to his old lifestyle.

"You'd be amazed at the changes that take place in a man's appearance, and his actions down the hot stretch of a close finish," Miller commented, but at the time nothing like that seemed to bother him. He loved to drive fast cars and motorcycles and often missed tournaments to pursue other sports and family outings. His skiing and tennis frequently resulted in injuries. In 1975 he compiled another enviable record, winning four times and finishing second twice. He won again at Phoenix, by 14 strokes over his nearest rival, and took the Tucson tournament by nine shots. He recorded rounds of 61 in both events. But only two years later his magical skills seemed to disappear. He was 48th on the money list in 1977 and won only $60,000. He failed to record a single victory, and a fellow pro said: "Miller lacks the tenacity and dedication of a Ben Hogan. If he had Hogan's determination, he might never lose."

Miller's boyhood instructor, John Geertsen, disagreed: "Johnny's a great believer in mental practice. He'll sit at home analyzing his game in his head for an hour and do more good than he could by hitting a thousand range balls." When told of Geertsen's comments, Johnny reinforced them, and was so vocal about his competitors and so distant from the social web of the Tour he gave offense to many players.

"A lot of people think I'm aloof," Miller said, "but I don't mean to be. I don't socialize much because I would rather be with my wife and kids. My oldest boy has started school and my family can't travel with me as much, and that bothers me."

Miller was a Mormon and like other members of his faith he stressed the importance of family life. This distracted him from spending as much time on practice and travel as many other stars. He had a contract with Sears that paid him about $200,000 a year in 1975 dollars. With his Prince Valiant hair and modish, colorful wardrobe, Miller was thought by some to be a younger copy of Doug Sanders. This was erroneous. His faith kept him in church a good part of every Sabbath, and he was no party goer during the rest of the week.

After his remarkable start Miller lived through an unusual four years from 1976 to 1980 when he was without a victory on the PGA Tour. "I was fighting the fact that I had sort of done all the things I wanted to do in the game," he said. "I was just content. I had lost that passionate love for the game." Then he won the Sun City, South Africa tournament and golf's all-time highest prize of half a million dollars.

During the dry years he had not lacked income, having become a one-man advertising industry following the U.S. Open victory at age 25, and a follow-up British Open Championship at age 28. He continued to drive race cars and motorcycles, and missed the 1981 PGA Championship when he fell while trying to do a handstand on his bike. He also continued skiing and playing tennis which led to a fractured wrist in 1981. The same year he sold his Napa property and returned to Utah and his Mormon roots, buying a new ranch in a rugged mountain valley. Yet he could play well enough to win the 1981 L.A. Open and the Tucson Open, followed by the first place prize in the 1982 San Diego Open. He also won the Honda Classic in 1983.

Mac O'Grady thought that a large part of Miller's success should be credited to his caddies. One of the best, John Sullivan, "is like Johnny Miller's adopted son," Mac said. "If he wasn't around Miller might be through on tour. Johnny has a tendency to pout — if he'd plugged it in the sand like I did he might have whined for four or five holes, but his caddie won't let him. He'll tell him, 'Relax, get back in the ring and see your own blood.' A caddie is so important!"

In 1989 Vin Scully left NBC and commentator Lee Trevino started playing the Senior Tour. The producer of NBC's golf program had worked with Miller years before and remembered how candid he was at that time. When Miller was contacted about joining the network he turned the offer down. When they called again, Miller's wife was present and he was surprised to hear her say: "It would be nice at this time in your career to get a regular pay-check."

When Miller looked at the schedule of events he saw that most of his work would be in the spring and fall when his kids were in school, and the summer would be free to spend with them at home. So he joined Bryant Gum-bel, and the feedback was favorable. But then Miller roused tempers with a comment about Mike Ditka, who was playing in a pro-am at the Bob Hope Classic. Describing the mercurial Ditka, Miller said: "He looks like Curtis Strange after a 3-putt!" Strange took umbrage and complained to the com-missioner. Later Miller explained,

> The line just popped out of my head. That's part of my spontaneity. It just came out of right field. It wasn't mean to be malicious, and it was pretty funny. Most of America enjoyed the line and didn't think anything about it. But I can see Curtis's side. It did hurt him a little, and I feel bad about that. I don't want to be taking potshots just to get humor. So I learned a little bit.

Miller's style on television drew accolades from viewers and critics alike. His comments about choking and other sometimes taboo topics were a refresh-ing change from other broadcasters. He occasionally took breaks from televi-sion to play in a tournament, and in 1994 he stunned the golf world by edging Tom Watson to take the winner's trophy at the Pebble Beach pro-am. At age 46, Miller had years to wait before he would be eligible to play the Senior Tour. But he could still play, there was no doubt about that. And he was as free as ever with analyses of tour players and of himself.

"My theory, when I was in my prime, was that I had three guys playing for me." Asserted Miller.

> I had three distinct swing images. I had Lee Trevino, where I opened my left foot and hit this low little squeeze fade. I had Tony Lema, where I took it out-side, sort of like Hubert Green with a light grip, and dropped it in and hooked the ball high. And I had Johnny Miller, who hit the ball pretty straight. So no matter what pin or what hole it was, one of those three guys had the perfect shot for that hole. And I learned to play that way. The advantage of it was I knew that on every day, one or two of those three guys was going to be playing good. No way that all three of them were going to be playing bad. The problem now is I see a lot of young players, they have one guy playing for them. They have one shot and one shot alone. If that one guy is having a bad day, there is no fall back. People don't know that, but that was one of the keys to my success.

Lee Trevino's family moved to Dallas when he was seven, into a house with a distant view of the 7th fairway at the Athletic Club Golf Course where he soon was caddying. Trevino never knew his father's name, and the little money he earned went to help his mother and grandfather who came from Monterrey, Mexico to work as a tenant farmer growing cotton and onions. Lee helped with the field work until the move to Dallas, after which his grandfather found work as a grave digger. After a full day of caddying, Trevino went along at night to help his grandfather with his assignments. His mother, whom he remembered as "loud, she talked a lot, and made a joke out of everything," toiled as a cleaning lady in more prosperous households.

Curtis Strange (author's collection).

Of all the ventures churning to make ends meet in the Trevino household, young Lee enjoyed his days at the Athletic Club more than any other. Soon he was wagering with other caddies to see who could hit a 4-wood the farthest, and often a member would allow him to forgo caddie responsibilities as soon as they got out of sight of the clubhouse, to begin playing the course toe to toe with someone 40 years older. Trevino looked back on his experiences at the caddie shack as "an education of hard knocks," as it was for generations of other golf professionals. He was a boy of ten in an in-your-face environment. He remembered many of the caddies as being violent older teens and men who carried guns and knives. There were frequent altercations of no precise origin, almost continuous gambling, and open drinking.

From the age of eight or so Trevino had been on his own. No one in the family had much respect for schooling, and if Trevino failed to arrive at class, no one seemed to care. When he did attend, however, he invariably was the best player on the football, soccer, and softball teams. At age 14 he saw the last of school. That year he was offered a full time job with the grounds crew at Glen Lakes Country Club. Before long he also was working for Hardy Greenwood's driving range. Hardy spotted potential in Trevino before anyone realized he was big enough to carry a golf bag. Hardy met him when he was eight, and encouraged him to practice and to develop the natural talent that was evident to the older man. Trevino had other ideas, and at the time very meager ambition. Drifting along he began to think of entering the Marine Corps, and on his 17th birthday was signed up and sent to California for basic training. The Corps sent him to Japan to the Third Division, where he became a machine gunner. When the division was posted to Okinawa in 1957, Trevino liked the island so much he asked for an extension on his enlistment. After arriving at his new company, the commander asked Trevino if he played any sports. "Yes sir, I play golf," Trevino responded.

"We'll put you in Special Services then," the captain replied, and for the final 18 months Trevino played golf. At noon a driver stopped at his barracks and drove him to the course, where every afternoon he played with a collection of high ranking officers. He also played for the base team which traveled throughout the Far East contending with other service units. He won the Okinawa club championship and the Okinawa Chamber of Commerce Tournament. He met the Army's Orville Moody, and was trounced.

Late in 1960 Trevino obtained a discharge and returned to Dallas, where he went to work for Louis Shawver, who had constructed a new course at the Columbian Club. Hardy Greenwood had not forgotten Trevino, however, and he persuaded him to start working nights at the driving range so days would be free for practice. Now he had plenty of time to work on his game and the ambition to join the PGA and begin playing local tournaments. Soon he was winning regularly. One year later he married a 17-year-old North Dallas High School senior and became a fixture at Tenison Park, the 36 hole Dallas course where Trevino said "a lot of wealthy people played, some for fun, some for money. Tenison was the only course I've ever seen where the parking lot was filled with Cadillacs, jalopies, pickups, and beverage trucks."

He met Arnold Salinas there. Salinas was regarded as the best Mexican-American golfer around Dallas, and he and Trevino soon were inseparable. Tenison was a gambler's nirvana, with Dick Martin, Titanic Thompson, and other high rollers in attendance. Trevino didn't have the money to play with that crowd, but play he did anyway, so much so that wife Linda moved out with son Ricky and filed for divorce. Less than a year later Trevino played in a pro-am at Glen Garden and shot a record 61. At the same time he remarried, to 17-year-old Claudia Penley. Some people, including Hardy, commented that Trevino did not seem to be maturing normally.

Now Trevino's game really began to progress. He surprised everyone by winning the 1965 Texas Open, set off for Mexico City and finished second in the Mexican Open, then continued south to play in the Panama Open. Moving next to El Paso, he took the job of club pro at Horizon Hills. Owned by Jesse and Don Whittington, the club was a modest private layout where gambling was as much a way of life as at Tenison Park. Trevino never had much money, and what he did have in his pocket usually was in play. These experiences doubtlessly were indispensable to the lack of nerves he displayed subsequently on tour. Playing against a pair of gamblers' best ball, he often was compelled to shoot 62 to win. And, "it was win or don't eat."

Prior to the memorable Ray Floyd–Trevino match, Titanic Thompson came to Horizon for a week's visit. Word soon got out that all-night games of poker and blackjack, interspersed with daytime golf matches, were drawing huge galleries and much money, but too much adverse publicity for the local folks who alerted the Texas Rangers. They notified club management that if the action continued a raid would be mounted to close down the club. Before departing for Dallas Titanic placed one last bet with Trevino. Titanic was halfway through a big money match when Trevino ambled by. "C'mon pro, you want to play this hole?" Titanic called out.

"Yeah," said Trevino, "But I don't have my clubs."

"There's mine," offered Titanic, who was playing this match left-handed.

"What do you want to bet?" asked right-handed Lee Trevino.

"I'll bet you just $5.00 on this hole," the legendary con man said.

Trevino used the left-handed 3-wood and 5-iron to reach the green, two-putted for par, and beat Titanic's score. "Here's your $5.00," said Titanic. "You're a freak."

Titanic took Trevino aside and talked to him for a long time in an attempt to recruit him to the hustler's life. "Forget the PGA Tour," Titanic insisted. "There's no money in it. Why don't you just travel the country with me? You play golf and I'll do the betting." Trevino declined the offer.

Later Trevino described how Titanic got his name: "He drowned everybody," explained Trevino. Thompson was a phenomenal poker and blackjack dealer, knew the odds on anything you could name, and at age 70 had the reflexes of a man half his age. Trevino and his friend Arnold Salinas were among a handful to beat him at one of his own games. One of Titanic's tricks was to sail a playing card 15 feet through the air and land it edge first into a slice of watermelon. Titanic loved games like this, and would spend all day gambling at them.

In 1966 Trevino played in a qualifying event for the U.S. Open, held that year at San Francisco's Olympic Club. The weather was 45 degrees and foggy, very different from the Kuwaiti heat of El Paso. The experience was beneficial, however, especially for Trevino's appreciation for accurate driving on the narrow fairways and pasture rough of Open courses. He finished in 54th place and won $600. The following year the USGA sent an entry blank, but Trevino wanted nothing more to do with Open conditions and he threw the application in the trash. Claudia retrieved it and invested the $20 entry fee for Trevino to qualify. He shot 67–69 to lead the nation's local qualifiers. Then it was on to Dallas to compete for the five Open spots available to qualifiers. He finished second at Dallas to secure a place at Baltusrol. Friends scraped enough money together to buy a plane ticket and off Trevino went to New Jersey for the 1967 U.S. Open Championship.

Arriving at Newark with bag of clubs and a small suitcase, Trevino had no idea where to go. A taxi driver listened, then drove him to the Union Motel on busy Highway 22. Possessing no sport coat or tie, Trevino found dining difficult. The dining room at Baltusrol was out, so Trevino returned to the motel each evening before venturing out for an expedition up Route 22 in search of a Chinese restaurant that reputedly did not require a coat and tie.

Everything about New Jersey seemed as strange as his first trip to the Far East, except for the golf course. Trevino loved Baltusrol. He shot outstanding practice rounds, and was befriended by a member named Chuck Smith who owned a nearby Cadillac agency. Smith offered to buy Trevino a beer after one round, and that led to another. Feeling more at home he could relax and play well, so well in fact he shot 70-72-71-70, finished in 5th place in the Open, and won $6,000.

Standard operating procedure for the USGA was to mail prize checks to the players at their homes at the conclusion of a tournament. No one realized that Trevino had only $5 left in his pocket by Sunday night. The next tour stop was at Cleveland, which Trevino had not thought about entering until his fantastic success in the Open. Claudia flew to Cleveland, paid Trevino's entry fee for the tournament, and paid his bill at a hotel. Trevino went on to finish in the money in seven of the next eight events. During that 1967 season he won a total of $29,000 in 14 tournaments and was named PGA Rookie of the Year. He returned at the end of the year to El Paso and bought an interest in Horizon Hills from the Whittingtons.

Trevino was a popular new star, a favorite of galleries and sports writers alike. He was very different from the new generation of touring pros who were criticized for being humorless and conformist. Trevino was a throwback to the days of Clyde Mangrum or Tommy Bolt. Always the supreme individualist, Trevino described how:

> I relax by staying away from golf pros at night. A lot of guys who play the tour room together, drive to the course together, eat dinner together, and all they talk about is naturally, golf. They never get away from the game, they're talking backswing, putting strokes, and this and that about the game and end up getting tight about the whole thing. Man, after six o'clock I charge caddie fees. I don't want to know about golf once I leave the course. I like to pal around with guys who fish and talk baseball or football or girls—anything but golf. You've got to get away from the game some part of the day otherwise it will eat you alive.

If fans and reporters enjoyed Trevino's presence on the tour, not all of his peers were equally complimentary. Many loathed his endless chatter. When Trevino and Tony Jacklin arrived on the first tee for the 1972 British Open, Jacklin turned to Trevino and earnestly implored: "Lee, we don't need any conversation today." Trevino replied immediately: "Tony, you don't have to talk, you just have to listen."

In 1968 Trevino got off to a slow start. He took 8th place in the L.A. Open and a 6th in the Bob Hope tournament, but he missed the cut at San Diego and did poorly in Miami. At the Masters he was high on the leader board at the beginning of the final round but shot 80 the last day. He was ahead at the Houston Open with only two holes left, but hit two bad approach shots and lost. The U.S. Open in 1968 was held at the Oak Hill Country Club in Rochester, New York. Trevino shot 69-68 the first two days to place second to Bert Yancey by one stroke. On the third day Trevino shot 69 and Yancey 70 as the two men pulled far ahead of the rest of the field. Paired together in the last round, Trevino and Yancey played indifferently on the opening holes.

But Trevino rebounded strongly on the back nine and finished with a 69 to make him the first man ever to score four rounds in the 60s in the Open. Lee Trevino was the 1968 U.S. Open champion.

After winning the Open, Trevino talked about what it meant to his family.

> I'm still conservative with my money. I just can't believe that I won the U.S. Open. I'm still not planning on going wild with my money. I'm gonna invest wisely. I'm not gonna start spending it everywhere.... Before I won I was working for $30.00 a week, plus lessons, plus repairs. We didn't have a bank account. We didn't have any money at all.

Trevino went on to win the 1968 Hawaiian Open, won the Tucson Open the following year, and again in 1970. His reputation really was cemented in 1971 when he won the U.S. Open again, defeating Jack Nicklaus in a playoff at Merion. In that year Trevino won the Canadian Open, the British Open, and the U.S. Open, all in the space of 20 days. Trevino ascribed his confidence to having played for high stakes for years on municipal courses: "It's a tough company out there. You really have to play good golf and you have a lot of nerve or those people will take your money. I learned how to play with some awfully good players, and this is probably what I owe everything to for playing so well on the tour."

As he accumulated a little money, Trevino and Claudia began to speculate in real estate. Establishing a company called Lee Trevino Enterprises in El Paso, Trevino let his cronies dive into the Santa Teresa project in New Mexico just across the state line from El Paso. Trevino and Claudia moved into an impressive home on the golf course, and the family company committed to building a clubhouse and nine additional holes. But rising interest rates made financing the deal a nightmare. Soon most of Trevino's winnings were pouring into the real estate commitment to save equity. The IRS arrived to ask why no taxes were paid on Trevino's bonuses. A lien was placed against his Santa Teresa house and the banks said they would foreclose on the golf course.

The Trevinos packed up their possessions and moved back to Dallas where Claudia assumed control of Trevino Enterprises. Fortunately Trevino had one of his best years on Tour and won a quarter of a million dollars, which made it possible to settle the New Mexico debts. He continued to win. In 1974 he bagged a PGA Championship, and also won at New Orleans.

The following year at the Western Open he was struck by lightning. Sitting on a golf bag with his back propped against a tree, Trevino was talking to Jerry Heard as they watched a storm approach Butler National. He had an umbrella stuck between his knees and relaxed as his caddie went off to buy a hot dog. Trevino said that he remembered watching the caddie leave, but in the next instant the former Marine heard a report like a cannon shot. The bolt's impact lifted him off the ground, passed through the steel shafts in the bag, and exited through Trevino's left shoulder before passing to Jerry Heard's umbrella and striking his legs. Then it knocked a golf club out of nearby Bobby Nichols's hands without seriously injuring him. Arnold Palmer's club also was knocked flying, but the only golfer to be badly injured was Trevino. He was in spasms, trying to breathe, left arm twisted below his body, and believing his shoulder must be broken because he could detect no feeling at all in his left side. When their ambulance arrived at the hospital Trevino wanted to know why his left side was numb and why he was having so much trouble breathing.

"I can't tell you a lot about that," the doctor replied. "I don't get too many lightning victims in here. They go straight to the morgue. The electrical shock stops the heartbeat, but the blood is still rushing and it takes very little for your heart to rupture. That kills you immediately."

Trevino was wheeled into intensive care where he stayed for two days. Jerry Heard went back to finish the tournament.

Upon arriving home in El Paso, Trevino could barely walk. Heart tests revealed no permanent damage but his nerves were raw. All his life Trevino had ignored thunderstorms. In Texas violent storms were so numerous he rarely paid any attention, going on with a round of golf through all but the most awful weather. Now the least aggravation, even a pop from a flashbulb, sent him into uncontrollable spasms. For a long time he experienced cold chills and goose bumps when he saw lightning on the horizon.

"I'm sorry it worked out that way," Trevino lamented:

> I used to love the rain. When I was a kid working in a golf shop we only got to use the course when it rained and the members didn't show up. We'd play all day. After I got on tour, when it rained in a tournament I always moved up. Not anymore. When it starts raining I get worried what will come next. I think about it a lot. I know now that the safest place to be in a lightning storm is in a deep bunker.

Doctors later discovered damage to vertebrae in Trevino's back. In May of 1976 he was lifting a potted plant at home for Claudia when he felt something snap. A doctor located a ruptured disk and commented that his bout with lightning may have been responsible by burning out the lubricant in vertebrae along his spine. The pain he experienced following the operation was almost unendurable, but following rigorous therapy Trevino came back eight months later to win the Canadian Open played at Jack Nicklaus's notoriously tough Glen Abbey.

He continued to win tournaments but his troubles also continued. Experimenting with traction, acupuncture, and standard medications did little to relieve pain. "I couldn't put my socks on in the morning," Trevino complained. "I couldn't chip or putt without intense pain. I couldn't hit enough practice balls to get loose." In 1982 a specialist discovered a pinched nerve in Trevino's back, and a new experimental technique was used to treat the nerve. It was successful. The following year he married for the third time, to another Claudia who was 25. Trevino was 44, and still winning.

Over the years Trevino had trouble with only one of the major championships. He racked up two victories apiece in the U.S. Open, British Open, and PGA Championship, but never was able to play well at Augusta National. His troubles with the Masters started when he was in the middle of a practice round one year and a security officer tried to evict his caddy because he was displaying the wrong identification ticket. Trevino told the officer that if his caddy went, Trevino was gone too. After a long meeting of club officials a go-fer arrived with proper credentials for the caddy. After the round Lee sought out Clifford Roberts and asked why the tournament ticket did not count for practices. Roberts answered that tournament tickets always were sold out in advance, so the club liked to keep the practice tickets separate and sell them on a daily basis. Trevino said that he would be happy to buy them, but no tickets were sold at the main gate where the players entered. Roberts's reply was: "Well, we just don't do it that way at the Masters!"

"I don't need this. I'll leave!" Trevino exclaimed.

He packed his gear and prepared to go. But after a few minutes he reconsidered and stayed to finish out the tournament.

In subsequent years Clifford Roberts tried to approach Trevino, but was rebuffed. "Roberts sent an emissary to the practice tee with an invitation," Trevino remembered. 'Mr. Roberts is having coffee in the clubhouse, and he'd like you to join him.'

'Just tell Mr. Roberts I don't drink coffee.' Lee answered."

One day Roberts waylaid Trevino after a round and offered to show off Bobby Jones's trophy room. Reluctantly Trevino trooped along as Roberts gave a 15-minute tour. His poor play, however, was an added aggravation, combined with the plantation atmosphere at Augusta which always preyed on Trevino's minority nerves. Finally he told friends and reporters that he had played in his last Masters Tournament. His mind was changed when Jack Nicklaus sat down with him on a locker room bench and talked him into playing once again.

"You just don't know how good a player you are," Nicklaus said. "You can win anywhere!"

Despite Augusta National, Trevino fulfilled the prediction by compiling one of the best records of any modern pro. Between 1967 and 1989 on the PGA Tour, Trevino won 27 tournaments and recorded 34 second place finishes. He played on six Ryder Cup teams, and won the Vardon Trophy five times. He worked very hard to get ready for the Senior Tour. At age 49 he played in 14 regular Tour events, finishing in fourth place at Hartford and in fifth at the Western Open. In late fall he started hitting 500 practice balls a day, then in

December when he passed 50 he entered the GTE Classic and finished in seventh place.

In the first senior event of 1990 he beat out Jim Dent to capture the Royal Caribbean Classic, then finished second the following week at the Suncoast Classic, won the next event at Naples, and won again the following week at Indian Wells. In his first ten Senior Tour stops Trevino finished in first place five times. Then he beat Nicklaus in the U.S. Senior Open. At the end of that season Trevino had recorded $1,190,000 in prize money, more than Greg Norman had posted as leading money winner on the regular Tour. The achievements brought in new endorsement contracts from Motorola, Cadillac, and Spalding that propelled Trevino into becoming a very wealthy man. He continued to draw the fans, and never lost his little-kid attitude at the novelty of his success. But for some Trevino's presentation to the outside world could seem contrived. A PGA official who watched him for many years commented.

> People think Trevino is loosey goosey. In fact, he's tight as a drum. They think he's relaxed. Really, he's so intense he has to talk and joke constantly to relieve the tension. The reason he plays so fast is because he has to. Trevino goes absolutely nuts if play is slow. It can destroy his game and other players know it.... Once he steps off the course, he's one of the least sociable, least out-going guys on the tour. He never, and I mean never, eats outside his room. He's the all-time loner when it comes to fraternizing with other players off the golf course.

Trevino agreed with the assessment:

> There ain't nothing relaxed about me on a golf course. I'm very tightly wound. All that jabbering is a pressure valve. I couldn't do without it. The competitor inside you knows what has to be done. If the game doesn't eat you up inside, you can't possibly be a great player. I still get made but not near like I once did. In the last ten years that's probably the biggest improvement in my game.... I can count on one finger the guys out here I've had dinner with. I never spend any time with golfers away from the course. I don't want to hear, "At seven I hit over the green." After six I charge caddie fees to listen.... Let me say that there's nothing wrong with the guys who aren't quite so outgoing. The tour needs all kinds of personalities. Besides I created a monster in myself, and I can't be on 100% smiling all the time. The most difficult day is the Wednesday pro-am, with people taking pictures around every green. By the time you get to sixteen, maybe you don't feel like smiling anymore, and some guy sitting by the green says, "Trevino ain't nearly what I thought he was. I thought he was a nice guy." But I've been smiling for five hours and have ink all over my hands, and maybe some fan has had a few beers and wants to grab me — so I get a little rowdy. It's not great all the time.

Trevino was very proud of his achievements in golf, and was never bashful about pointing them out to critics. Toward the end of his years on the regular circuit when he was struggling, he said,

Yes, I think I have the best swing on tour. Why have scores come down in the last ten years? Partly because they're imitating me ... open position, fade, lots of power and control from the right side. In the evolution of the game who says they invented the swing right back then? Maybe it's supposed to be flat like mine. The best swing is the one that repeats. And that's what I have. Years ago I had a one-iron that I could hit 260 yards through a doorway. Now I can hit it through the keyhole.

But what gave Trevino his greatest pleasure were memorable duels with Jack Nicklaus. He defeated Nicklaus in a playoff at the 1971 U.S. Open at Merion. He barely edged Nicklaus winning the 1972 British Open. He beat Nicklaus on the final hole at the 1974 PGA Championship, and repeated the trick in the 1990 Senior Open.

"If I've proved anything," Trevino claimed,

It's that you don't have to be born into the country club set. And folks should remember that I came up in the era of Nicklaus, the greatest. I'm the same age as the greatest player in the game, and I didn't handle him all the time but I did handle him some of the time. Somewhere along the line I'll be recognized as one of the top players in the Nicklaus era. That's all I want to be remembered for.

The 1980s

"We've taken fear out of the game. What you've got in a tournament now is 150 guys who have no sense of history and no reason to play safe. They just hit it long, find it, shoot at flags, and see you later!"
—Lee Trevino, 1985

During the 1980s American golfers began to suffer in comparison with foreign-born players, although from time to time Jack Nicklaus, Tom Watson, and Lee Trevino still were capable of beating any competition. But the American players who were expected to rise to superstar status, among them Curtis Strange, Ben Crenshaw, Tom Kite, Mark Calcavecchia, John Cook, Hal Sutton, Lanny Wadkins, and Fuzzy Zoeller, not only failed to attain the level of Miller and Watson, but also increasingly were dominated (especially in major championships) by foreign stars Greg Norman, Seve Ballesteros, Nick Faldo, Bernard Langer, Ian Woosnam, and Sandy Lyle. In 1986 foreign players won 25 American Tour events, and the top four Sony-ranked golfers in the world were Norman, Ballesteros, Langer, and Nakajima in that order. In the British Open that year only two American players—Fuzzy Zoeller and Gary Koch—finished among the top 12. Ten years earlier at Turnberry, in the memorable Nicklaus-Watson shootout, 11 of the top 12 finishers were American.

Some observers of the American golf scene attributed the American decline to the emergence of college-trained golfers. A new class of pros was replacing self-taught American stars of earlier decades who had fought their way up through the caddie ranks. It was pointed out that college players were trained to put their teams first, rather than to seek individual glory. Some critics also blamed the regimentation of college team-golf for the lack of colorful personalities entering the pro ranks. Players were instructed to dress alike, to play together, to go to meetings together, to live together. The individuality of a Tony Lema, Lee Trevino, Chi Chi Rodriguez, or Dave Hill was anathema to the new generation. Ray Floyd spoke for those in his generation who took a jaundiced view of the men who were joining the Tour in the 1980s.

"When you're going one on one," Ray explained, "there's no second, third, or fourth. You have to win. Many players through the years have said: 'I don't care about the money. I just want to win!' But that's chin music. That's lip service. Only a few players in history have ever cared about just winning."

Ray obviously placed himself in that elite, and he went on to regret that many young men would never experience the rigors of "pure competition" because of the safety net provided by the all-exempt tour, just as he wished his sons could have the memories of his 18 months of Army duty. "I really believe a kid will come along someday to whom the money won't mean anything," Ray predicted, "and he'll step out to be the next Arnold Palmer."

During these years many outstanding foreign players were spending more time on the American Tour. Seve Ballesteros might chafe at the restrictions the PGA commissioner instituted to compel attendance at tournaments, but other European and Asian players were only too happy to compete for bulging purses in the United States. Many took up permanent American residence, among them Norman, Price, Elkington, and Baker-Finch, so that travel did not interfere with participation in a large number of events. At the major championships a very powerful foreign-born contingent formed.

American players had dominated the majors for a very long time, in fact since the 1920s when they recorded victories in 25 of the 30 majors held in that decade. In subsequent years this pattern continued. However, in the 1980s and 1990s the pendulum began to swing back. Americans won 29 of the majors in the 1980s, while non–Americans won 11. In the early 1990s an abrupt reversal occurred. In the first four years of the 1990s foreign-born golfers whipped U.S. players nine to seven, with Bernard Langer, Nick Price, Greg Norman, Ian Woosnam, Wayne Grady, and Ian Baker-Finch succeeding at a pace unmatched since the days of Harry Vardon and Ted Ray. Foreign-born stars won three of the four Masters from 1990 to 1994 (and seven of the last 11, all four British Opens (nine of the last ten), and half of the PGA Championships. In 1994 Jose Olazabal took the Masters, Els the Open, and Nick Price won both the British Open and the PGA Championship.

Hale Irwin was quick to point a finger at the probable cause of American decline: "I don't see that Eye of the Tiger in many of the younger players," Hale complained. "I never finished number one on the money list, but I would have given anything if I could. It doesn't seem to make much difference to these guys one way or another. The foreign players have the discipline, ours don't."

A triumph for American players, and an astonishing feat given the age of the victor, was Jack Nicklaus's win at the 1986 Masters. Nicklaus surprised golf fans everywhere by winning at Augusta at age 46 after recording only one tour win in the previous four years and no majors since 1980. He shot a final round 65 and entertained the galleries and TV audience in a way rarely witnessed before or since. Nicklaus edged Greg Norman and Tom Kite by one shot, and Seve Ballesteros by two. Among the other top ten finishers were Tom Watson, Nick Price, and Payne Stewart, worthy rivals in any era. Nicklaus had trailed Ballesteros by four shots with only four holes left to play before logging eagle-birdie-birdie on 15, 16, and 17 to pull even, then assumed the lead when Ballesteros hit into the water on 15. When Nicklaus made par on 18, the championship was his.

The following year Nicklaus captained the American Ryder Cup team at his beloved Muirfield Village. The European team went home victorious, and a shocked Nicklaus reacted with characteristic bluntness. "I had twelve great players on my team," he said. "I couldn't have asked for better players, but winning breeds winning and these fellows don't win enough. I know those guys from thirtieth to two hundred on the money list will say: 'There goes Nicklaus again,' But I'm going to keep preaching. Without stars you don't have a tour. The tour is based on stars." When someone mentioned Payne Stewart, Nicklaus said: "How old is he? Thirty? He's won only three PGA tour events in his career. A player as good as he is should have won fifteen by now. You have to taste victory to learn how to win!"

Young players were as much amazed as angered by Nicklaus's criticism. It was a little like shooting all the foals of Secretariat because they failed to measure up to the sire's standard. Secretariat was not merely an exceptional thoroughbred. He was a champion for all time whose accomplishments might never be equaled. That was how Nicklaus's record was perceived by Tour players, as an amazing, probably unique record so far elevated above the sights of fellow pros as to be unimaginable. Who would question Nicklaus's preeminence as the greatest player in history, or his cachet to speak out in his waning years of glory on the sport's health and future? But to hear him draw such invidious comparisons between himself and lesser athletes seemed too much like General Patton taunting and humiliating convalescents, men who could not rise no matter how much they struggled. Such opinions required an ego of unusual size.

When Nicklaus was asked to explain his reasoning he often focused on the change in emphasis from winning to making cuts and a paycheck. He and Palmer and older stars were quick to denounce the tendency of younger players to be satisfied with top-ten finishes rather than championships. Nicklaus believed that a large measure of the blame for this attitude rested on the creation of what was called the all-exempt tour. When Deane Beman ascended to commissioner of the PGA Tour he inherited a system in which the top 60 prize winners earned exempt status to enter the following year's PGA tournaments. Everyone else endured Monday qualifying rounds in order to compete for a vacant spot in Thursday's first tournament round.

The non-exempt players, called "rabbits," lived on the edge literally and figuratively. "Rabbits" did not start their week on a Monday. They were compelled to show up at the next scheduled Tour stop on Saturday to work in practice rounds before the Monday qualifier. "You didn't exactly feel like the world's best," recalled Mike Nicolette. "First of all the club members didn't want you there. You either had to play late in the afternoon or go out with a member. Playing with a member isn't necessarily bad, but watching a guy shoot 100 doesn't build the feeling you belong on the PGA Tour!"

Then, when Monday arrived, the torture really started. Gary Hallberg contended that "to get into the tournament you had to play your best golf. Most of the time you had to shoot in the neighborhood of 66 or 67 since there often were one hundred pros attempting to fill ten spots."

If the young player shot a low round and qualified he had Tuesday to play another practice round. On Wednesday the pro-ams were held, but "rabbits" were not invited. So by the start of a tournament on Thursday the non-exempt player had been on site for five days, yet four days of intense competition would follow, days in which the player concentrated first of all on making the 36-hole cut because if successful he received an automatic exemption for the following week's event.

Beman made many changes in the way the Tour operated, and one of the most consequential changes was a doubling of exempt spots for each event. Beman raised the number of exempt players to 125, which ensured that a very great percentage of the players in any given tournament would be exempt. These golfers were now provided with a cocoon of security never before enjoyed by pro golfers. At the same time the commissioner was hugely successful at building up purses, so that by the early 1980s the Tour constituted a very comfortable existence for many scores of players, and immense riches for a handful.

The lucky 125 in the exempt category were able to fatten their incomes with additional revenues obtained from exhibitions, clinics, and endorsements. The days of the itinerant touring professional who would fight to make gas money to carry him and his buddies on collegial trips to the next event were relegated to memory. The pros were happy with their new-found prosperity, and very happy with Deane Beman. But there were a few dissenting voices allied with Nicklaus, who viewed the younger generation not as apprentices struggling to hack out a toehold in the ranks of self-sufficient pros, but as a class of landed gentry who fought their main battle to obtain exempt status and then relaxed in the certain knowledge that a spot always was reserved for them in tournaments where the prizes were so great a finish in the top 20 or 30 places might still earn a sizable check in any week's tournament.

This Nicklaus considered anathema to the best interests of golf, because in his opinion it sapped competitiveness from the sport. It created an environment of declining challenge, while simultaneously gilding a life of luxury for less skilled players. Nicklaus pointed to another problem as well. He believed that the all-exempt tour was instrumental in reducing the power of American participants in tournament golf, as players from other countries came to the United States to contend for the growing spoils. Gary Player echoed Nicklaus's sentiments:

> When I joined the Tour it was the win that counted. Now the players are obsessed with making the top 125 so they can keep their cards. The foreign players don't have this all-exempt system overseas. They have the determination to go out week after week and keep fighting. That is how you determine champions. In the long run, the tour's present situation will retard competition and offer more opportunities for the foreign players to excel.

The foreign-born golfers seemed tougher to Nicklaus. Certainly their competitive skills seemed sharper, and by the 1980s a glance at the leader boards reflected his concern. At the top of every major championship could be seen names from Scotland, Australia, New Zealand, South Africa, Germany, England, and other climes where the players sparked memories of earlier American pros, the former caddies and hard scrabble gamblers who viewed Tour purses with the glee of a Turk sacking Venice, rather than the calculating accountant's perspective that Nicklaus attributed to young American players. Nicklaus was not shy in offering up examples of that species, in naming names if anyone should fail to recognize the combination of self-satisfied congeniality married to immense talent. Anyone who visited a PGA Tour event could compile a list of fabulously talented American players who seemingly went through the motions week after week, and who lazed through U.S. Opens and Masters as if they were conducting a guided tour of their hometown arboretums.

Among the most gifted who seemed to fail on the final day during the mid–1980s were Freddy Couples and Payne Stewart, who like so many of their contemporaries made the golf swing look effortless. What then accounted for their failure to come up with more championships? Did the seeming effortlessness mask a lack of fiber? Were foreign players toughened by years of grinding out meager purses, so that by the time they qualified to play the richer American tournaments they acquired a fierce determination that produced victories? The contrasts were striking. Match an Ian Woosnam against Freddy Couples, Seve Ballesteros against Paul Azinger, Greg Norman against Payne Stewart, Nick Faldo against Curtis Strange. Who could say the physical skills of the former were superior to those of the latter? How measure the desire to win, rather than to place or show?

Mark McCormack thought he had the answer. He differed only in small measure from other detractors by attributing the problem to complacency. McCormack argued that younger pros were

> Spoiled by a lifestyle that pays them too much money for minor results. American pros are no longer the best in the world. They are consistently outplayed by foreign players who have learned to compete — and win — at the highest level

Payne Stewart (author's collection).

while coping with different countries and customs, strange foods and courses and officials with which they are unfamiliar. They are a hardy bunch indeed. But American pros? For the most part they are complacent. They are hard working on the practice tee but far from hungry on the course. Many are skilled but few are ingenious. Some pros would just as soon settle for a fifth place paycheck as summon the will to win. They no longer seem to care about being champions. At last year's Western Open, Fred Couples was an inadvertent spokesman for his generation when he claimed that if he won at Butler National he'd quit for the rest of the year. Can you imagine if, around 1957, Arnold Palmer had said he would quit because he didn't need to work beyond August? If Arnold had taken that tack then he would be playing constantly today just to make a living. In fact so might all pro golfers, for the golf boom would have fizzled out at the start. In those not-so-distant old days the great champions were obsessed with winning. Prize money was secondary. Nicklaus pointed out not long ago that his generation and those before him, played against the history books. Now the answer to the question, "How did you do at Greensboro?" is a proud, "I finished fifth." The scrapping and fighting for the victory seems to be a thing of the past.

Another unsettling development for the sport of golf in the 1980s, coincident with the lack of a dominant superstar, was the decline in television viewing. For example, from 1987 to 1988 the average audience for golf tournaments declined 15 percent. Television broadcast 50 events for the PGA Tour, Senior Tour, and the LPGA. Advertising agencies continued to admire the demographics of the sport with its high-income fan profile. Tournament sponsors often bought enough advertising time to ensure network profits. But the decline nonetheless was alarming. Some critics said that golf had grown boring. Dan Jenkins, who covered the golf scene for many years for a variety of publications, observed:

> We now have a situation that breeds boredom, not stardom. Brilliant, charismatic, legendary stars emerged in golf through those years of the 20's, 30's, 40's, 50's, 60's, 70's, when a player had to be among the best before he had a chance to be one of or the best. For the longest time you had to play yourself into the best sixty each year or win something important to be eligible to compete. If you weren't good enough to do this, you faced weekly qualifying. In short, you had to prove yourself to join the elite. The tour rewarded only excellence, and rightly so. Under these circumstances we produced a Ben Hogan, Byron Nelson, Arnold Palmer, Gary Player, Jack Nicklaus, Lee Trevino, and Tom Watson.

Purses and crowds grew enormously. With the all-exempt tour we now have a situation where it will be doubly hard, if not impossible to produce a superstar. The proven idol — a Watson — for example now finds himself in a shooting gallery with 150 players who have nothing to lose. It will be far more difficult for anyone to win consistently. Our bankable stars now have to play in the street with the rabble. On the "welfare tour" of today the full field fires at the pins for all four rounds. In the past, half of them needed to play safe for two rounds in order to make the cut and qualify for the next tournament. What is comes down to is that the stars have been forced to accept non-stars as equals...

"We've taken fear out of the game," Lee Trevino said at one point in 1985. "What you've got in a tournament now is 150 guys who have no sense of history and no reason to play safe. They just hit it long, find it, shoot at flags, and see you later."

The emergence of college golfers and the all-exempt tour drew caustic comments from many quarters. Of course, men like Sam Snead, Lee Trevino, and Ray Floyd would be recruited for college golf teams in the present era even if a tutor were necessary for every course they entered. Perhaps the vinegar in their personalities would be watered down as well after four years at Houston, Wake Forest, or Stanford. The devil-may-care attitude of Chi Chi Rodriguez, Tommy Bolt, Tom Weiskopf, and Dave Hill failed to leach away despite frequent remonstrances from fellow pros and tour officials who would have appreciated a dash of conformity in those anarchists of the fairways. College did not blunt the personalities of Arnold Palmer, Tom Watson, or Tom Weiskopf. They remained some of the most interesting men in the world of golf with ample competitive backbone and charisma.

Now they were yielding to a younger generation of players, and the entire financial and organizational structure of the Tour was changing so radically Walter Hagen and Gene Sarazen would find little that was recognizable. When Deane Beman succeeded Joe Dey as commissioner of the PGA Tour he was only 35 years of age and charged by many new ideas for golf. In years to come Beman transformed the Tour, not only in the way players qualified for competition, but also in business aspects of real estate development, licensing of ancillary products, increased revenue from television, and other opportunities his predecessors had ignored. During his playing days Beman had attempted to persuade the Tour to build golf courses for its championships. After becoming commissioner he immediately started to design Tournament Player Clubs (TPCs) that would come to be known as stadium courses because they were designed to accommodate much larger galleries than was possible with more traditional courses like Oakmont, Merion, Oakland Hills, and Pebble Beach.

In order to finance the building of such clubs, Beman participated in a number of real estate developments which eventually expanded to more than 18 TPCs, seven of which were owned completely by the Tour and the rest licensed for use through independent contractors. A new golf course design and construction company was formed within the PGA Tour, a for-profit enterprise that was intended to construct additional real estate developments. This led to Beman's first and most troublesome clash with many of his former playing partners who had architectural interests, and who saw the Tour's new emphasis as competition rather than advocacy for pros as had been true in the past. Nicklaus, Palmer, Weiskopf, and other stars were developing businesses of their own and resented Beman's visionary attempts to expand the interests of the Tour.

In 1983 matters came to a head. Palmer, Nicklaus, and a dozen other pros mailed a letter to the Tournament Policy Board stating that the Tour should concentrate on organizing events for its members, instead of "owning, managing, operating, or endorsing golf courses. The concept of spectator golf is valid, but having the Tour involved in it on a commercial basis is not a wise course of action." The critics complained that such plans were "unauthorized and ill conceived, and we will take whatever action is required to protect our individual and collective rights." The letter attacked Beman personally, charging that he was attempting to place himself as the "Czar of Golf."

Hale Irwin was another player who attacked Beman's program. "I have never felt that it was the place of the tour to be into the design-management arena," Hale said. "Our forte is staging golf events. That is not to say that you can't have a consulting role in the design process possibly. And they indeed say that they have brought in player consultants, but I am not so certain that has been the case when you see some of the ways the courses have turned out."

Beman won despite his heavyweight opposition. The Tournament Policy Board continued to support him, and Beman forged ahead with plans to develop still more projects. The first TPC was built at Sawgrass on 415 acres obtained from a local developer for $1. The developer was confident that a venture of the quality anticipated by Beman would substantially raise the value of contiguous land he owned near Sawgrass. He was right. Beman's plan was to establish a permanent club for the Tour's own championship, and he spared no expense in developing his treasured project. Pete Dye was hired as architect, and Beman got a loan of $3 million from a local bank.

The golf layout built by Beman and Dye at Sawgrass was completed and opened as the site of the new Tournament Players Championship, but it was such a difficult course the players had something else to crow about. Eventually Dye was forced to make substantial modifications based on player advice, but Beman learned another valuable lesson in the process. In the future he would hire prominent player/architects like Weiskopf and Crenshaw to serve as consultants for new projects, and thereby co-opt them to his designs.

When challenged about his obsession with tournament player clubs, Beman was quick to defend them on the basis of their importance to the future financial stability of the tour. Prior to the building of the TPC at Sawgrass the

Tour looked to television as its chief revenue stream. Beman wanted to lessen the Tour's dependence on television, which he thought was too volatile despite its lucrative contribution to the game. Television had a long and close relationship with golf, dating from the 1947 U.S. Open which was broadcast locally in the St. Louis area. In 1953 George May's World Championship was broadcast on the ABC network. May staged two tournaments every summer for men and women at the Tam O'Shanter club in Chicago.

May was a tireless promoter and innovator whose purses far exceeded those of other events of the day. He also introduced grandstands for viewers, press boxes, and identification of pros by assigning numbers to each participant. At the 1953 event Chandler Harper, a journeyman pro, birdied the 18th hole to take a one shot lead on Lew Worsham. On the final hole Worsham hit a very long drive, leaving only a wedge to the small green. Commentator Jimmy Demaret had a microphone for the audio feed and was standing behind the green with Harper. Worsham needed a birdie to tie Harper, and Demaret tried to reassure the nervous Harper by telling him the worst that could happen would be a tie and playoff on the following day. "It isn't over yet, anything can happen." Harper warned. Worsham took a pitching wedge and landed the ball on the front of the green. Jimmy Demaret called the action for his audience: "The ball lands on the front of the green, takes a big bounce, is rolling toward the hole, rolling, rolling…"

The shot fell in the hole and Worsham's eagle won the tournament and paid him $25,000, an incredibly rich purse for that era. The following year saw the first national telecast of the U.S. Open, in large part because of the attention gained by Worsham's miracle at Tam O'Shanter. The 1954 Open was a success with viewers and advertisers, and golf was on television to stay. Ratings would rise and fall from year to year, but companies like E.H. Hutton, Cadillac, Traveler's Insurance, and golf equipment manufacturers salivated at the economic portrait of the average golf fan. Demographic research revealed that the typical viewer was highly educated, ranged from 24–45 years of age, and was employed in professional and managerial positions that commanded higher than average incomes.

Although Beman insisted on diversifying so that television would not be the Tour's only cash cow, he could be no less magisterial than Clifford Roberts at the Masters when it came time to approve contracts. One innovation that Beman suggested was for NBC to place microphones on selected players during TPC events. Nicklaus, Watson, Player, and many others refused to cooperate, although they allowed their caddies to be miked. The experiment backfired when one of the miked players, Tom Kite, complained publicly about the slow play of John Schroeder. Kite was waiting on the tee for Schroeder to finish putting out ahead, and he commented aloud that Schroeder should be penalized or suspended. When Schroeder was told about the criticism he vented his anger in an interview with Jack Whitaker of CBS, whereupon Kite apologized.

Proof of how important golf was to the networks came in 1994 when the USGA asked for bids on the U.S. Open, the Senior Open, and the Women's Open. ABC had the tournaments under contract through 1994 for $7 million a year. NBC came in with the highest bid to take over the broadcasts in 1995, offering $13 million a year to the USGA. The organization allegedly wanted to avoid ABC for a number of reasons. Dave Marr's dismissal by ABC in 1991 still rankled among some officials, while others were annoyed by the presence of Jack Nicklaus as ABC analyst on golf telecasts. Nicklaus was never chary about voicing opinions, and when he publicly criticized certain brands of golf balls and square-groove irons some people considered it a conflict of interest on his part.

On the other hand, USGA officials liked Johnny Miller's work very much, and when Miller made a personal appearance to lobby for NBC's bid his efforts were rewarded with a new contract. The biggest loser in all this may not have been competitors CBS and ABC. The rival sport of tennis had a lucrative Wimbledon contract for five years at $65 million with NBC, which let the arrangement expire in favor of golf. To make matters worse for the racquet sport, Arnold Palmer initiated a new venture called the Golf Channel, which began coverage of instruction, news, player profiles, and tournaments in early 1995.

Considering all of Deane Beman's innovations with the PGA Tour, none seemed to have the impact or drew such strong reactions pro and con as did his policy on exemptions. He always started with the argument that during the 1960s only 30 to 40 pros were earning a good income from the Tour. The rest were eking out a living. After the system was changed to allow more exemptions, about 200 men began earning substantial annual incomes.

The sniping against Beman by Tour stars never ceased completely, but the revenues that poured into professional golf and fattened purses beyond anyone's imagining in the 1980s did much to solidify his grip on the Tour. Numerous controversies arose during his tenure, but he weathered them all, even the onerous settlement to Karsten Solheim over square grooves in irons, which could have caused severe financial damage to the PGA if allowed to go to trial. Beman survived the controversies that arose as a result of his single-minded pursuit of tournament player courses and ancillary real estate developments. As long as such projects continued to be demonstrably profitable enterprises for the Tour, most players were content to let the policy board handle whatever liaison was necessary and went about their primary business, the winning of golf tournaments.

If not looking for a win, they at least strove to finish in the top ten. Here again the majority of players were in Beman's camp. Only the superstars criticized the all-exempt format. Apart from already fabulously wealthy men like Miller, Watson, Trevino, and Nicklaus, few others wished to see a return to the days of the "rabbit" when golf was a survival marathon and new players were lucky to find sponsors who could afford to foot the expenses of incessant travel. Some players were fortunate to have family members with the means to provide financial support. Others went begging. If a season on Tour in the mid–1980s cost upwards of $50,000 in expenses and players received no salary, where could a rookie find assistance? When Trevino was young, members of his club were willing to gamble on his success. "We were partners," Trevino recalled,

> and we split everything three ways. We didn't have a contract. The first year all they had to do was take $400 out of their pockets because I won early enough. Then we got a lawyer and when he asked me how long I wanted to make a contract I made the mistake of saying "indefinitely." Things got real messy later on. Real messy. But finally I got the whole matter settled and I got out of the contract. I didn't get out cheap though.

After Roger Maltbie won the California State Open in 1974, he said that he would have signed anything in order to join the Tour full-time. He organized a group of sponsors and agreed to give them half of all his income on and off the course.

> It started off as an amiable deal and I had a couple of good years and negotiated to keep all my off-course money. Then I had another good year and started to add things up. After giving the government twenty-five percent of my winnings and my sponsors another half, I came out with only a quarter for every dollar I won. I had a hard time with that.... I was grateful they gave me the chance, but they didn't own me. So I decided, and maybe I was cutting off my nose to spite my face, that if I couldn't get a better deal they weren't going to make any money.

Maltbie essentially retired for the duration of the agreement, and the layoff almost ruined his play. When the contract expired he tried a comeback, but never regained his early form despite occasional wins.

During Tom Watson's early years on Tour he was backed by a group that included his father and father-in-law. In the last year of the agreement Watson won the Western Open and a huge check. The deal worked out very well for the golfer and his family. Mike Donald, on the other hand, formed a corporation and sold shares of stock in himself. There were no friends involved, only businessmen, and the proceeds were adequate to get him started.

After finding some success, many players shed their sponsors in favor of attorneys and tax accountants. For Jack Nicklaus and Lee Trevino, who met with early success, the burdens of arranging for endorsements, exhibitions, tax filings, and investments were gladly passed on to sports agents. Fred Corcoran had served several early pros well over the years, but it was not until Mark McCormack founded International Management Group (IMG) that the world of the sports agent assumed scientific management status.

McCormack had been an excellent college golfer at William and Mary before going on to law school. He and a partner began handling endorsements and exhibitions for a few golf pros. Touring pros frequently switched from one manufacturer to another in search of the best fit and the most money for endorsing products. The Spaulding Company originated endorsements in 1901 when Henry Vardon was signed to promote golf clubs. Television, however, was the catalyst for enormous growth in endorsements because advertisers could use logos and other symbols on visors, bags, clubs, and other accessories to reach a national audience.

The use of visors to advertise everything from banks to resorts started with Julius Boros, who wore a hat stenciled with the name of the Amana Company during the 1968 PGA Championship. Amana proceeded to sign up more than two dozen pros after the success it enjoyed with Boros. International stars like Seve Ballesteros would come to enjoy even greater opportunities. Seve signed with Ram Golf in North America, endorsed Slazenger in Europe, and played Mizuno clubs in Asia. For pure prestige of products, however, no one could match Palmer. He represented the crème de la crème — Rolex, Cadillac, Westinghouse, Samsonite, Hertz, United Airlines, etc. Clothing endorsements also were a lucrative source of income for many players, with Izod, Munsingwear, Sears, and Robert Bruce dominating the early days. Sears worked with Johnny Miller and Arnold Palmer, while Hart, Schaffner and Marx marketed many wardrobes on the back of Jack Nicklaus.

As for participation in clinics and exhibitions, players often could earn more in personal appearances than in tournaments. A typical corporate outing might involve spending a day entertaining employees on the golf course and bring in from $10,000 to $80,000 depending on the star status of the client. An agent working on such commissions was able to save the player much time and trouble, often seeming to be worth the cost even if it was as high as IMG charged.

McCormack's fledgling enterprise had flared into a supernova when he signed Arnold Palmer in 1960. Palmer's popularity was just beginning to explode. As he grew into the wealthiest athlete in American history he would make McCormack very wealthy as well. IMG expanded to become the largest sports management group in the world, as McCormack signed up Jack Nicklaus, Gary Player, and Greg Norman in golf, Bjorn Borg and Virginia Wade in tennis, and many superstars in other sports. He opened offices in New York, Los Angeles, Brussells, Sydney, and Tokyo, while keeping his home office in Cleveland, Ohio. Each client of IMG received comprehensive services for taxes, investments, bill paying, endorsement contracts, etc., for a service fee that ranged from 25 to 50 percent of derived income. Over the decade clients came and went, but the most important lucrative client, Arnold Palmer, stayed on.

The loss of Nicklaus did not deter McCormack from continuing to diversify. In 1986 he signed British Open victor Greg Norman, who went on to win more than a million dollars that year. IMG signed contracts for Norman with Quantro Airlines for $3 million, with a real estate development for another

$3 million, with Reebok clothing for $2 million, with an Australian brewery for $1.5 million, among many other smaller deals. Like Nicklaus, Greg Norman eventually left IMG. But McCormack was able to keep Arnold Palmer on the top rung of endorsement contracts regardless of his winning record.

A self-confessed workaholic, McCormack traveled more than 200,000 miles each year to meet with clients and his 500 employees. He signed as clients Martina Navratilova, Chris Evert, Herschel Walker, Curtis Strange, Ray Floyd, Hal Sutton, Bernhard Langer, Peter Jacobson, Hale Irwin, Nick Faldo, Sandy Lyle, and many others. The example of Arnold Palmer was an irrefutable sales pitch. Palmer had risen to superstar status by 1960 but was earning only $60,000. Under McCormack's tutelage, Palmer's income immediately shot up to $500,000 a year.

In time IMG signed on to manage many tournaments on the European Tour, oversaw the Sony World Ranking system, brokered TV contracts for the Royal & Ancient, and represented clients in virtually every major sport. Many of McCormack's most important clients left to manage their own affairs. But IMG remained more powerful than anyone else, and more clever at contracting for the television rights to Wimbledon tennis, the America's Cup, the U.S. Open, the British Open, and the Skins Game. IMG remained the most powerful sports management company because it vigorously pursued foreign expansion in an era when superstars like Martina Navitralova and Ivan Lendl were dominating tennis tournaments, and Greg Norman, Denis Watson, Ian Baker-Finch, Nick Faldo, Bernhard Langer, and Seve Ballesteros were atop the golf Sony World Rankings year after year.

Like Ballesteros, many of the foreign-born players toiled to prominence in tough, bare-bones environments in Europe or in Asia, where conditions often resembled the pre–1970 American Tour of Ben Hogan and Arnold Palmer. Ballesteros was a throwback to that era and in several respects he resembled Palmer. His unique charismatic style electrified the golf world beginning with his first days on the world stage as a 19-year-old when he came within a chip shot of winning the British Open. For the first three days of the tournament Ballesteros had played with the enthusiastic abandon of a young Palmer. Full-bore drives, every iron shot aimed for the flag, Ballesteros maintained the lead until the final round when Johnny Miller made a remarkable charge to take the trophy.

Ballesteros tied Jack Nicklaus for second, but his aggressiveness brought the galleries scrambling to watch him, and he rarely disappointed. Coming to the 18th green on Sunday, he found his ball in the rough behind two bunkers and a mound of earth. He needed to birdie the hole to tie Nicklaus, but birdie seemed impossible. The conservative approach was to play safely and hope for a par. Ballesteros chipped the ball between the bunkers, up over the mound, and watched it trickle past the hole to leave a short putt for birdie.

Seve Ballesteros was the fourth son of a Spanish peasant. All the boys

caddied at a golf course near their home in Santander, and they all eventually became golf professionals. Two were club pros in Spain, one became a
touring pro in Europe, and the fourth son was in a class by himself. Ballesteros won his home club's caddie championship at age 14, and received privileges to play the course thereafter from his uncle, Ramon Sola, the home pro.
Many years of apprenticeship as a caddie paid dividends. "When I was young,"
Ballesteros recalled, "I got tired of ordinary shots. I made the other caddies
play difficult shots for money. I put the ball against a wall. I put it against a
tree. I always win. That is how I learn to feel the club to know what it is
doing."

At age 17 he won the Spanish Young Pro Tournament, and two years later
he almost captured the British Open. He became the youngest player ever to
top the European Order of Merit by winning the Dutch Open and two other
tournaments. Golf fans thronged to watch him play, just as they had flocked
to Palmer. "People told me I should be more careful," Ballesteros said. "My
brother Maurice says I should be careful. Then maybe I wouldn't get so many
sixes and sevens. But if I was careful, I wouldn't get any birdies or eagles
either."

In 1978 Ballesteros won the Greatest Greensboro Open and got the attention of American pros. Super-sensitive as always about his status, a legacy of
his class-conscious Spanish heritage, he found Tour players to be reserved if
not unfriendly. His perceptions may have been accurate. American players
probably were unfriendly because of the commissioner's offer of an official
PGA Tour card to Ballesteros following his victory at Greensboro. There were
no strings attached to the offer, as was usual for other players.

At this stage of his life Ballesteros had no time for anything but golf. His
new wealth was piling up, depreciated only by the young man's fascination
with extravagant watches. Superstardom arrived when he won the 1976 British
Open. Only 22, he was the youngest Open champ since 1893. The following
year he won the Masters, the youngest man ever to win that championship.
Now he was lionized everywhere he went. No longer treated as a Spanish peasant's son, doors were open to him everywhere. The American Tour desper-
ately needed his presence. Ballesteros had trouble from the beginning in
reciprocating the affection fans felt for him and for the verve he brought to
the game. "Golf is the only sport in the world that has so much contact with
the public." He lamented:

> In the clubhouse, on the driving range, on the practice green, even when you
> play on the course, people are beside you. I always admired Jack Nicklaus. He's
> much better than I am at golf and at handling all those things. He looks very
> relaxed, very loose. Latin people, you know, have hot blood. Sometimes I have
> difficulty controlling myself. Sometimes I lose control. I don't show it publicly
> but inside I feel a little tight and a little claustrophobic. Jack never seems in a
> hurry for anything. I think he has the perfect character for this game.

The first of Ballesteros's many disagreements with the commissioner started when Beman was assigning home circuits to foreign-born players and he listed Ballesteros's home tour as Spain. Ballesteros insisted it should be the European Tour. Then, in 1983, Beman changed PGA rules to require foreign players to enter at least 15 events in the U.S. every year in order to remain eligible to play the American Tour. Previously a foreigner had to obtain an exemption from the commissioner to play in any event outside the U.S. unless it was in the player's country of origin. Ballesteros again argued that Europe should be listed for him because Spain hosted only one major tournament. Beman surprisingly acceded, due no doubt to Ballesteros's drawing power more than to the commissioner's magnanimity.

In exchange for the exemption to play in European events, Ballesteros agreed to play 15 tournaments in the U.S. each year. This he did in 1984, but the following year he participated in only nine. In 1986 the PGA Tour revoked his membership. Ballesteros restrained his temper, at least publicly, saying only that the Tour had made a "silly mistake." In response Beman said that Ballesteros could rejoin the Tour in 1987 by playing the minimum number of 15 events. If not he could play only in the Masters, PGA Championship, and the U.S. Open — all non–PGA Tour sponsored tournaments.

Ballesteros tried to explain the controversy to his fans.

> I started when I was sixteen. When I was beginning, I was enjoying everything so much. It was exciting going on airplanes, being in different places all the time, meeting different people. For two years I was happy just to play. I had nice clubs and enough balls, and gloves and shoes. Golf was everything for me. It still is. But after 1976, when I knew I had a good chance to be a champion, that is when I started to have big ambitions. Now, nine years later, it is different. I don't like flying. I'm tired of hotels. It's tough to be alone most of the time and also difficult to live like a little star. People are always coming to you with the same questions. Last year I played in twenty-nine tournaments. I spend thirty-four weeks away from my house. I made ninety-three flights, and I spent a total of eleven days inside an airplane. I miss my family, my friends, many things. But I like this way better than the other way around.

Despite occasional flashes of his old magic, Ballesteros's game declined rapidly after 1990. He remained a force in the Ryder Cup events and recorded wins from time to time on the European Tour, but his trips to America grew progressively less successful. Nonetheless his achievements stood out for all to admire. The European player and commentator David Feherty, who nicknamed Ballesteros "Old Blue Face" because of the way his face seemed to turn blue with rage, summed up his impact on the game perhaps better than anyone:

> Enormous Latin temperament. I never watch golf. The Ryder Cup is the first golf I've actually gone out to watch since I turned pro. But I would watch Seve.

He is just very special. He did for European golf what Nicklaus and Palmer did for world golf in the early 1960's.

A second charismatic and enormously successful foreign star in the 1980s was Greg Norman. In 1981 he finished in fourth place in the Masters Tournament in his first appearance at Augusta. Although new to the PGA Tour, he already had won 17 events in his native Australia and in other locales. At Augusta he awed the galleries with enormous drives and long irons, while mastering the difficult greens with a veteran's aplomb. His mother had been an excellent golfer but Norman, preferring surfing and rugby, did not play golf until he was 17. Within two years he was breaking par. He turned professional at age 20, and at the 1976 Australian Open was paired with Jack Nicklaus. Nicklaus's book, *Golf My Way*, had been an important primer for Norman, especially in course management and strategy. Nervous at the pairing in the Open, Norman shot an 80. The day after he played much stronger and bettered Nicklaus by a stroke. Afterward in the locker room Nicklaus went out of his way to reassure Norman, telling the much younger man that with continued hard work he could have an excellent career in tournament golf and that he should come to the States to play the Tour.

Interspersed with Norman's daily regiment of golf were frequent fishing trips off the Brisbane Coast, where he watched sharks take catches before they could be brought to gaff. Tiring of the losses he purchased a Lee Enfield rifle, the long-time infantry weapon of the British Commonwealth, and fired away at the sharks before they could dismember his fish.

In the late 1970s he graduated to the European Tour. Competition was keen at this time, with Nick Faldo, Bernhard Langer, Sandy Lyle, Seve Ballesteros, Christy O'Connor, and other young, noteworthy players competing for growing purses. Norman improved steadily, and rose to become the number one ranking European player by 1982. The next season he joined the American Tour and moved to Arnold Palmer's Bay Hill Club, where he tied for first in the local tournament, eventually losing the playoff to Mike Nicolette.

In his first appearance in America Norman differed from his contemporaries in ways more significant than merely his distinctive looks. When he traveled to Oakmont for his first U.S. Open, he went to the practice tee and was amazed to hear other pros talking about how they would love to finish in the top 20 places and receive an invitation to the following season's Masters. "I couldn't believe what I was hearing," Norman remembered. "I just can't think that way. I go into every tournament with the idea that I'm going to win."

It was Nicklaus who had informed Norman that he was talented enough to play the PGA Tour. Now settled in Florida, the men became close friends and neighbors. When an ocean front home near the Nicklaus's went on the market, the Norman family moved to North Palm Beach. From then on they

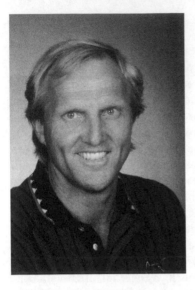

Greg Norman (©PGA Tour).

spent more and more time in one another's company, and Norman said that he benefited from the association. Other pros believed Norman would have been better off developing his own style.

In 1986 Norman came very close to winning at Augusta but pushed a 4-iron on the last hole to record a bogey and watched Nicklaus climb the hill for his last victory march at the Masters. In 1987 Larry Mize holed out on the 11th to edge Norman again at the Masters. In 1989 Norman bogeyed the 18th and missed the Faldo-Hoch playoff by one stroke. What hurt Norman more than anything at the Masters were mediocre first rounds. He always put together strong closing rounds, but the first one often was so weak it hurt his chances to win. Ken Venturi commented that Norman's first rounds were so bad because he put so much pressure on himself to live up to earlier predictions.

Norman signed with International Management Group and in 1986, at age 31, he had a sensational season. He won ten tournaments worldwide, becoming the first golfer to win a million dollars in one season. McCormack said his potential was unlimited. Norman led the four major championships going into the last round, but captured only the British Open of that year. Critics were fond of pointing to repeated examples of poor club selection when he was in contention to win. Sportswriters expected him to become Nicklaus's successor, as did the great man himself. But a series of bizarre mishaps befell Norman, dating from the shanks he hit under pressure on the 72nd hole of the 1984 U.S. Open and the 1986 Masters. He could be unpredictable in private life as well as on the golf course. With his fleet of Ferraris and other racing cars he was noted for racing against helicopters, and winning. He flew jet fighters, and of course was known early for a penchant for swimming in shark infested waters. "Anything that's dangerous he likes," said wife Laura.

In the 1989 British Open, Norman set a pattern for much of his career by shooting a tremendous last round at Troon. He birdied the first six holes to make up seven strokes and tie Mark Calcavecchia, then birdied the first two holes of the playoff only to watch Mark birdie one more and win. However, in 1993 at age 38, Norman won the Open again to record his second major tournament victory. It was in that tournament that Greg Norman and Nick Faldo fought one of the greatest duels of modern golf. Faldo came to St. George's with the superior record of the two. Number one in the Sony rankings to Norman's fourth place, Faldo had racked up five major championships in his career to Norman's one. In the 1990 Open at St. Andrews they had contested to no advantage in the third round, but on the final day Faldo humiliated Norman by shooting a 67 to the loser's 76.

In 1993 Norman earned his revenge. On the final nine holes he made a six-footer to save par on number 11, birdied 14, sank a ten-footer for par on 15, and birdied 16 to go ahead by three shots with only two holes to play. Then he missed a 14-inch putt for par on 17, and some of the fans began to think back to the frittering away of a four-stroke advantage at the 1986 PGA, the loss of a one-stroke lead with only two holes left to play at the 1989 British Open, and similar mishaps. This time, however, Norman did not disappoint. He hit two perfect shots on 18 to finish with a 64, the lowest winning final round in the history of the British Open. Watching the finish, Gene Sarazen called it the "greatest championship of my seventy years in golf."

After 11 seasons Norman had won 11 times on the PGA Tour, and 60 times worldwide. As impressive as the totals were, many fans remembered Norman for the series of disasters he endured, beginning with a 1984 U.S. Open playoff loss to Fuzzy Zoeller, dropping the Masters by one shot to Nicklaus, giving away a fourth round lead to Ray Floyd at the 1986 U.S. Open, watching Bob Tway sink a miracle bunker shot to win at the 1986 PGA Championship, and being beaten again by a phenomenal shot by Larry Mize at the 1987 Masters. In the 1993 PGA Championship at Inverness, Norman led after 70 holes, but Paul Azinger tied him on the last green.

Norman's 272 total tied the all-time PGA scoring record of 12 under, and he became the first golfer in history to shoot eight consecutive rounds under 70 in two consecutive majors, the British Open of 1993 and the PGA. The most amazing aspect of Norman's performance at Inverness was the number of pressure-laden putts he hit, at number ten, on the 18th, and on the second playoff hole, a stroke that looked as if it was dead in but spun out, because of, Norman complained, the white paint used to make the cups visible for television. He alleged that late in the day paint became crusty and repelled balls that should have stayed in. The men walked to the next playoff hole where Norman again needed a par to tie. Again Norman's putt lipped out. Paul Azinger won the PGA, his first major championship, and Norman became the first man in 50 years to lose playoffs in all four majors.

Although Greg Norman won only two major championships, he continued to command the galleries and television audiences. By 1994 he was earning nine million dollars a year, seven million from endorsements. He split with International Management Group to expand his own company, Great White Shark Enterprises, Inc., and hired more people to run Norman Yachts International and other family companies.

In spite of financial success fate continued to pursue him. The 1996 Masters was the scene of the most astonishing collapse in modern golf history as

Norman started the final day six shots ahead of the field, only to finish five strokes behind winner Nick Faldo! Reporters searched for an appropriate word. "Choke" seemed inadequate.

Another entertaining and competitive foreign player, whom no one could accuse of having been cloned from lackluster stock, was Ian Woosnam of Wales. At 5 feet, 4 inches, and 150 pounds, Woosnam was no less aggressive than Ballesteros or Norman. He hit the golf ball with everything he had, outdistancing Ballesteros to average 278 yards a drive, longest on the European Tour. Always tiny for his age, Woosnam had been bullied by his peers and had learned boxing skills as a remedy. In his first formal bout, Ian remembered:

> The first year I fought I recall being frightened before the bell went, so I tore into this boy and hit. His nose just splattered all over his face and his mother started crying and that was the end of it. I used to have to wear gloves that were bigger than my head and they laced up round about my elbows, but I could still do some damage with them. I'd just put my head down, get the other boys against the corner, and beat the crap out of them. In my second year they couldn't find anyone my age to face me so I took on one of the camp instructors who had to fight on his knees. He didn't enjoy that because he couldn't move fast enough, so I won again.

Woosnam displayed similar combativeness when he began playing golf tournaments. In order to stretch an inadequate budget, he bought an inexpensive motorhome with no heater and slept in his clothes. After five years he finally won the Swiss Open in 1982, climbed to eighth on the money list, and made an unexpected $200,000 that season, a huge reward for the poor farmer's son. Always welcome in the pubs, Ian cut back on his roistering and played much better after his marriage to childhood favorite Glendryth. His most impressive victory was the 1991 Masters, where he came to the last hole tied with Tom Watson and Jose Maria Olazabal. Ian sank an eight-footer to win the championship.

Not all the European golfers were as colorful as Ballesteros and Woosnam. Some, like Sandy Lyle, Bernhard Langer, and Nick Faldo could be as dour as an accountant facing an IRS audit even when playing Augusta National as if they owned it. Lyle won the Masters in 1988, and almost repeated in 1989. Langer won at Augusta in 1985, and again in 1993. Faldo took the championship in 1989 and 1996.

Bernhard Langer was such a methodical golfer he served as a ready caricature for his countrymen. He frequently used a surveyor's wheel to measure yardages at unfamiliar courses rather than rely on local caddies. "I agree that I'm methodical," he said. "I prepare very well. I feel happier when I'm well prepared. I do my yardages very correctly. I like to play a practice round or two and I like to know what I'm doing. Otherwise, it's a waste of time."

Son of a bricklayer who survived as a prisoner of war on the Eastern

Front, Langer began caddying and discovered he had an aptitude for striking golf balls. His 1993 win at Augusta was his second Masters victory, and gave him a total of 39 tournament wins worldwide. For a time he was the most consistent putter on the European Tour, but when the yips struck Langer resorted to an unusual grip whereby his putter shaft was braced against his left forearm. This served well on the terrifying greens of Augusta, although Langer never knew from one round to the next whether he could play unaffected by spasms.

"I was scared every day," Langer admitted:

> Every time you gave me the putter, I was scared. Even when you gave me an iron, or my caddie gave me an iron, I was scared I would hit it too far away from the hole and three or four-putt.... I can't recall what the yips felt like the very first time, but I've had them for so long. The first time lasted four years, then it came back two more times, so I know very well what it feels like. It's an uncontrollable movement of the muscles. It can go anywhere from a twitch, to a freeze where you can't move at all, to a sudden explosion. It's very confusing. Everything is totally out of whack, out of sequence, out of control. It's like your hands and arms are not part of you, not part of your body.

Despite his reputation for reticence, no one ever described the terrors of the yips better than Bernhard Langer.

One of the most dominant European players of all time was Nick Faldo, who remained atop the Sony World Rankings despite mixed reactions from his colleagues. Faldo was the only son of a London bookkeeper. He excelled at a number of sports. One day he watched a television broadcast of Jack Nicklaus in a golf tournament. From then on there was only one sport for Faldo. He turned pro at age 19. He won the British Open in 1987 and 1990, and the Masters in 1989, 1990, and 1996. Faldo acquired an unenviable reputation when he called a penalty on Sandy Lyle in 1980. Lyle placed some tape on his putter to prevent sun glare. Faldo noticed it, and after the round was completed he reported it to officials. Lyle was not amused.

Other players had been quick to notice that Faldo played most of his practice rounds alone, he seemed to constantly complain about course conditions, and he publicly ridiculed other players' swings. Of Greg Norman he was particularly scornful: "I have to be honest," said Faldo. "I look at his swing, and it's got faults. Under the severest of pressure will it hold up? It's way

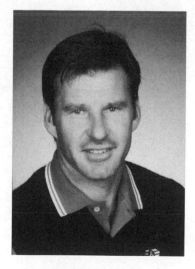

Nick Faldo (©PGA Tour).

too loose.... Some of what Norman does seems too obvious. Moving next door to Nicklaus, tying up their boats together. Design my back garden, Jack. But when he's playing with Nicklaus, he's always saying stuff like: 'Watch this, I'll fly Jack here. No problem.' I don't know if that's how you treat a friend."

In the 1990 Skins Game Curtis Strange showed obvious delight in beating Faldo. Curtis won $220,000, while Nick finished with only $70,000. Afterward Faldo told reporters: "I could not believe how nervous those guys were about it. I'd just won $350,000 in Japan where Curtis got shut out, and I never mentioned that. Yet Curtis actually seemed proud he'd won the thing."

Frequent comments of this kind did not endear Faldo to his peers. He appeared not to mind, sallying forth from his $2 million home on an 18-acre estate near London to joust with old rivals Lyle and Woosnam on the European Tour, and with many unfriendly adversaries on the PGA Tour. No one went out of his way to greet Nick Faldo or ask him how he was, irreverent David Feherty asserted, "because no one cared!"

The 1990s

"Remember that the life of this world is but a sport and a pastime."
— Koran LV II 19

The trends established in professional golf during the 1980s carried forward into the first years of the following decade. American players continued to be overshadowed by foreign-born stars like Greg Norman, Nick Price, and Nick Faldo, with the major championships of the early '90s dominated by European players Faldo and Bernhard Langer, South Africans Ernie Els and Nick Price, and Australian Greg Norman. John Daly, who suffered a series of personal mishaps, rebounded to win the 1995 British Open in a playoff. But Daly's contemporaries—Phil Mickelson, Tom Lehman, Davis Love, Justin Leonard, Lee Janzen, Paul Azinger, among others—while often winning flamboyantly, nevertheless failed to achieve anything like the presence or record of the leading stars of previous decades. The result? Fan interest in the 1990s increasingly gravitated toward the Senior PGA Tour and the charismatic elder statesmen of the game.

The Senior Tour had its genesis in the Legends of Golf Tournament, a two-man, better-ball event that Jimmy Demaret and producer Fred Raphael (founder of *Shell's Wonderful World of Golf*) organized in 1978 at Onion Creek Golf Club in Austin, Texas. The television audience tuned in to watch older players compete for rich purses. Sam Snead and Gardner Dickinson won the inaugural event, and when the team of Julius Boros and Roberto DeVicenzo went six extra holes to defeat Tommy Bolt and Art Wall in 1979, response from the galleries and television audience was extraordinarily favorable. Players age 50 and over were eligible to play, which attracted Gene Sarazen, Sam Snead, Jackie Burke, Ralph Guldahl, Gardner Dickinson, and other crowd favorites who were amazed at the interest the tournament engendered. In a magazine article Frank Beard remarked on the success of the event and pointed out that Arnold Palmer would be turning 50 soon. Arnie had by that time amassed some $55 million from golf and was the game's all-time spectator draw. The time was ripe for a Senior Tour.

Snead, Dickinson, and Boros met with PGA Commissioner Deane Beman and proposed a series of senior events to be open to any PGA member over 50 who placed high on the all-time victory list. Other players were to be admitted on sponsor exemptions and through special qualifying rounds. The commissioner approved the idea despite some misgivings, and he projected a high of 15 or 20 tournaments if sponsors could be found. He agreed to put up $350,000 as collateral, and when the new tour was announced older players deluged the commissioner with queries trying to find out if they were eligible. Officials limited the number of entries to the top 36 players, and in 1980 two events were held, at Atlantic City and Melbourne, Florida, each worth $125,000 in prize money.

The importance of Arnold Palmer to the success of the new tour soon became apparent. Palmer had sent a letter declining to play in the first PGA Seniors Championship for which he was eligible, despite the fact he had not won since age 43. For almost a year and one-half he passed up all invitations to play in official senior events. In December 1980 he had a change of heart and entered the PGA Seniors Championship at Turnbury Isle, which he won. The following year he played in several senior tournaments culminating in a victory at the 1981 Senior Open.

In 1980 the Open had drawn only 4,000 daily spectators without Palmer. With him, 43,000 fans gathered at Oakland Hills. This set the pattern for the next several years. Without Palmer tournaments drew few spectators. When Palmer arrived, so did the fans. Attendance for the Legends of Golf in 1979 had been 20,000. When Palmer played in 1980, 100,000 spectators showed up. His impact on the burgeoning success of the tour was incalculable. When one tournament organizer told sponsors that he could guarantee Palmer, Snead, Boros, Casper, and other leading lights for a senior event, but went on to ask if they would be interested also in hosting a regular PGA tournament, the sponsor said, "No. Who's playing on the regular tour??"

In 1981 sponsors began lining up to host events for the Senior Tour, and Miller Barber won three times. That season Barber won $50,000 on the regular tour, and $83,000 on the senior circuit. 1981 was a watershed year in more ways than one. A *Golf Digest* column expressed caution about the future of the Tour, as the players lobbied to have the number of tournaments increased. Beman was providing all the organizational apparatus for the seniors at the behest of Palmer, Snead, and other superstars, while Billy Casper, Gene Littler, Doug Ford, Bob Rosburg, and others helped draw the crowds. At the same time observers worried that very few name players would be turning 50 anytime soon. Gay Brewer, Dave Marr, and Doug Sanders were coming along, but there were no more Palmers or Sneads on the horizon.

This bothered the current players not at all. Bob Goalby banked $112,000 in 1981, which was $35,000 more than he ever made in a single year on the regular tour. In 1982 Barber finished first again, with $107,000 in prize money.

In 1983 the number of senior tournaments reached 18. Popular pro-ams scheduled for two separate days at each tournament site brought in a minimum of $1,000 per amateur and carried the Senior Tour along until gallery interest and growing television audiences caught up. The rivalry for roster spots grew contentious. Exemptions to play the regular PGA Tour were based largely on performance in recent tournaments. However, the senior circuit granted playing privileges based on how many tournaments and how much money players had won during their careers when younger. In any given senior event with 50 entrants, the top 20 career money winners and the top 20 in career tournament victories were automatic participants, leaving about ten spots for sponsor exemptions.

The first few years were especially lucrative for Miller Barber, Don January, and Jerry Barber. On the prize money list for the initial four years, Barber finished in top place twice, and second place twice, as did January in reverse order. Then Peter Thomson ignited, winning nine tournaments in 1985, the most any pro had won since Sam Snead captured ten in 1950. That year the success of the Tour provided ample resources to start a retirement plan for the seniors. Any pro who placed 40th or above was credited with a retirement unit valued at $500. The money was placed in annuities that were non-taxable until a player decided to withdraw his benefits.

The year 1985 was pivotal. Snead, Goalby, and the other founders of the Senior Tour persuaded Don Ohlmeyer to arrange televised coverage of six senior events. ESPN provided the coverage, and Mazda bought the time. Other advertisers examined audience demographics and quickly signed on. R.J. Reynolds and Cadillac were major backers. That year larger purses created larger entrant fields. In each event 72 players teed off, 28 from the all-time prize list, 28 current leaders, 12 from a qualifying test, and four from sponsor exemptions. Most of the men discovered they were having more fun than they ever had experienced on the junior circuit. They realized that to guarantee success it would be necessary to capitalize on the lucrative pro-am formats. Sponsors began to arrange social events prior to the start of a tournament, and an awards party on the final day. Other parties were scheduled whenever possible, and pros like Bob Goalby made them all.

"We had a tremendous amount of fun the first five years," Goalby remembered. "We all went to the parties. We were out to pasture, and to make it work we had to go to the parties and hobnob."

Goalby gave a lot of the credit for success to Sam Snead and Julius Boros. "Without them we would never have gotten to first base. Snead played every tournament for four years and went to every clinic, every dinner and every draw party. He said he had more fun playing senior golf those four or five years than he had had in golf anywhere else. The only thing he felt bad about was that he wasn't a little more competitive. He was 67 when he started."

Some of the seniors who were never crowd favorites as junior players now realized how important pro-am revenue was for the Senior Tour, and they went out of their way to make amateurs welcome. By 1985 the Senior Tour had become a separate division of the PGA Tour and had grown to 27 tournaments with more than $6 million in prize money. Don January's amazement was typical of many of his peers.

"If you had told me back in 1980 that we'd have this many events and be playing for this money," Don related, "I'd have said you were crazy!" Within five years, however, the seniors were playing in 42 tournaments, half of which were televised, and prize money ballooned to $24 million. Television ratings for senior events were very high, and some overshadowed the regular PGA, as with the 1990 Senior Open that featured a head-to-head duel between Jack Nicklaus and Lee Trevino. That drew twice as many viewers as the simultaneous broadcast of the PGA Tour event in Hartford.

The junior circuit was more than ever suffering the doldrums of cooler rivalries and fewer charismatic players, while Arnold Palmer, Chi Chi Rodriguez, Gary Player, Lee Trevino, and Jack Nicklaus were drawing a large, loyal audience at the course and on television. Trevino rolled to a remarkable rookie season, winning seven of the 28 events he entered and banking $1,190,000 in prize money. The success of Trevino and Nicklaus's entry on the Senior Tour pushed gallery attendance and TV ratings up 35 percent in one year. The other players benefited proportionally. Mike Hill, who had been rated a journeyman player on the PGA Tour, earned $895,000 in 1990 on the Senior Tour. His brother Dave was winning as well. Dave Hill wanted everyone to know where the credit for all this good fortune belonged.

"The Senior Tour had it made before Trevino and Nicklaus ever got here," he argued. "The man who put this tour on the map was Arnold Palmer, not Trevino and Nicklaus!"

Hill was just as feisty as ever. Frank Beard was playing with him again, and observed:

> I think it's fair to say Dave has not mellowed as a senior. Not one iota. Frank Beard he loves. He's not mad at me. He's not mad at you, either, or the guys he plays with every day. It's Nicklaus he wants to take on. It's the golf course architects, the corporations, the government, the world in general. Somebody once dubbed him "The Last Angry Man" and I guess that's true, since his brother Mike has calmed down.

J.C. Snead turned 50 in 1990 and said he had been looking forward for a long time to the Senior Tour, which seemed from a distance to be Nirvana. But he revealed that he soon discovered the opposite, that the tour was one

> big crybaby party. Everything bothers these guys. They complain about the birds chirping, the color of your shoes, the coin you use to mark your ball, the side of the fairway you drive your cart. It's just ridiculous. It takes the fun out of it.

> Some of these guys are almost mean. There's been more fights out here than in the last fifteen years on the other tour. We've had guys almost get into fistfights. They're like old dogs fighting over a bone.

True to form, the first publicized slugest occurred between J.C. Snead and Dave Hill, a donnybrook followed by Snead's launching shots toward Hill's group on a practice range.

Another tough guy from the past was Bruce Crampton. His character did not change on the Senior Tour either. Beard played with him and reflected: "He is such a stickler in life that if you want to change your ball in a tournament and you neglect to show the ball to him first, he might call a penalty. Not out of spite, not out of resentment — that's just the kind of person he is. So when I wanted to change the ball today I took it over and showed it to him. He took it from me, and he STUDIED it!"

Despite a few prickly personalities, the Senior Tour thrived, and its rejuvenated participants basked through halcyon days. In its 14th year, 1993, the tour grew to $28 million in prize money. Many new faces arrived to drink from this spring, colorful club pros like Larry Laoretti who captured the 1992 U.S. Senior Open and took home more than $900,000 in his first three seasons. Jim Albus and Mike Joyce joined Laoretti as the only non–PGA Tour regulars to win senior events in those years. Club pros faced a qualifying school that permitted only eight exempt positions among a field of 400 men.

If he survived, the club pro went head-to-head with veterans who had played the regular PGA Tour for as long as 25 years (Floyd and Nicklaus could boast even longer tenures). Staying on the senior circuit was very difficult, as only the top 31 money winners were exempt each year. This made the success of unknowns even more remarkable. Galleries loved to root for the underdog, and several unheralded players emerged to garner publicity and fan attention. Larry Laoretti, Walt Zembriski, Jim Albus, Tom Wargo, Jay Siegel, John Cain, Simon Hobday, and others became celebrities and wealthy. Albus won the 1992 U.S. Senior Open, and Wargo took the 1993 Senior Players Championship. Albus was a long-time club pro who had been victorious in many events in the Northeastern U.S., while Wargo leaped to fame after toiling as an auto worker, short order chef, and dairy farmer in Illinois.

Wargo qualified to play the Tour for the first time in 1992 and went on to win $70,000 in five events the following year. He came to the championship at PGA National without one commercial endorsement. In the final round of the tournament Bruce Crampton birdied the final two holes to tie Wargo and force a playoff. On the second playoff hole Crampton bogeyed while Wargo made par to pocket the $110,000 first place check.

Albus and Wargo truly were Horatio Alger stories, but the most improbable success story of all may have been Walt Zembriski. Starting as a caddie at the Out-of-Bounds Club in Mahwah, New Jersey, Walt alternated stints in the Army and construction jobs and a growing passion for golf. He won the 1966 New Jersey State Amateur and earned a PGA Tour card, but then won nothing for two years. He lost his sponsor and his spouse and wound up on the Florida mini-tour competing against youngsters like Paul Azinger, Bob Tway, and Mark Calcavecchia. In 1985 he became eligible for the Senior Tour and qualified to enter the U.S. Senior Open at Tahoe Country Club. Leading after two rounds, Zembriski fell back at the end but still tied for fourth place overall. In his first full season, 1986, he won over $100,000 then doubled that the following season. In 1988 he posted his first victory, the Newport Cup, and went on to win the Vantage Championship, the Tour's largest winner's check, worth $135,000. That pushed his winnings to $350,000. Walt recalled what it had been like to enter the elite environs of the Senior Tour: "At first I wasn't comfortable out here. I didn't go in the locker rooms because guys were sitting around telling stories about the old days and I didn't have any."

Most of Zembriski's memories seemed to evoke discouragement, like the time he had qualified to play in the U.S. Open and arrived to find his locker placed next to Tom Weiskopf. When the two men bumped into one another, Weiskopf tried to give his shoes to Zembriski to have them cleaned. "I don't work here!" Walt said testily. "I'm playing in the tournament. In fact, I'm one stroke ahead of you!"

One revenue enhancer that was not available to players like Zembriski was a system that was similar to the appearance money given to stars on the European Tour. Although appearance money was banned by the PGA, it was legal for sponsors to offer compensation for what came to be known as "outings that surround." Marquee players received large sums to give short speeches, to attend dinners, or to walk through a cocktail party. It was rumored that as much as $75,000 might change hands for these minimal chores. During the week of the Bell Canadian Open, top stars were offered $20,000–50,000 to play in a Monday outing prior to the start of the tournament. Many other tournament sponsors employed the same tactics.

In 1994 the season for the regular PGA Tour got off to an unusual start when the most popular American stars suffered early injuries, Fred Couples with a bad back and Paul Azinger with melanoma. Phil Mickelson broke a bone in his leg and fractured his ankle in a skiing accident as 46-year-old Johnny Miller won the Pebble Beach AT&T and 49-year-old Hale Irwin walked off with the MCI at Harbour Town. It would not be long before those two brought their considerable talents to the Senior Tour. That Tour had become so lucrative, several unheralded pros were angry about the attention given to famous but no longer competitive names, and the PGA was sued on the grounds that the Senior Tour was discriminating against talented players when it awarded exemptions to stars from the distant past.

Frank Beard, for one, defended established practice when he said the Tour needed people like Arnold Palmer, Julius Boros, Sam Snead, and Billy Casper for their nostalgic drawing power. He used the analogy of an old-timers baseball team composed of Mickey Mantle, Yogi Berra, Whitney Ford, and teammates from the past matched against a younger and unbeatable American Legion team. Who would pay to see the Legionnaires if the old-timers were not present?

Younger, less heralded seniors would have to be content with a qualifying school that admitted about 15 high finishers each year, plus the exemptions that were available from sponsors. Given the growth of the Senior Tour, officials were unwilling to tinker with the formula that had created success. Sponsors were lining up to host events, and senior tournaments frequently garnered higher television ratings than competing regular PGA events. As long as the most influential players continued to compete and enjoy the experience, no one was going to radically alter the organization of the Tour.

One of the most influential pros steamrolled the competition like a one-man tank army. Jim Colbert captured three tournaments in his rookie senior season and banked $880,000, a figure that was more than half his total winnings during 22 years on the regular PGA circuit where he had won eight tournaments. In the late 1980s Colbert had endured a number of physical aliments that redirected his energies toward managing golf courses and broadcasting work for ESPN. But when he turned 50 Jim sold his businesses and gave up the TV assignment to embark on the senior circuit. As with so many of his contemporaries, the Senior Tour for Colbert turned into a second professional career beyond his wildest imaginings.

Colbert's talent with money management backfired in 1994 when it was discovered that players were relying on him to act as a banker for purse splitting at senior events. Many golf fans knew that superstars frequently received appearance money to play in tournaments they might otherwise ignore, but few were aware how common purse sharing was in playoffs where two or more men would agree in advance to split prize money regardless of who the winner might be. The USGA had a prohibition against the practice, but the PGA was less stringent.

Jack Nicklaus liked to tell the story of how he was a very young pro when Arnold Palmer offered to split first place money as the two men were playing off a major championship. Palmer already was wealthy and Nicklaus needed the money, and considered it an act of charity on Palmer's part. It is doubtful if anyone in the gallery that day realized that an agreement had been made before the two men teed off on the first playoff hole. The fans assumed that both men were fighting for the first place check. In reality, at the conclusion of such a playoff the winning pro received a winner's check, after which he wrote a personal check to the second-place finisher for the difference between first place money and half the sum of the combined prizes. At income tax time the winning player declared the full amount of first place money as income, then deducted as a business expense the check paid out to the second place player.

When questioned about the ethics of this practice, pros had a ready argument, i.e., purse splitting agreements did not mean that one man would play with less commitment because what was most important in the long run was the title, not the money. The desire to win championship titles far outweighed the importance of purses because of the exemptions from qualifying that major championships granted and the many endorsement contracts that would be offered to the winning player, factors that far exceeded the value of tournament prize money. When he was the best player in the world Arnold Palmer was quick to defend purse sharing:

> A guy who's worked hard for seventy-two holes to gain a tie shouldn't have to throw it all away on one hole.... I believe that the two guys who have tied for a championship have a right to do what they want with the prize money. I know I'll go either way. If the other fellow wants to split, OK. If he doesn't that's OK too. I've always played for the title, which is very important. Where splitting is concerned, sometimes I'll bring up the suggestion. Some guys don't like to bring it up. I might ask them, just to get their feelings about it. I guess there is a little pressure in my case to be a good guy and split. But it isn't going to hurt me in any event, and it might really help out the other guy. The thing that's important is there's no lack of incentive. Everything depends on winning. The guy who finishes second in a playoff, or anything else, might just as well finish twentieth. I don't care what anyone says. Nobody ever remembers who finished second.

Gary Player seconded Palmer's opinion: "I'll be the first to admit that I've split in some playoffs. I'm in favor of it, especially in sudden death playoffs. There is too much involved to have it riding on one hole. I tell you, when it comes to a split I'm never ashamed to ask for one, or accept one."

Critics objected, however, arguing that it was one thing for Palmer and Player to say that splitting did not dilute the golfer's incentive, and that "everything depends on winning," but it is something else when a journeyman pro plays strongly enough to reach a playoff, may indeed have played beyond his routine capabilities and is savoring the triumph of finishing in a tie for the championship just as his competitor, a reigning superstar, deflates the balloon by offering to split first place money. This was the view of longtime USGA Director Joe Dey, who believed that a "player in any sport should do his best on his own and his best all the time. The USGA feels that if a player has an interest in another player's performance the opportunity is present for things to happen that should not happen in any sport."

Purse splitting seems to have been practiced as early as the 1920s. Walter Hagen described how in the early years of the century it was common for some players to divide winnings. If one man finished second, another fourth, and still another fifth, they placed their prizes into a pool and divided it at the conclusion of the season. Hagen, however, denied splitting any money at all, because as he averred, "I always figured I could beat all the others." By the time Byron Nelson was playing his best golf in the late '30s and '40s, purse splitting was widespread.

"In my time about sixty percent of the pros split playoff purses," Byron recalled:

> I would guess about the same percentage of them do nowadays. In my opinion there is nothing unethical about such arrangements. I never asked to split a purse after I had tied for a championship, but if anyone asked you to split with them before the playoff round the sporting thing to do was to agree. If you didn't you were apt to lose friends. I specifically remember the Tam O'Shanter Open in 1942. Clayton Heafner and I tied, and Clayton asked me to split with him. He said, "You're going to beat me anyhow, so why don't you be a good guy and cut the money up?" I didn't refuse.

Bob Rosburg, television commentator and former chairman of the PGA tournament committee, was another who believed that splitting was not unethical, especially in sudden death playoffs. Bob believed that dividing purses did not affect effort. "It means too much to win," he argued. "In most tournaments you get more in bonuses than you do in prize money. I'm not even a top echelon player, but every time I won I picked up bonuses from companies I'm associated with." Another contemporary of Rosburg's, Jay Hebert, agreed: "The sudden death playoff is partly responsible.... It's the title, not the prize money that really counts. There's hardly a player who wouldn't give away his first place check for a title. A sudden death playoff makes it all a matter of luck. Even Ben Hogan was willing to split a playoff purse. But he would always make you play for about one thousand dollars." Hebert and others pleaded with sponsors to hold 18-hole playoffs, as in the U.S. Open, which was a fairer test of talent with less likelihood of luck deciding the outcome. But the importance of television and the crammed schedules of most Tour players militated against long Monday playoffs.

In 1994 Deane Beman discovered that senior players had split the purse of the United Van Lines Aces Championship, and he fined the men who had participated $2,000 each. The players filed an angry appeal. The commissioner expanded his inquiries and learned that splitting was practiced frequently among the seniors. Dave Stockton, Isao Aoki, Dave Hill, Larry Laoretti, Miller Barber, Billy Casper, George Archer, Bob Charles, Mike Hill, Jim Dent, and Jim Colbert, among others were said to be participants. After some events players would send splits to Jim Colbert's accountant, who calculated taxes and divided up shares for other players. At the Merrill Lynch Shoot-Out, for example, ten players competed for $400,000 in prize money. It was alleged that the players agreed among themselves in advance to split the purse equally, and when later fined argued that the event was not a PGA competition but only a television event of a semi-comedic nature. Bruce Crampton had worn a wig and earrings at one event, and said: "I don't consider them competitions. They're hit and giggles. It was no big deal!"

Commissioner Beman disagreed. Despite his planning to join the Senior Tour after retirement and the fact that Jim Colbert was so prominently involved in splitting (Colbert was a long time friend and supporter of the commissioner), Beman decided to fine players for every incident of purse splitting. Because the events had been advertised and run as if they were bona fide competitions, it was prudent of the PGA Tour to take reasonable precautions against sullying the reputation of any senior tournament no matter how frivolous. So successful was the senior circuit, with so much money flowing into the pockets of even journeyman pros, that many of the pros no longer could judge an issue like purse splitting from the perspective of an ordinary fan.

As the Senior Tour climbed from one success to another, the regular PGA Tour was pinning its hopes for continued popularity on the robust shoulders but fragile psyche of John Daly. The galleries multiplied for Daly, and he attracted legions of new fans who did not even play the game. He also awed his playing partners. Tom Watson, paired with Daly at Blue Hills, Kansas, hit a very good drive only to watch John hit his 330 yards uphill to stop 80 yards ahead in the fairway. At the Skins Game, Curtis Strange was hitting what for him were long, drawing tee shots. Daly's ball was settling 60 yards past Strange's. Joey Sindelar watched Daly's ball land where Joey's had stopped rolling in the fairway and said: "What's different about Daly is that in the past the latest long hitter was always, say ten yards longer than other players. Not thirty yards!"

Tour statistics placing Daly longest with an average of 288 yards to Davis Love's second place 278 yards did not tell the whole story. At Spyglass Hill the first hole is 600 yards. Daly hit driver and 4-iron over the green. In the U.S. Open at Baltusrol, Daly reached the 630-yard 17th hole with driver and 1-iron. At the Players Championship, on the 336-yard dogleg 12th hole, Daly drove the ball past the green. At the 13th at Greensboro, a par-five requiring an extremely high, long drive to cut the dogleg, he hit a towering drive more than 320 yards, then took a 9-iron for his approach shot. At Castle Pines on the tenth hole, which plays to 525 yards, his drive carried so far he had only a sand wedge to the green. In a practice round with Jack Nicklaus prior to the British Open at Sandwich, Daly's drive rolled through the green on a 421 yard dogleg. The galleries loved every shot.

Daly's fame started at the 1991 PGA Championship. He traveled all night from Memphis to Carmel, Indiana unsure if he would get into the tournament until Thursday morning when Nick Price finally withdrew. Daly teed off at Crooked Stick having never seen the course and shot a 69, this on a layout that Nicklaus claimed was the most difficult he had ever played. Pete Dye had lengthened his creation to 7,289 yards, second longest in PGA history. Distance off the tee was a very big advantage, which Curtis Strange learned on his way to shooting a first round 81. The galleries moved to watch Daly, and the television cameras soon were trained on his every move. He birdied the 18th hole on Saturday to take a three-stroke lead, while Nicklaus told the television audience: "Good gracious, what an unleashing of power. I don't know who he reminds me of. I haven't seen anybody who hit the ball that far!" The television audience was further intrigued by a caller who claimed Daly should have taken a two-stroke penalty when his caddie helped show the line of a putt on number 11. After a mini-crisis the caddie was absolved of any rules violation, and Daly went into Sunday's round well ahead of Bruce Lietzke and Kenny Knox. A collapse by the unknown on Sunday would not have surprised veterans. Instead Daly made only two mistakes during the round and easily held on to capture the championship and $230,000.

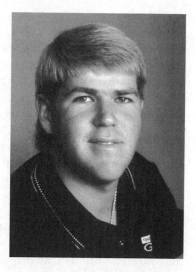

John Daly (©PGA Tour).

Soon thereafter Daly was invited to The Skins Game, where he won $160,000 and three cars worth at least another $60,000. He was the gallery favorite despite the presence of Nicklaus. On the third tee Daly told the fans: "I think it's time to pump up you all," and reached down to hit the inflator buttons on his new golf shoes. The plug brought joy to the manufacturer and enlivened the gallery. Plagued by a sore back and perhaps by the prowess of the youngster who routinely outdrove him by 60 yards, Nicklaus won no skins.

John Daly was the youngest of three children born to Jim Daly, a nuclear engineer who traveled constantly and switched jobs frequently. Daly was a loner who found solace at golf courses wherever he moved. He progressed rapidly with golf, playing so well at age 12 he won the men's championship at Lake of the Woods Country Club in Fredricksburg, Virginia, after which the adults changed club rules to exclude juniors from the championship. When he was a senior in high school, his parents moved once again from their current home in Arkansas, and this time the son stayed behind to live with his older brother in Dardanelle. With the added freedom for recreation, Daly's grades slipped badly from his customary As and Bs. The University of Arkansas came through, however, with a partial scholarship, and the coach turned Daly into a project. Constantly admonishing him to lose weight, coach Steve Loy rode Daly hard, treatment that Daly later found difficult to forget or forgive.

At age 21 he married Dale Crafton of Blytheville, Arkansas, a union that collapsed after two years. By this time Daly had left the university and was playing the South African Tour. Improving steadily, he gravitated to the Hogan

Tour and won a tournament in 1990. Then he qualified for the PGA Tour in 1990, and the following season won the PGA Championship.

During the following two years Daly suffered a series of misfortunes caused largely by substance abuse, and Commissioner Deane Beman notified Daly that he would be suspended from the PGA Tour if he did not immediately begin a recovery and treatment program. Afterward Daly and his wife Bettye moved from Castle Pines to Orlando, where his fondness for beer passed to Diet Coke, pack after pack of sugar rich M&Ms and ubiquitous Marlboros.

At this point there were many fans who believed that the commissioner needed Daly more than the unpredictable star needed the Tour. Bereft of superstars, the PGA Tour was quick to welcome him back from recovery. The only golfer capable of bringing more spectators to a regular PGA tournament than Jack Nicklaus, John Daly was widely believed by officials to be capable of attracting as many as 30,000 fans all by himself. If many of the fans were raucous and unfamiliar with the rules of the game, tournament sponsors nonetheless were compensated when they totaled their revenue. The 92-year-old Gene Sarazen watched hundreds of fans line up at the first tee to watch for Daly, and he said:

> I'm delighted that John is coming back into the fold. It reminds me of when the Yankees played in the 20's and 30's, and if Babe Ruth wasn't in the lineup there was hardly anybody in the crowd. Now comes the Babe Ruth of golf, John Daly. They don't care what he shoots, as long as they're watching John Daly.

However, Daly's behavior continued to worry observers. He was placed on probation by the Tour for failing to sign a scorecard at the Kemper Open and for quitting after nine holes at the Buick Southern Open. Then he picked up his ball after shooting three double bogeys at the Kapalua International, and the commissioner issued a suspension of four months. When he returned he further angered colleagues with comments about drug abuse. Off in the British Isles to play in the 1994 Scottish Open, Daly told reporters,

> I wish we could have drug testing on the Tour. There are certain people on the Tour who do the crazy stuff. They are never going to get exposed unless they are found out by the police and put in jail. I think it's unfair a lot of this stuff has been hidden. If we did introduce testing it would help the guys with problems, not hurt them. Plus, a lot of the guys would say, "No way I want to get caught, so I'll quit."

The remarks set off a firestorm, and the next day Daly offered a caveat: He personally knew of no one on the Tour using drugs. "But I've heard rumors," he said.

> I don't know it, but I believe it…. If we did have drug testing I'd probably be one of the cleanest guys out there. Drugs, cocaine, some of the other crazy things. If you're going to test everybody, athletes in the NBA and football players for steroids and stuff, test the golfers, let it come out.

Other players immediately fired back. Curtis Strange was quoted as saying, "Daly should crawl under the rock he came from. He doesn't realize it doesn't take much to tear down what it took Arnold Palmer and Jack Nicklaus and others thirty-five years to build!" And from the Senior Tour, Bob Murphy added: "I don't know how to react to Daly except to say, in my humble opinion, we saved the young man's life. We clamped down on him at a time when he needed it. He got help. He's a lucky, lucky young guy. He should be very happy that he's clean and he shouldn't be worrying about anyone else."

Other players publicly agreed by claiming that professional golf was self-policing because anyone using powerful drugs would self-destruct by missing cuts and losing playing privileges. The controversy died away as the Tour commissioner explained: "There may have been very isolated instances over the years in which an individual needed assistance, but our sport has been blessed because we have not had these problems. I look forward to talking to John and to anybody else, for that matter, who has any information on the subject."

Daly's erratic behavior continued through the 1994 season, culminating at the World Series of Golf in August. During the final round, in which Daly shot an 83, Jeffrey Roth accused Daly of hitting into him. In the previous week's tour event, both Andrew Magee and Greg Norman's caddies had complained of Daly hitting into their groups. As Daly left the clubhouse at Akron following his miserable last round in the World Series he was confronted by 62-year-old Bob Roth, Jeffrey's father. Remarks were exchanged and Mrs. Bob Roth alleged that Daly cursed both parents before Bob grabbed him from behind. They fell to the ground and wrestled briefly before being separated by caddies and bystanders. Neither man was seriously injured, although Bob Roth's elbow was scraped and needed to be bandaged. The newly installed commissioner of the PGA Tour, Tim Finchem, investigated the incident and met with Daly before announcing that the player would sit out the remainder of the 1994 season and would "prepare himself physically and mentally for coming back to the Tour."

The adverse publicity and enforced absence from the Tour proved to be much worse than a temporary inconvenience. Daly lost his multi-million dollar sponsorship deal with the Wilson Sporting Goods Company, to be resumed only if the golfer met specific behavioral and performance measures. The contrite golfer promised once again to reform. "Wilson has been very supportive of me during my career," Daly said, "so I understand and support the company's decision. I plan to practice and prepare myself as much as possible so that when I return to professional competition I will play and conduct myself at the level Wilson and my fans have come to expect."

Daly did return and played well for a time. But in the spring of 1997 he slipped into old habits. Arrested after tearing up a hotel room in Florida, Daly again voluntarily entered a center for treatment of alcohol addiction. His friends began to publicly voice doubts about whether his enormous talent for golf could survive and resurface after such a series of self-destructive actions. But he was befriended by Ely Callaway, who aided in his recovery and signed the troubled player to an endorsement contract to play Callaway clubs. When Daly returned to the Tour he resumed his competitive status and remained one of golf's premier attractions.

In 1996 the Tour entered a new age with the advent of superstar Tiger Woods, a heartening development for the future of the regular PGA Tour and for the sport of golf in general. In 1994 Tiger Woods had stunned the amateur golf ranks by setting two milestones. He became he youngest winner, at age 18, in the history of the U.S. Amateur Golf Championship, edging out Jack Nicklaus who had accomplished that feat at 19. In match play Woods recorded a two-up victory at Ponte Vedra Beach. Trailing badly in the early going, he rallied to win six of the final ten holes. In the same season, as a Stanford University freshman, he won the National Intercollegiate Tournament at Shoal Creek, where so much civil rights history had been made during the 1990 PGA Championship.

Just prior to the start of the 1990 Championship, the owner of Shoal Creek publicly stated that he was not interested in having African-Americans join his club because "That's just not done in Birmingham." The statement caused an uproar, and led to the issuing of new regulations on the part of the USGA, LPGA, and PGA Tour that required tournament hosting clubs to have integrated memberships. Thompson and Shoal Creek hastened to obey in order to save the 1990 Championship. Other clubs dithered. Of a combined total of 121 tournaments on three professional tours, five hosting clubs refused to conform to the new guidelines. Butler National, host of the Western Open, refused to admit women and the tournament was moved to Dubsdread, an outstanding public course at Cog Hill in the suburbs of Chicago. Also recalcitrant were Cypress Point, Merion, and the Saint Louis Country club. So when Tiger Woods became the first minority golfer to win a major amateur event, in a sport that had few non–Caucasian stars to boast of, the achievement was especially salutary when it occurred at Shoal Creek.

In the summer of 1996, Woods won an unprecedented third consecutive U.S. Amateur title. Immediately, speculation began that he would forgo his studies at Standford and turn professional. When the decision was announced a short time later and the financial details were outlined, the endorsement contracts finalized for Woods staggered the most jaded sports fan. International Management Group, the Nike Corporation, and Titleist won out over a host of competitors, and their combined payments would make Woods an extremely wealthy young man even if he failed to win a single PGA tournament. Estimates ranged upward to at least $10 million a year to be paid out by Nike and Titleist, even though Woods played with a mixed bag of clubs— Mizuno irons, a Cobra driver, Cleveland wedges, and a Titleist putter.

When the hullabaloo over Wood's endorsement contracts died down, media attention switched to whether or not he would be able to qualify for the 1997 PGA tour, given the fact that only a few scheduled tournaments remained to be played in the 1996 season. The first event Woods entered was the Greater Milwaukee Open. Tournament sponsors were delighted to see 10,000 more spectators show up than were expected, the surplus attributed to Woods's appearance. After having won 36 consecutive USGA championship matches, three U.S. Junior crowns, and three U.S. Amateurs, Woods expressed little fear about the PGA Tour. But the reality was different. He never had played particularly well in the PGA events to which he had

Tiger Woods (©PGA Tour).

been invited as an amateur. The constant media attention was also a major distraction for the new pro. Loren Roberts won the tournament and Woods faded badly, generating still more doubt that he would be able to win enough cash in the events remaining to qualify as one of the 130 exempt players for the 1997 Tour.

The breakthrough came in early October. Woods won the Las Vegas International with a first prize of $297,000. Two weeks later he won for a second time, at the Walt Disney World tournament, and pocketed another $216,000. Not only was his place on the 1997 Tour assured, but Woods had answered all his critics by winning an amazing $790,000 in his first two months as a professional. His achievements brought Woods the 1996 *Golf Digest* Rookie of the Year Award.

Woods started off the 1997 PGA Tour season in similarly grand style. He won the first event of the year, the Mercedes Championship, and finished second at Pebble Beach. As the Tour continued its trek toward the first major tournament of the year, the Masters, observers began to note the historical significance of having an African-American favorite on the tournament roster. When journalists questioned some of the competitors about Woods's chances at Augusta, they were skeptical. As if to confirm those doubts, Woods played his first nine holes on the opening day in 40 strokes, four over par.

That was the last opportunity for doubters. Woods proceeded to shoot 30 on the back nine, then fired a 66 on Friday, and a 65 on Saturday, to take a huge lead into the final round. There was no repeat of the year before when Greg Norman disintegrated on the final day. Woods shot 69 on Sunday to win the Masters by 12 shots over second place Tom Kite. Woods set numerous records. He became the youngest winner in history, with the widest margin of victory and the lowest total score of any Masters victor. His length off the tee created a formidable advantage over his peers, but equally as impressive was his work on Augusta's terrifying greens. "Tiger is out there playing another game," commented Jack Nicklaus, echoing an opinion that Bobby Jones voiced many years before when watching the young Nicklaus play Augusta for the first time. "He plays a game with which I am unfamiliar," Jones said at the time.

Woods's victory was so complete, and so uncontestable, his detractors were nowhere to be found at the end of the tournament. Golf fans were attracted to the young superstar in numbers and fervor unseen since the emergence of Arnold Palmer. Huge galleries followed Woods from the first hole, and television ratings—especially on the final day of the tournament — soared. The sponsors who had put up all the cash a year before now were ecstatic.

"I think Tiger will have greater impact worldwide then even Michael Jordan," said Nike's Phil Knight, who had signed Woods to a huge contract earlier. Others, like Charlie Sifford and Lee Elder, were excited about the enhanced possibilities for minorities now that Woods had somersaulted into national prominence. Not just the sports world would benefit from having a new and charismatic dominant player, but also many millions of inner-city children gained an idol in a sport which lacked notable minority role models.

At the time of Tiger Woods's debut, many golf fans could remember the days when sports were almost totally segregated in America. At one of the earliest U.S. Opens, Shinnecock Hills, in 1896, 35 entrants had appeared. One, Oscar Bunn, was a full-blooded member of the Shinnecock tribe. Another, John Shippen, was an 18-year-old whose father was African-American and mother Native American. Shippen received sponsorship from members of the Shinnecock Hills Golf Club where he had been a regular caddie and thus knew the course well. However, the other entrants announced that they would not compete if Bunn and Shippen were allowed to play. The president of the USGA, T.A. Havemeyer, responded that the Open would be played at Shinnecock even if Bunn and Shippen were the only participants. The tournament was held as scheduled. Bunn finished in 21st place; Shippen tied for fifth.

The salutary outcome at Shinnecock Hills unfortunately did not serve as a model for the future. Prejudice against minorities became ubiquitous in golf, and for more than half a century African-Americans met with discrimination. In response they formed their own organization, the United Golfers Association (UGA) in the 1940s. At the time very few golf courses were operated by minorities. A notable exception was the Wayside Golf Club in Illinois. Another minority-owned course in Stowe, Massachusetts became the site of the first UGA Championship. Many outstanding players went on to win this tournament, including Charlie Sifford and Lee Elder among professionals, and Joe Louis among amateurs.

One of the very best minority players of that era was Bill Spiller. Spiller lived in Los Angeles much of his life. He played well enough to easily qualify for PGA events, but time after time he was denied entrance, not only to locker rooms, but also to the tournaments themselves. In 1948 Spiller qualified to play in an event at Oakland, but at the last minute a PGA official canceled his entry. The PGA had inserted a clause in its constitution in 1916 that specified Caucasian membership only, and this was used to prevent many minorities from participating.

Spiller's attorney filed a $250,000 suit against the PGA, which settled out of court by agreeing not to discriminate in the future. However, conditions improved only marginally until 1960, when the attorney general of California warned the PGA that it could no longer use public courses in California if there was any hint of discrimination. Still recalcitrant, PGA officials responded that they would turn to private courses. That, too, was illegal, warned the attorney general, who wrote to other states and described what was happening in California. Finally the PGA gave in and dropped its Caucasians-only bylaw. Bill Spiller had a long career in the UGA, but he never received a PGA membership.

Lee Elder (©PGA Tour).

Many other fine African-American players failed to receive justice from the PGA. Pete Brown, Lee Elder, Cliff Brown, Ray Botts, Charlie Sifford, and Ted Rhodes had few opportunities to compete fairly. Ted Rhodes probably was the first to gain admittance to a tour event, the 1946 Los Angeles Open. Twenty years later, in the midst of the Civil Rights Movement, Cliff Brown could not make it past the locker room attendant at the Texas Open in San Antonio. Shortly thereafter he tried to order dinner at the clubhouse during a Memphis tournament and was escorted out of the restaurant. As late as 1962, African-American golfers in the UGA Memphis tournament were forbidden to stay in the same hotels as white players (Caucasians were welcome to play in UGA events), or even to play together in organized competition. At many public courses, for example the Baltimore Monumental Club, African-Americans were allowed to play only on Mondays. Minority golfers in Chicago banded together to form the Linksman Club in order to enforce integration of public golf courses in that city.

One of the most glaring examples of discrimination, the Augusta National Golf Club, home of the Masters, had engendered critical commentary from minority players for many years. In 1967 Charlie Sifford was a first time winner in a tour event and had finished 25th in the money standings, yet Clifford Roberts did not extend a Masters invitation to the African-American star. Lee Trevino also disliked the plantation environment at the Masters Tournament, and scorned the club's practice of avoiding black competitors. Finally, in 1975 Lee Elder received an invitation to play in the Masters after qualifying by winning the Monsanto Open. Once before Lee thought he would be invited for having won the 1971 Nigerian Open. He wrote to Clifford Roberts describing his achievement and requesting an invitation to the Masters. His response arrived somewhat later with the news that foreign championships provided entry to the Masters Tournament only if won by foreign-born players. In 1975, however, Elder was chaperoned by PGA Tournament Players Commissioner Deane Beman from Washington to Atlanta, whereupon the airplane of the chairman of the Coca-Cola Corporation was waiting to fly the two men to Augusta. Elder's wife sent a check for $2,000 to Roberts requesting admission tickets for scores of the couple's friends. They arrived with a considerable traveling party and rented out private homes in Augusta for the occasion.

Elder had seen many strange scenes over the years. He had entered his first UGA tournament at age 14, and had lost to heavyweight champion Joe Louis. After working as a caddie for Lloyd Mangrum for three years in California, Elder entered the service and captained the Sixth Army golf team. After his discharge in 1960 he went to work for an acquaintance of Mangrum's in Washington, and also began playing regularly on the UGA tour. During those years he was befriended by Ted Rhodes. Many contemporaries believed that Rhodes would have equaled the achievements of any white golfer of any era if given the opportunities. A fine player in his own right by this time, Elder had trouble earning a living from golf, but his talent was unmistakable.

Elder's problems were very similar to Charlie Sifford's early in his career. Sifford was capable of beating the PGA Tour regulars in the 1950s, but the only tournaments to which he could gain an invitation were in California and Arizona. By the time the tour moved on to the deep South, he was finished for the year. Sifford beat South African Harold Henning to win the 1969 Los Angeles Open, and he is believed to be the first African-American golfer to gain PGA-approved status, a rating he worked for years to achieve. He played regularly on the UGA circuit, the only full tournament schedule open to minorities at the time. Sifford won the UGA National Championship six times. The top prize never exceeded $800. At the few PGA events where he was welcome, he often changed clothes in his car and took meals away from the club. Usually traveling alone he had no sponsors, nothing to fall back on. "I'm just one black man against one hundred and fifty whites," he told the press, "and I've got pressures nobody ever dreamed of. If Palmer and Nicklaus had to play with the handicaps I have, they couldn't beat me.... Every time I go into a tournament

I'm strictly on my own. I know I'm playing for my bread and butter. The result is I try too hard. I can't be relaxed. I'm always pressing!"

During his first seven years of entering PGA tournaments, Charlie won only $17,000. As late as 1974, fate was cruel to Sifford. Growing tired of tour life he applied for the golf professional's job at three public courses in Los Angeles, and failed to get an offer. Finally he became a fixture on the Senior Tour and gained a grudging acceptance for his skills despite having advanced in age long past his prime playing days.

Charlie Owens, a contemporary of Sifford's, had a similar story to tell. His father had been the greenskeeper at a city course in Winter Haven, Florida, where Blacks could not play except on caddie day. Nonetheless, Owens was scoring in the 60s as a teenager before going off to Florida A&M with a football scholarship. He did not take up golf again until he was 36 years old, in the interim suffering an injury to his knee in an Army parachuting accident that resulted in fusion surgery. Discovering the knee did not handicap his golf swing, Owens qualified to play the PGA Tour at age 40, in 1970. Over the next seven years he experienced a series of physical aliments and earned little prize money. By 1977 he was working as a club pro in Tampa and whiling away the time until he qualified for the Senior Tour. He bought a 52-inch putter and won $80,000 in 1985, and increased that to $100,000 in 1986.

Another man who enjoyed better days on the Senior Tour was Jim Dent. A non-winner for 18 years on the PGA Tour, Dent banked $1.5 million and inked endorsements contracts with Cadillac and Bullet after only two years on the senior circuit.

Jim Dent was born in Augusta, Georgia. Working at the Augusta National Golf Club, he caddied for Bob Rosburg and Bob Goalby in the Masters. Not welcome at Augusta National as a player, Dent became a fixture at the local municipal layout and nearby Fort Gordon. Moving to Los Angeles he became a regular at Rancho Park and finally passed the Tour Qualifying School in 1971. Although he was always one of the longest hitters in golf, Dent's chipping and putting failed to complement his driving. He earned but $7,000 in 1971, and finished among the top 60 Tour pros only once thereafter, in 1974. The remainder of the time he was compelled to qualify on Mondays with the rabbits.

After the number of exempt players were raised to 125, Dent did better, but still failed to qualify during his final four years as a junior. Nearing 50 and looking to the seniors, he knew that his short game would have to improve. Homero Blancas worked with him on skills around the greens, so that by his 50th birthday Jim had the confidence to finish high in the inaugural event, the Bell Atlantic Classic, where he won $22,000, the biggest paycheck of his entire career up to that point. In his first five years on the Senior Tour Jim Dent won $3,620,000. In 20 years on the PGA regular tour he had banked only half a million.

An African-American player sometimes mistaken for Jim Dent, although younger, was Jim Thorpe. He was the ninth of 12 children, and his father said they ran out of names when Jim arrived and had never heard of the first Jim Thorpe. Thorpe was an outstanding high school athlete and earned a football scholarship at Morgan State College in Maryland. Like his namesake, Thorpe was a runner. He also was an excellent basketball and baseball player. While in college his older brother Chuck was a PGA Tour player with vast talent but an ungovernable temper. Lee Elder remarked that Chuck Thorpe was one of the finest ball strikers he had ever witnessed, and when Jim Thorpe began playing golf, Chuck gave him considerable assistance.

Jim Dent (author's collection).

Thorpe quit Morgan State and worked at the General Motors assembly plant in Baltimore earning $6 an hour and working the six a.m. to two-thirty p.m. shift. The schedule left ample time for golf at the city's many municipal courses, and for gambling. "There were big money games all the time," Thorpe recalled. "Guys would play from dawn to dusk with galleries and everything. There would be bets flying all over the place — side bets, presses, garbage. Thousands would change hands. Man it was great." Thorpe gradually began wagering, first for $300 a round, then $500, and it escalated from that. As he got better and better, backers persuaded him to go on the road in search of even larger winnings. This he did successfully until earning a tour card in 1975. Playing inconsistently at first he moved to the UGA Tour, stayed for a couple of years, then returned to the PGA. Driven now by greater confidence, he was able to tie Bruce Lietzke and Tom Watson going into the final round of the Tucson Open in 1979.

"I was a wreck," Thorpe admitted. "I couldn't sleep. I couldn't eat. It was all I could do not to faint dead away. Lee Trevino came up to me just before the round and told me to try and relax. He said Watson and Lietzke both felt the same way I did. If that's true there was three sick dudes standing on that first tee."

Despite his anxiety, Thorpe played well enough so that by the last hole he needed only a par to tie for second place. He hit a solid drive and was 160 yards from the pin. Adrenaline flowing, he chose a pitching wedge for the shot. The ball flew 180 yards. The long approach putt stopped four feet short of the hole and the world started to crumble before his eyes. "I started to ask my caddie what he thought," Thorpe said, "but I was stuttering so bad I barely got the words out. When he tried to answer he stuttered so bad he couldn't get the words out. He was choking worse than I was. I started laughing and it broke the tension." Thorpe sank the putt and pocketed $19,000.

Now Thorpe knew he was capable of beating the Tour's best players. He always played strongly on the toughest courses, Merion in the U.S. Open, and Butler National in the Western Open. At the 1985 Western he engaged in one of the oddest confrontations of modern golf when amateur Scott Verplank tied him for top place. Scott, from a country club background, shot 68, 68, 69, 74, and defeated the African-American former caddie in a playoff. The amateur's victory entitled him to play in at least ten events in following years, and he became exempt from having to weather the qualifying school.

Meanwhile Thorpe was happy believing that his low professional's finish at Butler National meant that he could enter the upcoming PGA Championship at Cherry Hills. The PGA skipped over Thorpe, however, and handed an exemption to someone else. Thorpe was vocal about his displeasure. The slight was a reminder of all the indignities minority players had suffered in golf, and it may have spurred him on to greater efforts that year in which he captured three first place finishes and rated as the Tour's fourth leading money winner. At the end of the season he had a much more positive attitude about his career.

"I love golf," Thorpe commented,

> because nobody gives you anything but nobody takes anything away from you. I know that in golf I'm a black face walking through a white man's world. It can make you jittery. But I've reached the point I don't feel like an outsider. I know half the people I meet. When your back is turned and the other players still speak to you ... or when they're fifty yards away and yell, "Hey Zorro, that's not a sword! Slow that swing down!" You know you are accepted.

Thorpe injured a wrist that required surgery in 1988 and returned to the Tour the next year on a special injury exemption. Afterward he played so poorly he lost his Tour card and was forced over the following four years to rely on sponsor exemptions to enter tournaments. In 1994 he regained his card after winning $185,000. That season he was the only African-American player on the regular PGA Tour.

"It's a shame," Thorpe said:

> Except for Tiger Woods, we don't really have anybody in sight. I don't know what the answer is. Somewhere along the line, we — that is people like Michael Jordan, Magic Johnson, Julius Erving — we have to do something for our kids. We can't keep turning to Coca-Cola and Pepsi-Cola for help. Unless we open our eyes up and do something for our kids, then I don't see anything changing.

One of the most unusual success stories on the PGA Tour belong to Calvin Peete. Born to a family of 19 children in Detroit, Peete worked as a farmhand

and as a salesman before taking up golf at the age of 23. He had suffered a childhood injury to his left arm which could not be fully straightened, and which resulted in his becoming a very strong right-sided golfer who always fought a pull hook. Nonetheless he became an extremely accurate player, turned pro in 1971, and went on to win the 1979 Milwaukee tournament, then followed it up the following week with a second place finish at Quad Cities. Winning a tournament was qualification to play in the Masters in 1980. "I had no desire to play," Peete recalled:

> I thought it was an overrated tournament because Augusta is a big hitter's course. And because of the restrictions the Masters put on so many good golfers, particularly Blacks. Lee Elder was the first Black allowed to play at the Masters, in 1975, while other Blacks like Charlie Sifford and Pete Brown who were before him had won tournaments and should have been eligible to play but weren't. But I thought, "Well, I guess a lot of Blacks are depending on me to represent them." So I went to the tournament and finished nineteenth or twentieth.

Five years later he had his worst round at Augusta National. He shot an 87 on Saturday, which made him the first player to tee off on Sunday. Since there was an uneven number of finishers, Peete played alone. There was something symbolic about the solitary figure, statistically the best player on tour, and a Black man, teeing off first and playing alone on the Augusta National Golf Club.

It was only after achieving considerable success that Peete began to suffer an odd form of stress, one that differed only in degree from the pressures of tournament competition. His wife offered a description of what it was like for the golfer.

> Calvin is a very, very private person. He needs time to himself, time to practice. He can't stand schedules and appointments. When you make plans for Calvin, he looks at you like you're trying to steal his life from him. But now it seems like everything is appointments, and schedules, and interviews. Everybody wants something from him. I never knew what invasion of privacy meant until the last few months.... For seven years on the PGA Tour I don't think Calvin ever said no to anybody, because he really believes that when you take something out of a sport, you have to put something back.

Peete offered further insights of his own:

> I love to sweat, I feel like I'm doing some honest work.... I've never been one to get ahead of myself. I do everything in stages. When I start forgetting that, my father reminds me. Your reach and your grasp should be the same. That's the way to be happy. Reach for the furthest thing you think you can get. Then reach again. Sooner or later, the things that looked way beyond you are the next natural goal to reach. Sometimes you can't believe how much you have to go through to get to the end thing, but one day it's there.... When I first joined the tour I

didn't think I was as good as I was. Now my mental has caught up with my physical. I'm as good a player as I think I am. If you can't win in your dreams, forget it!

Peete won the Tournament of Champions and the New Orleans US&G in 1986 at age 42. He held the position of the tour's straightest driver for five consecutive years and won 11 tournaments and two million dollars over that span. Despite those achievements he experienced severe problems— recording an 87 at the Masters, passing out from heat exhaustion in the U.S. Open, withdrawing from several tournaments for a bewildering variety of causes that prompted the Tour to enact a rule that disqualifies a pro from the Vardon Trophy ranks if he unjustifiably exists any tournaments during the year.

Peete already had suffered indignity at the PGA's hands when he was barred from playing in the 1981 Ryder Cup competition because PGA regulations included the requirement of a high school diploma for membership and Peete lacked that essential document. Working diligently with his wife, he studied until he passed the equivalency test, then played for the Ryder Cup team in 1983 and 1985.

Peete kept three large bureau drawers packed with diaries and notes culled from practice and competition. He often locked himself away in a room and studied those notebooks for hours. Turning 50 in 1993 after enduring several years of injuries, including back trouble and a torn rotator cuff, Peete believed it was more important to work on the mental aspects of golf rather than brood over his physical aliments. His father, a Baptist minister, recommended meditation. The practice helped. He won $175,000 in 1994, and he founded the National Minority Golf Foundation to promote golf among children in the inner cities, a project that included scheduling 12 to 15 clinics a year for some 1,500 aspiring golfers.

As he began his second career on the Senior Tour, Calvin Peete maintained that his winning swing was still on call, that "it's just a matter of whether my mind is strong enough." Surprising not a few of his peers, he quoted Sigmund Freud: "If the subconscious can conceive it, the mind can achieve it," a philosophy that every pro would enjoy putting into practice.

The limited success that minority golfers achieved was hard won, but Charlie Sifford, Lee Elder, Jim Dent, Calvin Peete, and Jim Thorpe witnessed profound changes in American sport and society. When tournaments like the Masters, and course memberships at clubs like Augusta National once were closed tight to minorities, now amateurs like Tiger Woods were welcome even at Shoal Creek. Not all golf clubs were color blind by any means, but the fondness for golf displayed by stars from other sports created a situation where private golf clubs competed to attract Michael Jordan, Charles Barkley, and other minority players as members. This was a far cry from a generation before, when admission to public or private links was an issue of color, as it was in so many other aspects of American society.

As the sport grew in popularity golf gradually became accessible to everyone. Once a game for aristocrats, now anyone could play. There were new courses to meet every level of talent, from the novice to the touring pro, and it seemed that one new club opened every day. By the mid–1990s, there were more than 14,000 golf courses in the United States. Professional golfers played the regal courses, but that did little to mute criticisms of conditions or design. When the first TPC courses were opened, tour players were virtually unanimous in their disparagement, and the commissioner acceded by completing alterations suggested by individual player-architects.

Later, superstars Palmer, Nicklaus, Watson, and others lamented the effects of new golf equipment that threatened to make older layouts obsolete for tournament competition. Always there were sporadic outbursts directed against architects who went against the grain by building too tough a test even for the touring professional's skill and courage, as when Robert Trent Jones redesigned Oakland Hills or when Pete Dye built the first TPC facility, whose incongruity bedeviled touring players. The pros were quick to castigate anyone who dared tinker with classic designs like Oakland Hills, even if time and technology were catching up with the grand dames of the game.

When the players were polled, their favorite courses invariably were venerable Pinehurst, Pine Valley, Pebble Beach, Oakmont, Winged Foot, Baltusrol, Olympic, Inverness, and other works of architects like Donald Ross, who started his career in golf working for Old Tom Morris at St. Andrews as a greenskeeper. In 1899 Ross emigrated to America to a position at a country club in Watertown, Massachusetts, where the members asked him to redesign their inadequate course. The job was admired so much the new owner of a North Carolina resort heard of it and hired Ross away to redesign the first course at Pinehurst, and to build another two treasures as well.

What golfers admired about Ross then, and still do today was his use of wide fairways with few water hazards. He liked to incorporate two or more extremely long par fours, with at least one short hole demanding an accurate drive and an unerring pitch to a small, heavily bunkered green. Many of his greens were elevated with danger at the edges. After leaving a Ross course players usually realize they were compelled to carefully plan every shot and to use every club in the bag. These are the same requirements necessary to play a classic early design of American golf architecture, the incomparable Pebble Beach.

History of Golf Course Architecture in America

*"I wanted them to look as if they went through a battle coming off
the eighteenth green!"*

—Architect Pete Dye,
extolling one of his creations

The first golf course built in the western United States, Del Monte at Pebble Beach, was constructed in 1897 by railroad tycoons Huntington, Hopkins, Stanford, and Crocker. They paid $5 an acre for the property in 1880, and built a railbed to carry tourists from San Francisco to the new resort. Samuel Morse was the manager of the resort hotel, and he quickly spotted the potential of bluffs above Carmel Bay as a perfect site for a second golf course. Morse enlisted the aid of Jack Neville and Douglas Grant to formulate a design. When the railroad consortium unexpectedly put the resort up for sale, Morse obtained financial backers and tendered $1.3 million in 1919 to buy what came to be known as the Del Monte Properties. In that same year Morse opened the Pebble Beach Golf Links.

California players knew what a gem they had in Pebble Beach, and in 1929 the rest of the country discovered it as well when the U.S. National Amateur Championship was scheduled west of the Mississippi River for the first time. Bobby Jones was part of the strong field. Although he lost in the first round of the tournament, Jones so enjoyed Pebble Beach and its new cousin Cypress Point, he decided to stay on for several more days of vacation. Jones was so impressed by the design Alister MacKenzie conceived for Cypress Point that when he later began to dream of a course of his own in Georgia, it was MacKenzie whom Jones hired as architect.

During the 1920s Morse's fortunes at Pebble Beach prospered. Land prices rose, palatial homes were erected in Del Monte Forest, and the resort was overflowing with guests. The advent of the Depression, however, severely tested his management skills. Struggling to hold his company together, Morse resorted to sand mining at Spanish Bay, which destroyed the sand dunes in that area of the bay. He survived the Depression and lived until 1969, continuing to add refinements to the resort and to its golf properties until the end of his long life. Following Morse's death, the company was purchased by Wedron Silica Company, then by 20th Century–Fox, then by Marvin Davis, who reaped a bonanza when Japanese investor Minoru Isutani paid $841 million for Pebble Beach in 1990. The deal soured for Isutani almost immediately as a recession worsened in that year.

Isutani proposed to turn Pebble Beach into a semi-private club (a virtually private club, critics contended), where memberships would sell for $777,000. Approval of the plan was solicited from the California Coastal Commission and the Monterey County Board of Supervisors. The Board approved the plan, but a California law that guaranteed access to coastline gave opponents an issue with the Coastal Commission, which returned a negative decision. Local residents were outraged at the prospect of tourists appropriating most of the tee times at a membership fee that was a pittance compared to costs in Tokyo. Isutani's alleged ties to the Japanese Mafia did not help his public relations. When the economy worsened, Isutani grasped at other straws to generate quick profits. When a story was published in Japan that he had sold ten times more memberships that promised at two country clubs he owned near Tokyo, Isutani's financial backers deserted enmasse. He was pressured into relinquishing control of Pebble Beach in January 1992. He transferred management to a popular Japanese resort owner who promised to shelve plans for sale of memberships and to bring Pebble Beach to perfection for the soon-to-be-held United States Open Championship, which was won in dramatic fashion by Tom Kite.

Pebble Beach awed generation after generation of golfers and architects alike. When Bobby Jones went home to Georgia after his 1929 California vacation, he shared his dreams of building a new course with friend Clifford Roberts, who know of a nursery that was for sale at Depression prices in Augusta. The 365-acre Fruitlands had been conceived as an indigo plantation, but was purchased by a Belgian horticulturist who turned the property into one of the country's finest nurseries. He planted azalea, camellia, redbud, magnolia, dogwood, apple, pear, peach, and other varieties of trees and shrubs. Augusta was Mrs. Jones's hometown, and the city rested in a valley with mild winter weather.

Clifford Roberts arranged the financing, and Jones brought Alister MacKenzie east to prepare the design. The creation became one of the most beloved courses in the world. Roberts was credited with proposing Augusta for the Masters Tournament, and for persuading Jones to come out of retirement to host the event that would become a casual stop for the last event of the professional winter Tour. The inaugural year was 1934, and the Masters became the first to change the traditional tournament format from a 36-hole

event to four 18-hole rounds, the first to rope fairways and establish successful one-way flow for gallery control, first to erect scoreboards around the
course and to give spectators fast breaking information via underground telephone cables, and the first to televise action other than at the 18th green.

Augusta always had been a popular layover for sportswriters returning
North from baseball spring training in Florida. Jones suspected he could trans-
late his huge popularity with the press into favorable coverage for the new
tournament, an accurate assumption. Reporters not only wrote favorable
reviews of the new Masters Tournament, but also rendered glowing accounts
of the new course's beauty and difficulty of play. Jones handed over day-to-
day control of the tournament to Clifford Roberts. Roberts surprised the touring pros by handing out free lunches, free tournament entries, and much free
advertising for the Tour.

Roberts with his prickly disposition ruled the tournament like an emperor,
and for years withheld invitations from deserving African-American players.
No African-American played in the first 38 years of the Masters, until Lee
Elder was invited. But Roberts was a keen student of public relations, and he
always sent gifts to every reporter who covered the Masters. One year he sent
address books, and in his inimitable way he wrote out a set of instructions on
how recipients should use the gifts.

"Use a number two pencil," Roberts commanded, "because its lead is
easy to erase changes of address, and make a note of wives' names if you aren't
any better at remembering names than I am."

The detailed instructions continued in this vein. Throughout his life
Roberts exercised an ironclad grip on events at Augusta National, but in time
a system of 24 committees oversaw assignments for a total of 1,300 general
volunteers. There were committees on transportation, on pairings, on pin
placements, and on rules and presentations, among other matters. The pairings committee kept statistics on all the players so that stars could tee off later
in the day, slow players went off late so as not to delay others, and long hitters were paired with other power drivers. Whatever the committees recommended, the final decision was always Roberts's. It was Roberts who was a
major figure in the election of Dwight Eisenhower to the presidency, and it
was Roberts who saw to it that President Eisenhower became a member and
frequent visitor at Augusta National.

Ike had made an initial visit to Augusta in 1948 for a two-week vacation,
the first long vacation he said he had enjoyed in ten years. He liked golf far
better than any other sport, despite the fact that he had excelled at baseball,
shooting, poker, bridge, and football, in which he severely injured a knee that
hindered his golf swing. Clifford Roberts was Ike's usual partner in bridge and
in golf, and there were some who wondered if the imperious Roberts did not
consider himself superior in rank to the commanding general and subsequent
president.

Married three times, Roberts sired no children. His first wife was the switchboard operator at the Bon Aire Hotel. That union lasted six months. He met his second wife, Latitia, in a doctor's waiting room. That ended a half dozen years later. His last wife, Betty, survived him by two years. Always restless, Roberts maintained an apartment in New York City and personal quarters at Augusta National. In addition he added a home at Grandfather Mountain, North Carolina, a condo in Freeport, and a house in Beverly Hills, California.

He acquired a reputation for ruthlessness, yet curiously remained blind to pranks played at his expense. Every year there was a huge party and special tournament for members. One of the participants was an accomplished photographer, and he was given the task of preparing a film to show during tournament week. Roberts became a featured player in these films, which skillfully poked indirect and sometimes direct fun at the chairman. One year the filmmaker persuaded Roberts to hold a rubber duck and explain to the audience why there were no ducks in the ponds of Augusta National. The film was advanced in speed so that Roberts's motions became comic, like an early Charlie Chaplin movie. Meanwhile Roberts was delivering a long, carefully prepared exposition he had prepared about why golf courses are not compatible with waterfowl, but the talk was not recorded. Instead, the technician dubbed in a child's voice singing "Rubber Ducky."

At the highlight party the filmmaker showed the movie to a room full of members and recalled:

> When that hit the screen that night there was a tremendous suppression. You could look around the room and see tears coming down the members' cheeks as they tried to keep from laughing. Finally the dam broke and there was a he burst of laughter. Mr. Roberts didn't take it too well. He was still waiting to hear his comments about ducks at Augusta National. He never said a word about it, but he did give me a stern look.

Where Augusta National was concerned, Roberts saw little humor. Nothing took precedence over his beloved Masters. When Charlie Yates became president of the Georgia Chamber of Commerce, he told Roberts that he would not be able to attend the next meeting of the Augusta National Board of Governors because he had to preside over a Chamber meeting. Yates was a longtime Augusta National member and acquaintance of Roberts, and an amateur golf star in his own right. But nothing could help Yates on that occasion. Roberts fixed Yates with a contemptuous stare and said:

"Well, which is more important, the Governor's meeting, or the Chamber of Commerce?" Yates gave the right answer and remained an Augusta member. When Bobby Jones's health began to fail, Roberts assumed dictatorial control over the Masters. At Augusta a member recalled that "In the old days Cliff used to follow Jones around like a puppy. And the same with Ike later. Then he eventually reversed the role with Jones but not with Ike, who was as irascible as Roberts."

When Eisenhower died, Roberts failed to attend the funeral, which occurred during practice rounds for the Masters. First things first, and nothing could induce the chairman to leave Augusta at such a crucial time. He also came to treat his old friend Bobby Jones with the same icy disdain shown to so many strangers. On occasion Jones authorized Masters tickets for his friends. When the tickets failed to arrive Jones was asked for an explanation, whereupon he called the club and discovered that Roberts had overruled his requests. Later, as Jones rapidly declined in endurance, he still summoned all his resources to attend the Masters each year and to appear on television with the winner at the conclusion of the tournament. In 1968 Roberts bluntly told Jones that he was so alarmed about the health of his old friend that he was worried Jones might die during the telecast, and so Roberts would no longer schedule him for the wrap-up broadcast. Jones was incredulous. Jones died in 1971. During the next Masters Tournament his name was not mentioned at the prize-giving ceremony.

CBS acquired the rights to broadcast the Masters in 1956, but there were many days when network staffers regretted the acquisition. Clifford Roberts enacted many strictures governing what could and what could not be broadcast from Augusta. There was to be no mention of prize money, not even the winnings of individual players on tour, nor could any player receive fulsome praise for achievements. The size of the gallery was never an object of speculation, nor would the chairman acknowledge having precise figures for same. Bill MacPhail was in charge of the Masters broadcast for 18 years, and he recalled the toll the event took on his nerves and life expectancy:

> My first year at Augusta an official came up and announced that Roberts wanted to see me. I was on the seventeenth hole, and I said fine. I would just follow this threesome up and then see him. Well, they made me aware that when Mr. Roberts wants to see someone he means now. So I marched up to the Eisenhower Cabin and there was Roberts pointing to a little tiny tire track on the lawn and it was so infinitesimal that you could shake it out with a rake. He insisted that a CBS golf cart had made the mark, and holding his finger as close to my nose as he could without touching it, he proclaimed that this carelessness would not be tolerated.... Eighteen straight years I went down there and I dreaded it. I had to be chewed out at least eleven times in the course of four days. Roberts would sit in his suite and watch our rehearsals and there were just tons of things he didn't like. He was hypercritical and calculating. I think it was his intention to have me scared to death for the sake of the Masters. If one of the sportscasters said the wrong thing I was immediately summoned and told that if he ever said that again he'd be gone and so would I.

During the 1966 Masters, announcer Jack Whittiker made the fatal mistake of calling the gallery around the 18th green a "mob." Roberts notified

CBS that in the 1967 Masters the services of Whittiker would no longer be required. Later Gary McCord was banned for irreverent comments about the speed of Augusta's greens.

Clifford Roberts's health rapidly declined when he reached his 70s. Fighting heart aliments, he continued to live at Augusta National but turned over the chairman's job to William Lane, who later was succeeded by Hord Hardin. On the last day of his life Roberts ordered the Augusta National barber to come to his apartment where they talked for more than an hour. Then he called in a Pinkerton guard and brought out a gun to show him. He needed instruction on how to fire the weapon, explaining that he had heard someone prowling about his quarters. Late that night Roberts walked to the course's lower pond and ended life.

PGA Tour players enjoyed the beauty of Augusta National, but they came to dread the greens. MacKenzie and Jones designed diabolical contours in many of the putting surfaces, and the speed was much faster than at other tournament sites. To play well at Augusta it was necessary to hit accurate approach shots and leave uphill or level putts. Distance off the tee was important, and to win a player had to have his nerves under control and solve the intimidating greens. First-time players in the Masters were teamed with stars, and it was traditional for amateurs to play with former champions. If it were not difficult enough to be a young amateur in one's first Masters, there was the added weight of playing in front of Arnold Palmer, Jack Nicklaus, or Ben Hogan as a green Ken Venturi did in 1954.

"On the first hole the gallery trooped off after Hogan holed out," Venturi recalled,

> while I still faced a three-foot putt. On the way to the second tee Hogan told me to go ahead and putt out if I wasn't in his line so I wouldn't have the gallery distracting me. I said, "Thanks Mr. Hogan!" And he said, "Call me Ben." I felt great. On the fourth hole I hit first and put a three-iron six feet from the hole. Then Hogan hit a three-iron into the bunker short of the green. As we were walking to the green Hogan said, "Let me see that three-iron." He looked at it and said, "My God, you've got a bag of one-irons." I was in the Army at the time making seventy-two dollars a month and told him this was my only set and that I couldn't afford any other clubs.

After the tournament a set of new clubs arrived at Venturi's home, a gift from Hogan.

In the 1970s complaints began to circulate about the quality of the putting surfaces and methods of maintenance at Augusta. The greens had lost much of their reputation and were becoming much softer and slower. Augusta brought in a cadre of agronomists and finally made a decision to kill off the old Bermuda and rye grasses, and to plant bent grass instead. Bent grass varieties are favored in the Northern United States and are considered cool weather grasses. Augusta National had the capability to allow for extremely hot weather. The club closed in mid–May of every year, and reopened when temperatures in Georgia began to ameliorate in mid–October.

The experts believed that bent grass could survive the extreme heat of a Georgia summer if allowed to rest, and so the old grass was destroyed and the sod was sterilized by fumigation followed by aeration and sowing of new seed in late summer. Nothing went as planned thereafter. In September of that year Georgia sweltered through one of the worst months on record. The temperature passed 90 degrees 19 days that month and on eight of those it was above 95 degrees. Downpours in October washed seed out of many greens, then unusually cold temperatures hit and a fungicide application misfired and burned out swatches across the course. Some blamed the trouble on the failure of Augusta National to alter the sod composition of its greens before reseeding, but consultants dismissed those charges and went ahead with their original plans.

Club members hoped to see the speed return to pre–1970 days when players said they could hear balls strike the greens from far out in the fairway. Just treading on the putting surfaces for the first time was enough to cause jitters. "It sounded like you were treading on cellophane," said Frank Beard. "And they putted that way too." That was the way club officials wanted it at the Masters Tournament. Hord Hardin, chairman after Roberts, bragged: "You've heard of putting down a marble staircase? That was Augusta!" In the 1950s it had not been uncommon to see tour stars take 40 putts in a typical Masters round, as Ben Hogan did in 1952. On the 14th hole the average number of putts to get down was 3.5 for the entire field. Number five averaged three putts per golfer.

These were the conditions Augusta was trying to recreate in 1980. When an Augusta member was quoted in Golf Digest about the worrisome switch from Bermuda to bent grass, Hord Hardin summoned the offender, read him the riot act, and put him on probation. According to the chairman, the transgressor would have been immediately expelled if Clifford Roberts were still alive. He had been fond of exiling members by using the expedient of discontinuing their monthly club fees— no bill, no check, no membership. The new chairman may not have mirrored Roberts's ruthlessness, but he still enjoyed life at Augusta as an absolute monarch. The members always preferred leaving one person in control of everything, and so it remained.

The chairman was very lucky in 1981, for favorable weather returned that spring and the greens responded. The players at the 1981 Masters had nothing but accolades for conditions at the course. Work went on apace. Four greens were subsequently restructured, overseen by a newly appointed superintendent. The club also installed a heating system under the 12th green, which always presented problems because of its low, shaded location. A heating pump insured that green would never freeze again.

During Hord Hardin's tenure as chairman, there were occasional incidents that reminded visitors to Augusta of an earlier time and a former chairman. For example, on the Sunday before the start of the 1988 Masters Tournament, Bernhard Langer was playing a practice round by himself and a ball came whizzing by his ear. At the time Langer was slowly pacing the fairway with a special measuring wheel he carried with him on Tour. He picked up the wheel and hurried on to the next hole, teed off, and walked up to hit his second shot when he suddenly remembered leaving the measuring wheel back on the tee. Back went his caddie to retrieve the wheel while Langer prepared to hit his next shot. At that moment the foursome on the tee hit their drives, all four of which rolled toward Langer. The four men jumped into their carts for a fast run up the fairway, and when they stopped the first man to get out was Hord Hardin. "Hi Bernhard," the chairman inquired. "How are things?" "How is everything going?" the chairman wanted to know. "Oh, the golf course is good," Langer replied, "and everything's great, but I don't appreciate you hitting into me!" "…Oh, we didn't know you were down here," replied Hardin.

Langer recalled later how he wanted to say something else at the time, because he believed everyone knew that he had been standing in the middle of the fairway when the balls came flying by. But he bit his tongue, and the foursome of members sped off with the alacrity of Ty Cobb in his prime. Some months later Langer received a letter from Hardin, who suggested that just because the German star was a past Masters champion did not mean that he would be welcomed or could play any time he chose at Augusta National. Furthermore, it did not mean that he would be invited to play every year in the tournament.

Langer, not a little bemused, decided not to reply to Hardin's missive. But he did share his perceptions of Augusta with friends, and explained how the Masters had changed from the days of genial Bobby Jones:

> The Masters is one of the tournaments where they treat us quite different from most of the other tournaments. In many respects or in some respects, that's why Lee Trevino stays away. To mention one of the things. It's the only tournament where we don't get any free badges. Not that that bothers me, but I notice it because it's different. I mean, at the British Open you get two or four badges. At any of the other majors you get two or four. At Augusta you have to buy them. That's a small detail. All the guys that play there can afford it. But there are other things, you know. It started off with the caddie problem We couldn't bring our own caddies. There is a whole list.

The issue of badges aggravated many of the participants at the Masters, and was just one of the sparks that ignited Lee Trevino's powder. In 1987, speaking of his conflicts over the years, Trevino remarked:

> It has always been tickets. I like Augusta. The course is about as beautiful as any course you'll ever play. I stayed away twice and Nicklaus said: "Don't, Lee. You're too good a player, you're too good for the game. Come back!" So I did. I'm the

first to criticize and the first to eat crow. I said then that Nicklaus had talked me back into playing the Masters and that I was sorry. I made my peace with Augusta National. But then last year they charged me ninety dollars for my son's ticket because he was twenty-one. I didn't say anything at the time, but I didn't think it was right. When I got home I wrote a letter and said if the rule wasn't changed I wouldn't use my invitation for 1987. I got a letter back that said rules are rules, and we'll miss you but we'll just have to do without you. So I wasn't going back. But then they announced that the rule had been changed, and that I had been sent a letter to that effect in December. My office never received it.

In 1988 Trevino missed the cut at Augusta. All of his frustrations dating back many, many years seemed to find an outlet now, as he erupted in scorn:

They've done five hundred dollars worth of innovations on the greens, but I'll bet in the books it's seven hundred thousand dollars. A good husband on a weekend could have done it. Naw, they don't make any money here. They damn sure don't give anything to charity. I hope to God they don't send me another invitation. I don't want to be here. I'm going to pray they don't. If they send me one, I'll have to come....

When reporters repeated Trevino's comments to Hardin, the chairman was quick with a response.

Trevino's a very interesting man. I was with Lee, as his referee, in the last round at Oak Hill in 1968 when he won the Open. I presented the trophy to him. At that point, Lee regarded himself as a "minority." He may still, I don't know. He shouldn't. And I shouldn't put words in his mouth, but he acted as though he felt Augusta was opposed to minorities, and he wouldn't come here. But it wasn't so. Anyhow, Lee was finally persuaded by Nicklaus, as I recall, that it was foolish to say he couldn't play this kind of golf course — Lee had said that. So he started coming and he wasn't comfortable and I think it affected his game. He hasn't played anywhere near his best here. Now before I give you the wrong picture, I think Lee is one of the great, entertaining golfers and telecasters. I like his style. But he does spend his time being critical of us. It would probably be better for us if Lee said, "I tried, I'm not happy there. I'm not going." But if he would like to play, we'll treat him just like we treat everyone else.

Reflecting on the past, Hardin described how:

Roberts lived here, but his wife wasn't here much. He didn't mind being alone. It didn't bother him to stay in his room and eat his meals by himself. That isn't my style. I have I think, more friends and a more varied social life.... We have about three hundred members, with only twenty-five from Augusta. That's the maximum. We take members once a year. This year we took four. Last year was the same. We try to scatter members geographically. One doesn't apply. A man is brought to the club by a member and meets other members. If he's a fun guy — and that's before, during, and after golf, a lot of guys aren't so fun after golf if they haven't played well — then we take a good look at him. The average member probably comes in twice a year, bringing three friends and spending

Lee Trevino (©PGA Tour).

two, possibly three days. The club is open only from mid–October to mid–May. January and February are not busy months. So we're talking about six good weeks in the fall and eight in the spring. One of the charms of the place is that there's practically no one out there.

Visitors to Augusta were much more candid with their views of Hardin and the golf course than in comments ventured in Roberts's day. For instance, after the greens were changed to bent grass, Arnold Palmer was one of those who thought they were far too severe. In 1990 Palmer said that bent grass makes for a beautiful putting surface with a true roll. So what's the problem? Well, Augusta National's greens already are among the most undulating in the world. That's part of the Masters tradition. Bent grass greens are lightning fast. When that speed combines with the severe sloping of Augusta's greens, they can get out of hand. It's changed the character of the golf course. I've had putts at Augusta in the past few years that I couldn't do anything with. That puts the player in a position where he can't afford even to think about making a putt — all he can do is putt it to where he can make the next putt. Some people say that such conditions put a premium on iron play because the player faces an extremely difficult putt unless he avoids certain areas of the green. There's certainly something to that argument. The ability to put the ball in the proper position on the greens traditionally has been an important factor at Augusta. That's what makes the undulations of the greens such an outstanding feature of Augusta National. But with bent grass the penalty for leaving a downhill putt has become unfairly severe.... Not only does bent grass create a faster putting surface, it also gives a different bounce on the shot into the green. When Augusta first went to bent grass if softened the greens considerably. They've gotten firmer in the last couple of years, but I don't know if they will ever get firm enough to yield the same results as Bermuda.... Augusta should soften the severest slopes. They did that to some extent on the ninth and eighteenth greens, but more should be done on those two holes and others. Second, they could simply slow down the speed a little bit by not cutting the greens quite as close. Shaving the greens to practically nothing, as they've done in recent years, is going too far. I've witnessed players gently tapping ten-foot putts and watch them roll forty feet past the hole.

The 1994 Masters, won by Jose Maria Olazabal, was noteworthy for the incredible speed of greens and difficult pin placements. Many other golf clubs write to Augusta from time to time inquiring about the Stimpmeter readings of its greens, but receive no reply. In 1994 the greens were frightening. Some observers said that the members were angered by low scores in the previous U.S. and British Opens, and the same would not be repeated during the Masters. Lee Janzen tied the scoring record in winning the 1993 U.S. Open, and Greg Norman broke the British Open record. Then Norman recorded a 24 under par total in winning the Players Championship at the TPC at Sawgrass only two weeks prior to the start of the 1994 Masters. So when the Tour regulars showed up at Augusta they immediately began to howl about impossible pin placements set in environs they had never before seen on very hard putting surfaces.

"I left what looked more like a burn mark than a ball mark on one green," Tom Kite complained. Augusta officials countered that the set-ups were no different from any other year, but Bernhard Langer disagreed.

"It's almost tricked up," Bernhard alleged. "Mickey Mouse miniature golf." Yet, Olazabal's winning score of 279 was good enough to have won 16 of the previous 30 Masters tournaments, and he did not suffer one bogey from the 16th hole of the opening round to the next-to-last hole of the final 18 on Sunday. Loyal Augusta members explained that pin placements for each day always were selected from a master chart factoring in the wind and weather for that day. There were four preferred pin placements on the chart for each green, and the cups rarely varied more than three feet from one of those spots from year to year. The committee in charge of placements strove to create six easy, six medium hard, and six difficult placements for each round. If scoring was unusually low, the placements could be varied the next day to make them more difficult but not impossible.

The fact that an impersonal committee decided pin placements at Augusta National did not lessen the pros' resentments, nor did they view with equanimity even minor changes to bunkers, or lengthening tournament tees, or accentuating doglegs— all met fierce protest when they occurred at a treasured jewel like Augusta, or at any course of exceptional longevity and reputation. This altering of original designs, or what the pros considered to be tinkering with masterpieces, was the cause of much grief for one of golf's greatest architects— Robert Trent Jones.

The young Jones was a fine amateur golfer at Rochester, New York, but a duodenal ulcer made competition a nightmare. Donald Ross had designed a course at Rochester when Jones lived there. Jones had opportunity to watch the master at work, and he decided to follow in Ross's footsteps. Enrolling at Cornell University, Jones persuaded a dean to allow a hand-crafted curriculum tailored to the student's interests—courses in engineering, agronomy, chemistry, drafting, and other specialties to prepare him for a career in golf course architecture. Jones became famous for the severity of his designs, especially Hazeltine and Spyglass Hill. The pros were scathing in their denunciations of Hazeltine during the 1970 U.S. Open. After playing a round at Spyglass Hill, Lee Trevino remarked: "They just ought to hang the man who designed this course. Ray Charles could have done better."

Other pros reiterated complaints about Jones's designs, in general, as being too severe, too long, overly contoured, etc. Jack Nicklaus hated all the blind shots he faced in the Open at Hazeltine, and when the star publicly voiced his criticism, a seldom bashful Jones answered in kind: "Maybe Nicklaus is blind."

Jones had been similarly miffed at the 1951 U.S. Open at Oakland Hills when members hired him to renovate that classic but vulnerable course, and the pros reviled him for meddling with what they considered a timeless design. Undeterred by negative reviews, Robert Trent Jones continued to rack up one of the most impressive rosters of designs ever achieved, and two of his sons also became architects. Robert Trent Jones, Jr., studied at Yale and Stanford before taking up architecture, while Rees Jones attended Yale, the University of California, and the Harvard School of Design. The sons entered their father's firm and apprenticed with the master before setting off on their own. Many observers believed that Robert, Jr., was closer to his father in philosophy. Junior was fond of blind shots and sloping fairways, while Rees was more straightforward and generous in providing clear lines of sight on virtually every hole. At the Mauna Kea course in Hawaii, Junior was hired to redesign the extremely difficult greens originally built by his father. The putting surfaces presented so much contour and were so difficult to hold with long irons, the course's owner insisted on changes.

Robert Trent Jones, Jr., was said to be a very competitive businessman. "I don't like his ethics," complained Tom Weiskopf, after the golfer began devoting more time to architecture than to Tour competition. Name any subject, Weiskopf usually was willing to express an opinion, and when the work of Robert Trent Jones and Junior was discussed Weiskopf was acerbic. Robert Trent Jones, Jr., responded in kind:

> Golf architecture is very competitive. You're competing for the canvases and for the money to express your art, your craft. Anybody who has put enough work out there is going to be criticized for something. I really don't like to talk about hostile criticism such as Weiskopf's, because to do so is to give it a legitimacy it doesn't deserve. I mean it's one thing to say I am a preschooler. That's Tom's opinion. Of course I don't agree with him, but then to go ahead and apply the same words to my father is plain stupid. I don't think I have to defend my father's contribution to golf against Weiskopf's. They aren't in the same world. I just don't know what Tom was thinking. But you have to understand Weiskopf. He had great playing talent, yet has a volcanic personality and he explodes from time to time. Our new name for him is "Tom Pop-Off." I personally think that Tom and Jay Morrish have done some very fine work. Although I've seen the Troon course in Arizona, and Waikoloa, I haven't played any of their courses, and I wonder if they've played any of mine. Maybe he hasn't played some of our new courses such as the University of Wisconsin course in Madison, Highland Springs in Springfield, Chenal in Little Rock, or Wedgewood in Columbus, Ohio.

Robert Trent Jones, Jr., concluded by calling the work of many star golfers "production architecture," as a team of designers put together courses that would receive the star's name in order to sell attached real estate. In the end he seemed more mystified than angered by Weiskopf's comments. However, Tom got along fine with Rees Jones, and went out of his way to compliment his designs. Rees returned the accolades. "I like Tom Weiskopf," Rees acknowledged. "And he likes me. I think it's that simple. The real problem in this profession is that nobody wants to concede that anybody else is doing good work."

Despite various criticisms, many of Robert Trent Jones's courses came to be revered for their beauty, for harmonious use of water, trees, and natural landscape features. "I was probably the first to use the water hazard as a dramatic form consistently," the architect believed.

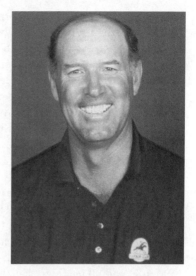

Tom Weiskopf (©PGA Tour).

Bobby Jones [no relation] chided me for putting in too much water on my courses. He told me the difference between a bunker and a water hazard is like the difference between a car wreck and an airplane crash: One you might survive, the other you can't. But bunkers were still an effective hazard in Bobby's day because he never carried a wedge. Once Sarazen's sand wedge became popular anyone could get up and down from a bunker so the designer had to introduce water if he wanted to make a really dangerous hazard.... Today's pros play on carpets, and the putting is much truer and easier. But equipment is the biggest difference. Architects always have had to compete against improved balls and clubs, but this forces the older clubs to be updated all the time. The USGA needs to do something about this before all of today's courses become obsolete. If something isn't done about the new golf ball soon, I may have to go back and move the fairway bunkers and tees on every course.

If the pros were repelled by the tough designs of Robert Trent Jones, the protests they sounded were whispers compared to the outcry when architect Pete Dye's work was chosen for major tournament sites. Pete Dye was born in a small town near Columbus, Ohio. His father had been a low handicapper who turned a family farm into a nine-hole golf course. The elder Dye had attempted to hire Donald Ross and other prominent architects without success. When they turned Dye down, he decided to do the design on his own. The course was ready in 1927, and young Pete started to play it when he was six years old. He also started to work at odd jobs as soon as he was old enough to handle a mower, and by the advent of the Second World War Pete was supervising the maintenance of the entire course.

At war's end Dye moved on to college in Florida where he played excellent amateur golf against tough competition, including a very young Arnold Palmer. During those years he won the Indiana Amateur title, and his wife Alice went on to even more notable achievements by winning the Hilton Head Senior Women's Tournament, among others. During the 1950s, Pete Dye's insurance business flourished. He and Alice raised two children, and he continued to be interested in course maintenance without actually being engaged in any related business. Then, in 1959, two acquaintances decided to build a golf course and they asked Pete if he would be willing to help. For years he had been keeping an eye on the research in progress by horticulturists and agronomists, particularly at Texas A&M where laboratories were testing new compositions of grasses and soils. He called the people he knew at those labs, and they responded with specifications for the design on nine greens. Pete followed their instructions to the letter and ordered 2,500 cubic yards of sand and 300 cubic yards of peat and top soil.

Not realizing how much material this would be, he watched with amazement when trucks arrived with enough sand and peat to fill a barn 100 feet long, 60 feet wide, and 30 feet high. He raced to call Texas A&M again to ask for help and was told that no one had ever tried to mix such large amounts of materials by hand. With no large earth moving equipment Pete and his friends laid the drainage tile and gravel base, then mixed in the sand, peat, and top soil using three farm tractors with endloaders. The correct composition was transported to each green site, wheelbarrows were lined up to move the mix to the green, and all the rest of shaping and contouring the greens was accomplished with shovels and sweat. The result? When completed and opened for play, the putting contours and grass composition of every green were remarkably good, so admirable in fact, the owners soon expanded the club to 18 holes.

In the following months a number of course remodelings near home dropped into Pete Dye's lap. Nothing of major importance came his way, however, until the University of Michigan commissioned him to build a second course in Ann Arbor, a plum assignment because the first university course was an Alister MacKenzie design. Dye completed that work in 1962. He was proud of the rugged contouring and routing of that layout at the time, but later spoke disparagingly about the greens, huge putting surfaces with too much elevation and unimaginative contours that he would like to rip up and mold all over again.

On a subsequent trip to Scotland, Dye and his wife made a tour of notable golf courses and returned home won over by the naturalness of what they had seen — non-artificial golf links that required minimal maintenance. He also was forming a realization that satisfactory collaborations between golf architects and construction companies were improbable objectives. The construction work at Michigan helped convince him of that, so he decided to undertake projects where he could be a combination designer and builder. He came to believe that it was necessary to wear both hats in order to achieve ideal results, even though the dual responsibility would restrict his career to working on one project at a time, unlike most successful architects, and this would necessarily constrain his income.

Unlike the artist who enjoyed working on several canvases simultaneously, Dye applied himself to the everyday tasks of moving dirt until one job was finished before going on to another. With that method he produced masterpieces. Crooked Stick, Harbour Town, Kingsmill on the James, Oaktree, and many other creative designs spilled from his hands. Crooked Stick was the first course where Dye combined design and construction responsibilities. He spun vast, heavily contoured greens like those of Alister MacKenzie, but also used planking and railroad ties similar to those he had seen on the 1963 Scotland adventure. He turned a cornfield near Indianapolis into a work of art. Day after day he stripped away all the topsoil, routed the holes, and conjured deft undulations before bulldozing the topsoil back into place and planting several different varieties of grass on fairways and greens.

The notoriety of his conception at Crooked Stick, plus a follow-up design at The Golf Club, in New Albany, Ohio, brought many favorable reviews and a flurry of offers to Dye. He soon was busy with more work than he could easily handle, and went on to construct many more notable designs, but in the future he often thought back to those early works that had been so much trouble while yielding such rewards:

> Basically, I don't think there's been very much change down through the years in strategic golf design — the elements that make a hole play. You try to deceive the golfer, to lead him astray, to create optical illusions that will make the better golfers think they have to go one way when they probably have to go the other. Take the second at Harbour Town. That's a par-five just under five hundred yards reachable in two for the pros if they play it correctly. I've watched those guys play that hole year after year. Off the tee what you have is a shallow bunker on the left that can't be eighteen inches deep. It's packed with hard, flat sand, the easiest stuff in the world to hit a ball out of. The fairway is wide open on the right, so they go for that side. After they play the hole once, they know they shouldn't drive down the right — from there you're shut off from the green, you've got no shot at all for it. Still, those experienced players keep hitting their drives down the right side time after time because of the way the hole appears to set up off the tee....
>   Again, on most greens there's a troublesome looking hazard on one side or the other. On the sixth at Cajuiles it's a big bunker on the left. On the right side you've got smooth mowed grass. What you don't see, what you don't keep in mind, is the way the green is contoured. If your approach ends up to the right of the green, you'll find there's no way to stop your chip close to the pin because the green falls away from you. On the other hand, if you put your approach shot in the bunker on the left you have a relatively easy shot. The green slopes toward you, and all you have to play is a little flip from a shallow bunker. Well, good golfers who know the course often continue to play their approach to the right of the green, though they know better. The severity of the look of the left keeps that sense of indecision at the back of their minds.... You know what Earnie Vossler says? He says the way to play a Pete Dye course is to aim for the bunkers.

When planning a new course, Dye often thought back to the day in the late 1940s when he was playing with a friend at the Indianapolis Country Club. The friend hit his drive into what should have been an unplayable lie in a drainage ditch. Refusing Pete's advice to take a drop, the man took out a 2-iron. Blasting the ball cleanly out of the ditch, he watched the ball bounce up to within a few feet of the green, and was so elated on making what seemed to be an impossible shot that he could not stop talking about it during the remainder of the round nor, indeed, during the following weeks of golf.

Pete began to note how many average golfers seemed to enjoy playing courses that tested their luck as much as their skill. In time, he incorporated increasingly difficult fairway undulations, heavily tiered greens, water hazards, and deep bunkers into his designs. He also discovered that the touring pros could play his early designs with ease, not so much because they were superior to the generation that came before them, but because golf equipment technology had leapfrogged course design to such an extent many traditional layouts were rendered defenseless. So when an opportunity came his way to design the first Tournament Players Club, Sawgrass at Ponte Vedra in 1979, Dye unfurled his full bag of tricks to create a course that demanded not only length off the tee, but also precision on every shot.

When the course opened for the first TPC event, the pros loathed Dye's conception, contemptuously dismissed it as "target golf," and made sure that Deane Beman heard detailed critiques of every hole. When Jerry Pate won the tournament he entertained his compatriots by pushing Dye and the commissioner into the pond fronting the 18th green.

One aspect of the design pros disliked above all others was the extreme contouring of greens and their convex (as opposed to concave) shape, whose tendency was to repel rather than to absorb approach shots. Some of the greens had a "runaway problem," where balls might hit on the fringe, go wildly forward, and run far away from the green. Jack Nicklaus, who had worked with Dye on the original designs of Harbour Town, now was overseeing a thriving architectural business of his own and was building concave greens that contained approach shots with the help of mounds placed parallel to the fairways. Dye's TPC design was vastly different from Nicklaus's and other contemporary architects with its unkempt appearance and lavish use of waste areas, steep bunkers, and blind shots.

So much criticism was leveled at Ponte Vedra that a committee composed of Ben Crenshaw, Jim Colbert, Tom Weiskopf, Ed Sneed, and Nicklaus requested a meeting with Beman and Dye to express their concerns. Dye complied and made many significant changes to the course, but his philosophy remained unchanged. He intended his work to demand tests of the pro's emotional talent as well as physical expertise.

"I wanted them to look as if they went through a battle coming off the eighteenth green!" he remarked, because he believed only the greatest players could survive witnessing the ball take insane bounces after making what should have been flawless shots. Dye's greens, with remarkable speed and contour, always followed this philosophy. The design at Kingsmill saw greens so fast at tournament time, only magicians like Ben Crenshaw were unintimidated. The same was true of blind holes. Dye loved them even more than Robert Trent Jones had, believing they were true tests of character and intelligence.

On the short, par-four, 12th hole at the Tournament Players Club, Dye built a fairway where the golfers' view of the green was totally blocked by 20 foot high mounds. On the next hole, a 170-yard par-three, he designed a high mound in the front of the green that hid the bottom of the pin. The coup de grace was the par-three, 132-yard 17th, the famous island green. "Never in my life did I think that hole would psych those pros," Dye chortled. "I realize now that it's the mere fact that they know they shouldn't miss it that makes it so tough." Unlike the players, spectators loved watching action at the island green. Arguably, it earned a reputation as the signature green of the Tour.

Relations between Dye and the touring pros were further strained when PGA West was constructed and the Bob Hope Classic was scheduled. To build PGA West, the architect moved two million yards of earth, shipped in 5000 railroad ties, planted 250,000 yellow cassia plants, and dug eight lakes. Then he concocted a witches' brew of water and sand hazards. Some bunkers plunged 20 feet deep and meandered for 200 yards along the edge of fairways.

"Spiteful, hateful!" Raymond Floyd erupted, when he was asked for his impressions after leaving the 18th green during his first round.

"Silly," echoed Bernhard Langer.

"Awful, artificial," bemoaned Tom Watson.

Ben Crenshaw sought out the architect and talked with him for 90 minutes about hole number five, alleging the design was horribly unfair because it took away skill from the game and put in luck. "Well, that kind of luck is one of the things that makes golf different from bowling," Dye rejoined.

Ray Floyd would not let it go at that: "Twenty-five years ago the pros would have refused to play these stadium type courses," Ray alleged:

> You can watch a good approach shot carom off the side of the green and wind up on one of the gallery mounds. Now you are hitting your third shot off a downhill lie out of high grass over a bunker onto a platform green that is tilting toward a pond. That is a shot that was never ever seen in golf until we started all this earth moving to build gallery mounds. I certainly wouldn't want to play a stadium course every week. They get monotonous and repetitious; in fact, they get ridiculous. If I miss the green I should be able to use my skills to put the ball close and save par, but the TPC courses force you to play defensively and not even attempt to get the third shot close. A lot of short game touch has been taken away. The same is true with the bunkers on some of these courses. I'm a fine bunker player and I have trouble getting out, let alone putting the shot close. I've started using a sixty-two degree wedge on some of these courses

just to get the ball up fast enough. So after eighteen years on the tour I had to learn to play a different type of game.

Peter Thomson echoed many of Floyd's opinions, and went on to describe how TPC courses were

Raymond Floyd (©PGA Tour).

born in commercialism as part of Deane Beman's bold plan to make the Tour self sufficient by the staging of Tour events in its own stadiums. Built into these arenas are the features that make for colorful television — the horror stretches of water and wilderness, railroad ties and savage sawgrass, areas wherein it might be hoped a front runner will come to grief to the sniggers of the multitudes watching from the high mounds. The mixture of these patterns makes for the photogenic aspect that magazines and calendars encourage, the reflection of green grass and trees in calm blue water (out west you can even have snow capped mountains mirrored in the hazards) — It sells a load of real estate but has little to do with golf, and more often than not it gets in the way. What we are seeing in these courses are not practical innovations but distortions of dimensions — not works of art but caricatures.... The whole sorry business stems on the one hand from the silly attempt to keep winning scores up at around par for four rounds, about 288. Winning scores in the early 1900's were near the 300 mark, but they steadily declined with the advancement in clubs and balls and the tremendous improvement in course maintenance.... The more notorious the course the higher the surrounding land prices. The luck for the developer, as devised through his architect, is to build something that is photogenically stunning, however impractical, extravagant, or absurd.

Dye usually had a twinkle in his eye when he listened to comments like the above. But occasionally he responded with heated defenses of his work and the philosophy behind it. One of his chief objectives, as he explained it, was to restore golf to the game it was in the glory years of Hogan, Snead, and Nelson.

The guys on tour today are so long they take holes that Hogan played with a driver and two-iron and play them with a driver and seven-iron. Maybe they are bigger and stronger, but the biggest change is equipment. They hit each club about nine percent further, which means that a hole that players in Hogan's era played at four hundred and forty yards must now measure four hundred and eighty yards to demand the same kind of shotmaking. It's a question of maintaining the integrity of the game.... Ideally a course should have four long par-fours that require approach shots hit with long irons, and six others that are shorter but feature very demanding landing areas. I don't see what the challenge is to hitting a wide open fairway with a one-iron. I love short par-fours but all I'm saying is if a hole is short it better be tight to make it a true test.

When thinking of deep bunkers and railroad ties as examples of what traditionalists hated about his work, Dye was quick to credit his wife with originating the ideas:

> Alice pointed out that pros get out of greenside bunkers ten out of ten times. Put them up against a nineteen-foot bunker with a one million dollar tournament on the line and it will give them something to think about. The idea is to make the course mentally frustrating. You have to look at tournament golf as excruciating pain. It's when you start thinking about what can go wrong next that the course will beat you. Golf isn't a fair game. People play under different weather conditions and different course conditions during tournament play. Is that fair? Do players forced to contend with bad weather or spiked up greens get any special breaks? No. It's just the breaks of the game. The best you can hope for is that the breaks eventually even out.... I'm trying to make these guys heroes! Do you think if Ben Hogan had hit that famous one-iron approach to the eighteenth green at Merion in the U.S. Open with an eight-iron it would have been as famous? No, not a chance! I'm trying to bring the long irons back into the game so these guys can get their pictures in magazines. The problem is, they don't realize it.

One of Pete Dye's greatest achievements was his ability to work with marginal locations that many other architects might have dismissed or avoided. He claimed that he never enjoyed having a "normal" piece of ground to design. In West Virginia he was faced with an abandoned strip mine and in Florida drained a marsh to build the TPC. One real estate magnate confided, "When you have a sow's ear for property, you hire Pete Dye and he'll work a miracle. You don't give him a silk purse to start with or he's liable to hand you back a sow's ear."

Throughout the 1980s, television had an increasingly important role in course design. Dye remarked that it was crucial to concentrate on the last five or six holes of a tournament-quality course, because not only would large galleries be congregating there, but also— the most significant factor of all — the television cameras would feature the closing greens. The architect should concentrate above all else to create the conditions for two-shot swings among the leaders on the closing holes.

"The holes must be so challenging that anything could happen," Dye explained:

> There should never be a routine par, where every player will be hitting the same driver, three-iron, and wedge to the green. The architect wants to provide a setting where golfers can gamble, tempt fate, and make shots that no amateur viewer in the easy chair at home would ever dream of attempting. If we want to threaten with a sudden two-shot swing, we have to give them some place they can't recover from, and the only thing I know like that is water. I've always hated

water, but now I have more water around my courses than you can shake a stick at.... The players say to me, "You're just trying to run up the scores!" Well, no I'm not. I'm trying to bring out the great shots. That's what television fans want to see. If you go back you'd find that the great shots in history were made with long irons. Hogan's great shotmaking at Merion and Oakland Hills took big drives and demanding long irons. Those are the ones we remember. Today's tour pros hit the ball so far we can't make them hit a long iron.

By the end of the decade even Deane Beman was beginning to have second thoughts about what he, Pete Dye, and other architects had wrought. Since the first TPC at Sawgrass had opened at Ponte Vedra in 1980, the commissioner of the PGA Tour had created 18 TPC facilities, and the pros seemed not to enjoy playing any of them. The commissioner had named Sawgrass "the Yankee Stadium of Golf," but Tom Watson swore he wanted to bulldoze all the greens at Sawgrass, and Greg Norman was heard to recommend dynamiting the ninth green at the TPC at Avenel.

"I don't want to be too harsh," Beman admitted.

I don't want to minimize my respect for the architects' talents, but I believe today that golf course architecture is overdone. And unfortunately, we helped push architecture toward the extreme with the original TPC, which I regret. The influence of Sawgrass, the heroic philosophy, has led to disaster holes at every turn. You either make a birdie, or you make a six or seven. We think we have a responsibility to change that trend. From this day forward, our philosophy, when we have complete control, will be to build traditional golf courses.

If this was a recanting of somewhat lesser importance than Galileo's during the Inquisition, it nonetheless shocked the commissioner's subjects. It was Beman, after all, who had taken credit for the stadium course concept dating back to the 1960s when he planned several layouts in Maryland and Virginia with Ed Ault. Beman was a top amateur at the time, and he encouraged the USGA to build tournament sites across the country that could serve as U.S. Open venues and as centers of research for turf grasses. His partner Ault had drawn up plans for golf holes that were sited in actual stadiums, and he argued for roadways and automatic people movers to move galleries around a course.

Later, when crowned commissioner, Beman deplored the limited space for parking, concessions, and spectators at so many tournament sites. He dredged up the plans from the 1960s and hired Pete Dye to build the TPC at Tour headquarters in Ponte Vedra. At the time, Dye's Harbour Town was earning accolades from players, many of whom thought it was the best new course in the country, and Beman hoped for something equally impressive at Sawgrass. If Dye went at his assignment with a vengeance, it was only because he had carte blanch from the top. When the players said they hated the completed Sawgrass, the commissioner was quick with an explanation: "When Pete got in there [Sawgrass] he didn't build a Harbour Town," Beman said, "I spent half my time toning down what he was imagining. I don't know what was in Pete's mind. The product we opened was very severe, particularly the greens. But it was toned down a lot from what it would have been if I hadn't been alarmed."

Dye's memory was quite different.

> I assure you that when we built the greens at Sawgrass, Deane and everybody looked at them and approved them. I didn't go out and build eighteen greens and they caught up with me. And when I built the island green, nobody disapproved. Maybe I should have said, "This is very severe!" but I thought we were all in accord. Anyway there wasn't a green at the TPC as severed as the seventeenth green at Medinah. And we were thinking about Bermuda grass at that time, which would have been slower. It was built when there was still a nebulous hope that courses wouldn't go toward faster and faster greens.

Whatever the truth, architects hired by Beman to design post–Sawgrass TPC sites began pushing to extremes. Beman had permitted reconfiguring and softening of the greens at Sawgrass, among other alterations, but ironically Dye's brotherhood adopted many of his initiatives when planning other stadium courses. And when those courses were finished the pros arrived at new tournament locations to discover, to their horror, the same severe greens, prominent spectator mounds, cavernous bunkers, and forbidding approach shots over water to multi-tiered putting surfaces. "They kept trying to outdo one another," Beman sighed. "The extreme became the norm as they tried to one-up each other."

At the same time that the TPC courses were being pilloried by pros and second guessed by the commissioner, the real estate developments that were so much an integral part of the overall concept were by and large hugely successful and were bringing added wealth to the PGA Tour. With mansions paralleling the fairways and huge galleries forking over admission fees, all but a few of the developments finally were thriving. The Phoenix Open, held at the TPC of Scottsdale, sold 109,000 tickets for one weekend day in 1990, a D-Day invasion force by the standards of most traditional courses that ideally accommodated perhaps 25–30,000 spectators for a major championship. Several of the TPC courses had been modified to address criticisms of touring pros, many of whom signed as consultants to Beman for remodeling work and for new course designs.

The assignments seemed to fan dormant fires in more than one pro. Not only was architecture challenging and lucrative, but also it was a natural sideline for aging stars who frequently had strong views on architecture and enjoyed putting them into practice. After suffering a neck injury in 1982, Jerry Pate hooked on with Tom Fazio to build a new course in Fort Walton Beach, Florida, and with Ron Garl on another in West Palm Beach. Then he joined talents on a project with old nemesis Pete Dye. Here were sublime apprenticeships, studying on the one hand with traditionalist Tom Fazio, and on the other with abstract expressionist Pete Dye.

Another former tour regular, Bill Rogers, debuted in architecture with Ron Pritchard at the TPC at San Antonio and with another assignment outside Houston. "This is not the result of my being burned out," Rogers explained. "I love being out in the field, doing the actual nuts and bolts work. It's something that has always interested me. Hopefully, with my energies concentrated in this direction maybe my desire to play golf will return. It came at a perfect time. I'm interested in actually pursuing architecture, and not just as a figurehead."

The golfers usually concentrated on routing holes, while engineers, agronomists, and other specialists handled the nitty gritty details of construction. The pro also was indispensable when the time came to start selling real estate. Gary Player, Lee Trevino, Arnold Palmer, and Jack Nicklaus ran thriving architectural businesses. Nicklaus, especially, built a prolific design company. His interests spanned four decades, dating back to the days when Pete Dye constructed a course in Nicklaus's home town of Columbus and the architect asked a very young Nicklaus for his opinions. The golfer's suggestions were incorporated in Dye's final routings. Later Dye asked him to consult on several projects, including the one at Hilton Head. "I made twenty-three visits to that site," Nicklaus remembered, "probably as many as I ever have made to any course, and although Pete should get total credit for the Harbour Town course I was involved a great deal. I know I learned a lot from him about how to use the terrain."

In 1973 Nicklaus was ready to launch his own architectural firm. He hired Bob Cupp and Jay Morrish as senior designers, and the contracts rolled in one after another, year after year, all over the world. Looking back to those early jobs with Pete Dye, where it all started for Nicklaus, the Golden Bear offered up insights into the characteristics that differentiated him from Dye:

> The only problem with Pete Dye is he falls in love with the land. He does his work purely as a labor of love, and he doesn't care whether he makes any money or not. I've told him, "Pete, you're the most talented guy in the business, and there's no reason why you shouldn't make a profit from your work." On the jobs I did with Pete, we never made a dime, which was OK with me because I learned a lot. But that's no way to run a business.

Jack followed his own advice. He built up a design company with a staff of more then 300, to provide financial planning, landscaping, and legal services for the real estate projects associated with most of his course designs. His architectural work gained renown. Five of his designs became part of *Golf Magazine*'s list of the 100 Greatest Courses— Shoal Creek, Muirfield Village, Glen Abbey, Bear Creek, and Desert Highlands— and were frequent hosts to tournaments and to special events like The Skins Game. Later Loxahatchee and Castle Pines added to Jack's reputation, and developers lined up to pay Nicklaus's $1 million fee.

The superstars reaped financial bonanzas from their design businesses. In the 1980s other tour pros flocked to architecture — Howard Twitty, Hubert Green, Ed Sneed, Mike Souchak, Tom Weiskopf, Mark McCumber, Bruce Devlin, Jim Colbert, Jerry Pate, Ben Crenshaw, Fuzzy Zoeller, Tom Watson, and a lesser stable of thoroughbreds joined the steeplechase. As Hubert Green said, "All golfers are architects, or so we think."

One of their number, Ben Crenshaw, would design courses only in the traditional mode. Above all he admired the works of Tillinghast, MacKenzie, and Ross, and said that his designs were intended to replicate courses from the 1920s. He loathed blind shots, island greens, and railroad ties. "I'm sort of a throwback," admitted Crenshaw. "I believe that older architecture is the best and the most natural. Target golf is not part of my scheme."

Crenshaw had been a member of the committee recruited by Beman to implement changes to the TPC at Sawgrass. This was the impetus for Ben to begin design work of his own choosing, based on very fixed philosophical guidelines. "Now there's a lack of personal attention," he lamented:

> I mean day by day. There's no secret to the fact that in the old days, the golden days of architecture, a tremendous amount of personal attention was given to each project. Today, when we move hundreds of thousands, millions of cubic yards of material, things can get lost pretty easily. And what's lost more and more these days is why the golf course was designed in the first place. Golf courses have become no more than an extension of somebody's backyard surrounded by condos and townhouses! The reason for the golf course boom is simply that golf sells lots. Only in a few cases have developers and architects done the sport justice. Golf was meant to be played in a natural state. The more natural the better — not with condominiums and golf holes on top of each other.

The iconoclastic Irish golfer, David Feherty, echoed Ben Crenshaw's opinions.

> People always talk about the great architects— MacKenzie and Ross and the old timers," Feherty bemoaned, "but no one copies them. Why doesn't anyone build courses like that anymore? It's because of people like Jack Nicklaus and Pete Dye. They have their own ideas and everyone is jumping on their bandwagon instead of using land to make beautiful places to walk around. We've now got parking lots, concrete strips all over the place with huge, monstrous, rolling greens. These guys like landscape gardeners on acid. To me the game has disappeared. I really don't think we're building courses right now. First, they're taking walking out of the game. You can't walk golf courses in America. Kiawah Island had three-quarters of a mile between the ninth green and tenth tee, and there are so many beautiful things to see out there when you're walking that you'd miss in a cart. The only way you'll see a wild fowl or whatever is if you happen to flatten it in your cart. It really depresses me. I fear for the future of traditional golf, where people get out, have a bit of a stretch, hit a few shots, and

walk around a nice place. That is the first thing a golf course should be. A nice place to walk. Most of the courses we play these days, you might as well be walking around the parking lot at Piggly Wiggly. There would be no pleasure in this game at all if it wasn't for walking.

The Trent Jones, Nicklaus, and Dye courses have got enormous fairway areas to hit it into, so you don't have to drive the ball particularly well. But fairway traps and greenside traps are incredibly penal. Like the Nicklaus course at PGA West — an elderly person or a youngster couldn't play those courses because if you hit it down fifteen or twenty feet below the surface of the green you're not going to get it out. And an elderly person may not get himself out, never mind the ball. What we need are hazards that allow the experienced and skilled player to show that he is skilled and experiences. Reducing him to the level of an absolute dummy benefits no one. There's no need to build a golf course seventy-eight hundred yards long despite the equipment changes, if it is designed properly. You should be encouraged to drive the ball off the tee even though it is narrow. You should have to drive the ball as often as possible, but if you do drive it off line you should be afforded the opportunity to display you skill as a recovery artist All of that has been driven out of the game. It's become one grand, sort of "Drive it anyway you like, thrash it onto the green with ten elephants buried under it, and then we'll have a crazy putting competition." Robert Trent Jones makes me mad faster than most things. Pete Dye's pretty close as well. He's the father of the TPC — the totally pointless course. Jack Nicklaus doesn't make me mad but almost bemuses me. I just don't understand why on earth, he of all people, is building golf courses like that. In general, I love player-golf courses. In general, I love player-designers. Arnold Palmer is absolutely magnificent, and Gary Player's probably the best in the world!

Critiques by players like David Feherty could be scathing, indeed, but no more dismissive than those of pure designers such as Robert Trent Jones, who frequently belittled the work of fellow architects. "Pete Dye made a huge mistake when he teamed with Nicklaus at Harbour Town," Jones confided after the course had earned renown with most players and other architects.

Up till then Dye had made challenging, medium length courses. Influenced by Nicklaus, he started lengthening fairways and changing the basic proportions of his courses. Harbour Town is famous for ushering in a move back to small targets. That's all right as long as you shorten the course. But an average golfer can't hit a small target from a long distance. True golfers don't like playing Pete Dye's courses that much because there's no easy way out. They're too penal.... When Nicklaus started designing courses, I said: "Jack, you're designing courses around your own game." He disagreed and began to lecture me. So I showed him how at Muirfield Village you have to hit very long tee shots up a hill, then play to a narrow green guarded by bunkers or rough. If you can't hit the ball over the hill you'll have a much harder time making it to the green.... What Nicklaus is doing is heroic golf — only heroes can play it. What Dye is doing is penal. I'm doing both and much more!

Golf fans are exposed to many of Pete Dye's designs, and Nicklaus's because of the number of times they are used for PGA tournaments and other televised events. At the same time classic designs on the order of MacKenzie, Ross, and Tillinghast are routinely chosen to host U.S. Opens overseen by the USGA, not the PGA Tour. While it may seem that the Open rotates among a small number of courses—Merion, Oakland Hills, Pebble Beach, Medinah, Baltusrol, Winged Foot, Oakmont, and Inverness, for example—the impression lingers with fans more as a result of dramatic contests at those historic layouts than as a conscious effort on the part of USGA officials to keep using the same tracks.

Courses are selected for the Open on the basis of very few criteria. They have to be capable of hosting 15–25,000 spectators each day; spacious grounds must be available for parking, concessions, and related activities; a strong club membership must be available to provide volunteers; the membership must own equity shares in the club; and the location should be near a major metropolitan area. There are exceptions from time to time, but most of these criteria apply year after year.

It doesn't hurt a club's chances of being selected, however, if members are officials or past presidents of the USGA. Hazeltine, for example, was selected when it was a relatively new course, at a time when its president was a former head of the USGA. It also doesn't hurt to be located in the Northeast or Midwest. Very few Southern courses are selected because of high summer temperatures. In the West, Pebble Beach and Olympic are favorite venues, but other famous clubs like Riviera and the Los Angeles Country Club are not, the former because it is a site for a regular PGA event (the USGA is not noted for sharing sites with the Tour), and the latter because it enjoys a very elite membership unimpressed by movie stars, wealth, or the cachet of hosting a major championship.

Year in and year out the USGA honors tradition, while the PGA Tour is capable of experimenting with the avant garde. But if the comments of many tour players are taken at face value, they would choose to play traditional courses at the expense of many new designs. Jimmy Demaret, always noted for fresh perspectives whatever his age, blamed his successors for part of the trouble when he said:

> They built better courses forty and fifty years ago that they do now. Golf wasn't meant to be a real estate promotion. We used to play some great courses—Riviera, Pinehurst, Los Angeles Country Club, Merion, San Francisco Golf Club, and Lake Mercer. They were marvelous courses, and still are. Then the new crowd of pros started griping about the grass, the trees, the bunkers, the locker rooms, and everything else, and the wheels come off. Fine clubs didn't want the tournaments. Before the pros knew it they were playing on public courses. Some players would complain if they were playing on Dolly Parton's bedspread.... The great course architects like Ross, Plummer, and Tillinghast built FAIRWAYS and GREENS. They didn't dig holes for one hundred sand traps. It's all cosmetics now. Helena Rubenstein and Max Factor could build these new courses. But they get away from golf. Palmer and Nicklaus might be able to play them, but the members can't.

Demaret agreed with golfers of all ages who, when polled by *Golf Digest*, chose Donald Ross as the all-time greatest architect, with Alister Mackenzie and Tillinghast close behind. Of architects, working in the 1990s, poll respondents admired Tom Fazio almost two to one over Pete Dye, while Jack Nicklaus, Jay Morrish, Tom Weiskopf, and Rees Jones finished in the top six. All of the top architects decried the influence of new equipment technology on modern golf, because it had the potential to make famous older courses obsolete.

Advances in Technology and Equipment

"High tech is affecting performance. I've never hit the ball so far. I've never gotten so much spin. The game is easier, and all of a sudden everyone is confident! We're almost to where you can put a computer chip inside the golf ball!"

— Mac O'Grady

Golf equipment in the 1990s had evolved to such an extent, both in design and composition materials, that architects and PGA Tour players alike were alarmed at the way technology was transforming the sport. The new balls are "ruining the game, period," Tom Weiskopf insisted in 1991:

I know the ball goes substantially farther. Look, I'm forty-eight years old, and I hit the ball longer than I did in my prime. I'll give you a perfect example. I've played thousands of rounds on the Scarlet Course at Ohio State. Today I hit one club less on all the par-3s. There's a par five there that I never reached in school. This summer, on watered fairways, I hit it easily with a driver and a one-iron. Now you tell me the ball doesn't go longer. And it goes straighter. That doesn't bother me as much as the distance, though. The ball is making the great courses obsolete. How can that be good? How about Merion? Do you mean to tell me that the Open can never go back to Merion, but we shouldn't roll back the ball?

Weiskopf criticized the length and flight characteristics achieved with modern ball designs, as did Raymond Floyd. "The guys who have the capability to be world class players," Raymond alleged,

the guys who can elevate themselves above the others and win majors, who can have above the rest kinds of careers — the equipment and technology are hurting some of the those guys. The golf ball goes through the wind so well everybody tends to play the same kind of game. In the days when the golf ball, if it started curving it kept curving, and if you mishit it off the center of the clubface of an old fashioned traditional iron it was a bad shot — then the best players emerged. But the equipment has created parity. The better players cannot

163

distance themselves as much from the mediocre players. That's not right....
When I face a certain shot that requires some movement, I remember how I used
to play it with the old balls. You had to cut it, or hit it low into the wind. Now
you just bang it at the flag.

It is a fact that between 1980 and 1990, PGA Tour statistics show that the
top drivers of the golf ball increased average length of tee shots by ten yards.
The percentage of fairways hit also rose, from 50 percent in 1980 to 60 percent in 1990, and greens hit in regulation increased from 56 percent to 63 percent. Similar advances occurred in other relevant categories. Greg Norman,
one of the longest off the tee, believed that things were getting out of hand at
the start of the 1990s:

> The effect of equipment advances on today's PGA Tour is enormous. It has
> served to lump everyone closer together and created what amounts to near par-
> ity. It's unhealthy for the game to have no superstars or heroes, nobody out in
> front to carry the flag or be the acknowledged spokesperson. Sure Curtis Strange
> deserves to be looked on as the best player in America [after his back to back
> Open wins], Seve as the best player in Europe, Nakajima in Japan, and myself
> in Australia, but there are no real challengers to our thrones. Everybody else
> seems a distant second, and it is the equipment that has caused the muddle.

The USGA created a test facility to which manufacturers submitted new
balls and clubs for approval. Adjustable clubs, with the exception of putters, do
not conform to the rules of golf established by the USGA. The shaft and grips
of clubs must be straight, the clubhead must be longer from heel to toe than
from front to back, and clubfaces cannot be concave. If the USGA technical staff
is unable to make a ruling, the cub in question is sent to the Implement and
Ball Committee composed of five USGA members and ten representatives of
the golf manufacturers industry. The committee makes a final determination.
   Each year about three hundred new clubs, half of them putters, are submitted. Odds for approval are only 50-50 from year to year. In 1992 an unusual
putter designed by Dave Pelz and used by Tom Sieckmann in several tour
events was declared illegal. The USGA's Rule 4-1d requires that putters must
be generally plain in shape, which Pelz's putter ignored. Occasionally even
golf shoes are ruled non-conforming. John Huston's shoes, for example, were
ruled non-conforming because of the addition of built-up supports at the margin of each sole. If the USGA gave up testing and no standards were maintained for clubs and ball composition, average drives would soon exceed 300
yards and regulation par at a typical course could decline by five or six shots.
That would drastically lower the prestige rating of courses, and in time economic value also would decline. If 1,000 yards were added to a course to
lengthen it, 15–20 acres of new land would be needed. Many new courses already
are surrounded by million dollar homes. With real estate in high demand,
prices undoubtedly would be prohibitive and expansion impossible.

One revolutionary leap in technology occurred around the turn of the century when gutta percha balls were replaced by three-piece Haskell balls. Skilled players immediately added as much as 50 yards to their tee shots. When steel shafts arrived, drives lengthened by another 20 yards or more. Many courses of that era acquired another 1,500–2,000 yards of fairway to compensate, but those days are far, far in the past. In 1931 the USGA set standards for the legal ball minimum diameter of 1.68 inches and maximum weight of 1.62 ounces. Ten years later a velocity limit of 250 feet per second was established. These limitations prevented development of a ball that would render courses obsolete overnight. The overall distance standard later was set at 280 yards (including roll) as measured by the Iron Byron testing machine.

With the robot, a clubhead speed of 160 feet per second (109 MPH) was required to average 280 yards. With a 4 percent tolerance to allow for variables of wind, flat ground, and soil texture, the legal distance could be extended to 291 yards. At the time the distance standard was set, very few players could attain clubhead speeds of 109 MPH, exceptions being Jim Dent, Jack Nicklaus, and Tom Weiskopf. Test results were kept secret to prevent competitors from gaining an edge on one another, but from time to time officials admitted wide variances in results. The head of the testing division revealed that the highest trajectory ball occasionally tested 50 percent higher than the lowest trajectory ball. Consistency varied widely as well, with some balls slicing or hooking off line even when struck squarely with the infallible robot.

In 1973 Titleist developed a revolutionary ball on which 324 dimples were distributed around 20 triangle regions. This design was a marked improvement, because Titleist balls presented a uniform surface in flight, thereby lessening drag. At the same time Spalding was testing various substances in an attempt to find a substitute for balata ball covers. The Dupont Corporation had developed a process of using surlyn to coat electrical wiring with great effectiveness. Dupont doubted that the same materials would work with balls, but Spalding persevered and came up with a surlyn cover that solved the cold-cracking problem of balata while improving overall durability and greater distance. Spalding marketed the new product as the Top Flite, and it was so successful other companies rushed to market with similar balls. Spalding sued for patent infringement and forced many competitors to pay licensing fees.

This was an era of experimentation for golf pros who had grown accustomed to hitting 3-piece, soft, balata covered balls. With the soft finish and rubber windings, balatas dispersed over the club face at impact to supply excellent spin, soft feel, and long carry. The 2-piece, solid plastic-centered, surlyn covered products introduced by Spalding and other manufacturers gave the pros a ball that seemed cutproof, and one that appeared to roll farther in dry fairways. The surlyn balls also seemed to fly better into the wind, and to perform better with metal drivers. Soon PGA Tour pros were switching balls from one make to another depending on wind and fairway conditions; for example using a surlyn ball on shots into the wind and balata around dry, fast greens. The USGA and PGA Tour responded by enacting a new rule permitting only one make and model of ball during an 18-hole round.

Lanny Wadkins, who was always experimenting with new balls and equipment, explained in 1993 that:

> One of the biggest things I've had to get used to in the last ten years is the difference in the flight of the ball as the dimples change. You grew up with the ball curving one way, and now with the dimples changing you have to get used to it. The ball flies straighter than it used to, which means you don't have to work the ball as much. If there's anything the USGA has missed, it's control over the ball. I am not against technology making golf more fun for the masses. But since we're trying to identify the best players every week, I think the equipment should be regulated to the extent that the guys with the most talent, the guys who really are the best players, emerge. If you've got more ability, then you don't need the equipment to make a difference. A lot of guys are getting by because the equipment brings them closer to the good players. They don't have the ability to be there otherwise.

According to records kept by the USGA, in the early 1990s the average handicap for male golfers in the U.S. was 17, the same as 25 years earlier. However, that was the amateur end of the sport. With pros, new technology could be utilized to an extent unobtainable by amateurs. Noted teaching pro Jim Flick explained: "The better the player the more the equipment becomes an advantage. It's like you and I trying to drive a race car at Indianapolis. We wouldn't know what to do with it. For the real expert, technology has made a measurable difference, particularly in the so called scoring clubs, the driver and wedge."

PGA Tour statistics reinforced the views of Flick. The average length of drives on Tour increased in the 1980s, fairways hit increased from 61 percent to 65 percent, and scoring average improved from 72.06 to 71.09 per round. Anecdotal evidence from pros was overwhelmingly in favor of much greater performance from new golf balls and high tech clubs, compared to the equipment used in the early days of the Tour. The first American touring pros were fond of building their own equipment, just as Scottish pros historically had done. The best known example probably was Gene Sarazen and his creation of the sand wedge. Many years after he invented the club Gene commented on its impact:

> Everyone was happy. Bobby Jones was a terrible sand player. Hagen used to chip out of bunkers because he didn't know how to explode with a niblick. That club helped popularize the game. The average player was making 7's and 8's when he hit into a trap. He'd come home crabby. But with the sand wedge he'd make no worse than bogey and come home smiling. There were fewer divorces after I invented that club.

One of the earliest American manufacturers, MacGregor, hired Tony Penna in the 1930s, and set him to work on a club design that Tommy Armour played and promoted. Penna not only was MacGregor's chief designer, but chief talent scout as well. He enrolled Jimmy Demaret in MacGregor's stable of professionals for $500 in 1937, added Byron Nelson in 1939 for another $500, and bagged Hogan in 1940 for $250. In decades to come, Jack Burke, Bob Toski, Dave Marr, and George Bayer joined MacGregor, as did Jack Nicklaus and Chi Chi Rodriguez.

Continuous development of new and better equipment seemingly should affect scoring, yet comparison testing frequently produces ambivalent results. In one test Titlist supplied top condition K-2 Achushnet balls of the kind played on Tour in the 1970s, measured against the performance of modern Tour balatas. In addition, Wilson supplied a classic persimmon Staff II driver and a Staff Dynapower 5-iron, popular clubs of the pros in the early 1970s, matched against the new Killer Whale driver and Ultra 45 5-iron played by John Daly and other modern pros. The balls and clubs were tested at Titlist headquarters using an Iron Byron machine, after which Mark McCumber repeated the exercises at a driving range.

With Iron Byron, both old and new balls were hit much higher with the new driver compared to the 1973 Wilson club, and also sailed eight to 18 yards farther. But the 1973 driver, with its lower trajectory, generated up to 20 yards more roll with either ball than did the new Killer Whale. On heel hits (one-half inch off center) the new driver hit either ball straighter than the older club, but the older of the two produced up to nine more yards of roll. Because of the larger heads and perimeter weighting of new drivers, it appeared that many new drivers hit somewhat straighter shots than older clubs. When a new 5-iron was tested against a 1973 edition, it was found that the new club hit new balls much higher. Into a head wind, the new balls flew about four yards farther than 1973 balls when hit with either club. On off-center hits with 5-irons (toe hits, one-half inch off center) the new irons hit the ball five to eight yards shorter into a head wind because the ball went much higher, but accuracy was better.

When the balls and clubs were turned over to pro Mark McCumber, he also discovered that the new driver and 5-iron hit balls much higher with less roll. It was much harder to deliberately fade or draw balls with the new clubs. Factoring in roll and trajectory, both old and new clubs and balls produced nearly identical distance and dispersion patterns. This surprised not only McCumber, but also most of his contemporaries, who were convinced that technology was changing the sport. Superstars were especially vociferous. Lee Trevino claimed that:

> Balls today are more forgiving. You can still work them, but not as much, and that's a tremendous disadvantage for guys who like to fit shots to rough positions

the way I do. It takes away one of my strengths. What it also does is equalize everyone. Just as you can't intentionally fade or draw a shot as much, the balls today tend to make a bad shot not quite as bad. As a result you tend to see the fields bunch up more, and whoever has the hot round or two generally wins. That makes it hard for someone to dominate the game.

Jack Nicklaus was quick to agree: "It's harder for the cream to come to the top," Jack alleged. "The equipment is putting everyone at one level. Good golf is not necessarily rewarded."

Tom Watson was equally emphatic:

There used to be a greater separation between the talented and not so talented. The new equipment is reducing the element of shotmaking and consolidating the talent. Yes, equipment advances are part of the game, but I think there has got to be a point where you say, no more.... Golf is today a power game, not a shotmaker's game. You see a lot of big, strong guys on tour now who can kill the ball but not as many who can shape shots. This is true of both foreign and American players. Part of that is a reaction to the courses we play, but a lot has to do with the ball.

Tom Kite was more assertive on the equipment issue than almost anyone else:

The reality is that equipment advances will always bring the less skilled closer to the more skilled. It's the history of golf. Equipment has always been an equalizer. If you played really primitive clubs, the best player would have an even better chance of winning. If everybody played with just one club, the guy with the most shots would win. But golf isn't like that.

The superstars were especially critical of the square-grooved clubs designed by Karsten Solheim. From the early 1940s until the '80s, the USGA maintained three rules for the configuration of grooves on irons. They were to be V-shaped, no more than .035 of an inch wide from edge to edge, and not closer together than three times the width of the adjacent groove. During these years most irons were manufactured using a forging process that stamped, milled, or rolled grooves into the iron face. Then, a new process was developed. Innovators began employing what was called investment cast processing, a technique that could produce U-shaped grooves.

The USGA responded to the new technology in the early 1980s with a ruling that allowed grooves to be configured like three-sided boxes. One manufacturer in particular, Karsten Solheim, was happy with the decision because he believed it would result in greater repeatability in shot making. Solheim's father had emigrated to Seattle from Norway. As a teenager Solheim delivered newspapers every morning, saved his money, and attended the University of Washington to study aeronautical engineering. After exhausting his savings, he became a repairman for a shoe store, then sold shoes for eight years. Taking up golf and beginning to tinker with clubs, he soon invented a putter of revolutionary design. He welded a shaft onto the sole of a blade to reduce twisting, and added lead onto the heel and toe to enlarge the sweet spot.

The result: Solheim's first Ping putter. He built the putters in his garage until the business began to boom. In 1966 he erected a small factory in Phoenix and began churning out 100 clubs a day. When Solheim's new Ping Eye 2 clubs went into pro-

Tom Kite (author's collection).

duction, they were snapped up by amateurs and pros who liked the effect the new design had on spin rates. Solheim continued to tinker with the clubs and submitted a set to the USGA for testing. In 1985 officials decided that the improved clubs had been rounded to the point where the grooves were so close together they did not meet rule stipulations. Anyone playing out of light or moderate rough could obtain spin rates that were better than V grooves could produce. With V grooves, balls hit from tall grass often turned into flyers, shots having minimum spin and unpredictable trajectories. Square grooves, on the other hand, produced shots that performed much as if hit from fairway grass. They landed softly and stopped more readily. Greg Norman claimed that he never would use square grooves, even though he

> could knock off six shots from his score in each tournament. The game integrity must be upheld. When you get into a situation where the golf club is making the shot easier and not the player's ability, then I think that's wrong. I really think square grooves are ruining the game. They are taking the shotmaker and putting him in the same category with the player who never learned to play the shots. They've eliminated the risk of catching a flyer from the rough, so the clubs have, in effect, made rough meaningless.

Solheim continued to insist that the Pings were within the rules if measured from the wall of each groove rather than from the rounded edge. Neither side compromised, and in June 1987 the USGA ruled that the Ping Eye 2 irons were non-conforming. At this point the Pings arguably were the most popular clubs in the history of golf, having sold more than 500,000 sets. Solheim fought back, and gained a partial victory. The USGA would rule Pings legal if only Solheim would agree to place the grooves farther apart in the future. The PGA Tour, however, was not so amenable. In 1990 the commissioner of the PGA Tour decided all square grooved clubs to be illegal for use in Tour events. This precipitated an angry rebuttal and subsequent lawsuit from Solheim, who insisted that his clubs conformed to the rules of golf. Many client players supported his stand. Mark Calcavecchia, the object of much criticism because he refused to give up his Pings, stated:

> They think the only reason I'm winning is because I'm playing Pings. That's their problem. Equipment might help a very small amount, but 98% of it is that the young guys out here are just better. If everybody used the same clubs and the same ball, you'd still have the same results—the young guys winning.

And USGA scion Frank Hannigan agreed:

> The fact is these kids are just terrific players. Calcavecchia for one, putts like God. I can remember when Nicklaus first came out. Guys were saying "Ah, he's just a big, fat kid. He can't work the ball. You know, he can't hit that knock down shot." Ridiculous stuff, but it's always been this way.

Nonetheless, the PGA Tour maintained its stand to the chagrin of some members who were taking a close look at the liability danger if Solheim should win his $100-million lawsuit, which as the months and years passed seemed more and more likely. To the relief of many PGA members, Karsten Manufacturing and the PGA Tour finally settled out of court in April, 1993. The agreement specified that square grooves would be allowed on Tour, and a five-man advisory committee would review golf equipment and make recommendations to the Tournament Policy Board.

The decision was seen as a victory for Solheim, who won an admission that the Tour could not prohibit Pings unless the USGA went along. The PGA also agreed to pay part of Solheim's legal fees, which totaled millions of dollars. Some believed the Tour settled so quickly with Solheim because lawyers warned Deane Beman about the complexity of the case. The Tour's position had been tested on a focus jury, and the results were not encouraging. In addition, the Tour's insurance company preferred that Beman seek a settlement rather than a possibly costly trial. Solheim had filed a conspiracy suit against the Tour and its officials. Insurance in place to cover PGA officials totaled $10 million, but a jury was capable of assessing much higher damages than that. If Solheim's suit had been successful, the Tour and its personnel could have been faced with a liability of $50–100 million. Beman had other worries. If a trial were held, the USGA official in charge of testing, Frank Thomas, undoubtedly would have been cross-examined, and he might have been forced to testify that Beman could have a preconceived opinion about square grooves.

Very early, Beman had told Thomas that all the USGA would need to find during testing was a small difference in the performance of square grooves over other designs in order to prove the Tour's case. Thomas's testimony in open court would have been revealed that in tests of Ping clubs the USGA found no significant differences in spin rates. Despite the opinions of many, many golfers, including some of the premier players in the world, no scientific evidence existed to prove that square grooves were superior to other designs. The imbroglio was summed up by Paul Azinger:

> The players were outraged because of the advantages of square grooves, so the tour had to pursue it. Then everyone got upset about how much it was going to cost, and the players forgot they were the ones who started it. Everyone got cold feet. In the end we had more to lose.

"Nobody won except the lawyers," concluded Mark O'Meara.

Karsten Solheim believed that he had triumphed. Solheim had made golf history with the innovations of perimeter weighting, offset hosels, and investment casting. When Solheim started in the business, golf manufacturers used skilled workers to carve designs from flat back steel forgings. Solheim developed a process of casting club heads from molds. He had developed the first Ping putter by constantly tinkering with one model after another until he hit on the idea of heel-toe weighting, a configuration that enlarged the sweet spot of the putter to enhance solid hits.

Continuing to experiment, Solheim moved from heel-toe weighting to perimeter weighting in his first investment cast irons, whereby a generous measure of the club's overall weight was located on the outside edge and at the bottom edge, not in the hitting area of the clubface. Solheim discovered that irons built with perimeter weighting suffered lower rotational torque and twisting. He became adept at weaving intricate patterns and cavities with his casting process, and simplified replication wrought a revolution in the industry. His clubs became so popular a host of imitators entered the market.

"Ironically, it took time for other manufacturers to catch on," Solheim explained after his company became enormously successful. "I made such ugly clubs that they left me alone for years. They didn't start knocking me off till they saw I was getting most of the business." Ping knock-offs flooded the golf equipment market, and Solheim hired a stable of patent attorneys whose task was formidable. One explained that "patent laws are so much in favor of the infringer and so difficult for the fellow with the patent. If somebody in this business has something that you want to manufacture, you go ahead and manufacture. It's just an accepted business risk."

A small manufacturer agreed: "It's the only way you can survive in the golf business," he claimed. "The products have such short cycles, and you have so many small-to-moderate sized companies out there. All you can do is see what's hot, knock it off, and go to market."

Several countries in Asia had acquired unenviable reputations for printing pirated editions of books, published and sold without regard for copyright and royalty payments customary in North America and Europe. The same illegal trade was repeated with golf equipment. Especially in Taiwan, manufacturers of knock-offs mass produced duplicates of Ping Eye irons and many other popular American golf clubs and paid no compensation. At the same time reputable manufacturers carefully noted changes in one another's designs. What worked well for one soon was available in slightly modified form by others, providing much new legal business for companies as lawsuits proliferated.

This situation was just as true for the golf ball industry, which had grown to exceed a $500 million annual marketplace, and particularly evident in the marketing of metal drivers. The Taylor Made Company began to experiment with perimeter weighted drivers in the late 1970s when the firm brought out a radically new metal driver whose head was filled with foam. Players immediately discovered they were hitting more par-5s in two shots, and because of the improved weight distribution they could make solid hits with the driver off fairways. In the 1979 U.S. Open, only three pros were seen playing metal drivers. Ten years later more than half the field had discarded persimmon woods for a plethora of metal drivers. Among them was the Yonex ADX built in 1989, with a graphite head 60 percent larger than standard drivers, as well as the immensely popular Callaway Big Bertha, whose manufacturer by 1995 was boasting of having sold two million copies.

The controversy over new clubs and balls continued unabated through the 1990s, as players experimented with specially designed low trajectory balls, jumbo irons, and longer-shafted drivers. Longer shafts produced faster clubhead speed at impact, ergo, longer carries. The long shafts increasingly were seen on the professional tours, especially on the senior circuit. Meanwhile, the Lynx Company produced a driver with a cobalt, chromium head and guaranteed golfers they could add ten yards to their carries. Cobra introduced a driver called the Ultramid, which was manufactured from thermoplastic, the material in bulletproof vests. Nearing the close of his tenure as PGA Tour Commissioner, Deane Beman was seen hitting new metal-headed woods, perimeter weighted irons, and surlyn balls. He confessed: "There is no question in my mind that the technology is allowing me to do things with the ball that I couldn't do fifteen years ago."

Despite some scientific evidence to the contrary, most of Beman's contemporaries agreed.

Great American Golfers and Golf Rivalries

"When there are 30,000 people waiting for you at 2 p.m. at Augusta National on Sunday in the Masters, a lot of them are there to see if you vomit all the way down the first fairway. The player is very much aware of this. You've got a four-shot lead and they want to see if you faint somewhere over the next five hours."

— Jackie Burke, Jr.

Looking back to the earliest decades of professional golf, it is obvious that equipment for players of that era was far inferior to the balls and clubs of the 1990s. It also is clear that Bobby Jones, Gene Sarazen, Walter Hagen, and other superstars were physically overmatched by subsequent generations of bigger, stronger, and better conditioned athletes. Over the years PGA Tour pros often were polled on various subjects—their likes and dislikes, and opinions about such topics as best ball strikers, best putters, best drivers, and best playing partners. Voluminous statistics maintained by several organizations supply decade-by-decade rankings of individual players on scoring averages, length off the tee, driving accuracy, and other comparisons. The information provided by such statistics telescopes the attributes of great stars from one generation to another, as golf fans argue the merits of Bobby Jones vs. Sam Snead, Byron Nelson vs. Jack Nicklaus, Ben Hogan vs. Arnold Palmer.

Of course the personalities of the great stars varied enormously, from the congenial charm of Jones, to the prickliness of Snead, to the taciturnity and implacable competitiveness of Hogan. Those men, Palmer and Nicklaus included, exuded a magnetism that attracted even non-golfers to tournaments and exhibitions, in the same way that a charismatic star like Michael Jordan drew fans to watch him play golf or baseball. But in the late 20th century, stars like Jordan were in short supply. In pro sports the presence of a dominant team or dominant star was increasingly rare. Basketball had the Bulls, but tennis no longer headlined Bjorn Borg and Jimmy Connors, hockey was witnessing the final displays of Wayne Gretzky and Mario Lemieux's fantastic gifts, and football missed Joe Montana and Walter Payton. Dilution of talent was pervasive, as teams and players melded indistinguishably one into another. Franchise owners in many sports preferred parity, where every team in the league had a good opportunity to win titles. Parity was achieved through drafts, where the worst teams year in and year out selected the best young players.

Because the talent was much more fairly distributed throughout each league compared to earlier decades, few teams were able to dominate their competition in the way the Yankees dominated baseball in the 1950s, or the Packers football in the 1960s, or the Islanders hockey through the early 80s. In the early 1990s it was difficult to find a sport in America that was as glaringly lacking a dominant superstar as golf, something of a paradox for a non-team sport where supreme individualism once had thrived. There seemed to be a different tournament winner each week, with no one able to command the respect of his peers the way Hogan, Palmer, and Nicklaus had done.

There were as many reasons offered up to explain this state of affairs as there were winners on Tour. Some claimed there were far too many excellent pro golfers to allow anyone to dominate as in generations past, while others argued that the all-exempt format and infusion of spectacular purses eliminated the drive that propelled many former notables to achieve superstardom and great wealth. If second place were worth more than $100,000 and fifth place $50,000, there would be more than enough money to go around without having to win tournaments to succeed on Tour.

Although a number of young players were exciting to watch, most of the Tour regulars by the mid–1990s had become indistinguishable from one another. Older fans dismissed them as bland conformists, preferring instead to watch more colorful actors on the Senior Tour. Young men entering the PGA Tour directly from college earned enough money from making cuts and giving clinics to live comfortably, and they went about their business quietly and anonymously. Winning was no longer a necessity in order to survive on Tour. Lack of motivation was noticeable even among the super talented, and especially noticeable among sons of superstars. Gary Player's and Jack Nicklaus's sons were particularly outspoken about what it was like to follow in their father's footsteps. Gary Nicklaus said: "I know this is not what my dad and mom would like to hear, but it's not the end of the world if I miss a cut. I can still pay my bills. My father has set all of us up in a way that we really don't have to worry. I thank him for that, but at the same time, if I said it didn't make a difference I'd be lying."

Identical sentiments were voiced by Wayne Player. Speaking about Gary Nicklaus, Wayne said: "He's been given all kinds of things. Like me, he's never really had to suffer, and when tough times come along maybe you don't hang in there like some other guys."

Contrast those experiences with the striving of an earlier-day Tour player like Jackie Burke, Jr., who said his big break came when the old Scottish pro George Fotheringham offered him a job.

"If you ever work for a Scotsman, you never forget it," Burke recollected. "He was the most difficult man who ever lived in the world.... Nothing you did was right. He was tough, but he was good. I learned a lot by him."

A player from the generation following Burke had a similar work ethic and perspective on life. Dave Stockton, who combined a so-so swing and flawless putting stroke into a long series of ups and downs in golf until finally achieving financial security on the Senior Tour, started off with an attitude that was a feminist nightmare. Prior to Dave and Cathy Stockton's marriage, he told his prospective bride that golf would be the first and most important thing in their lives; family would come second. Stockton's son developed into a fine player in the mid–1990s, long after the father's battle for success came to a successful conclusion.

Another son of a golf pro, Davis Love, achieved early fame with the apparent nonchalance of a Freddy Couples or Payne Stewart. As a rookie, Davis led the field in driving distance, a record 285.7 yard average, 25 yards above the Tour average for drives. He also set the Tour's mark for longest measured drive in 1986, a 389 yard cannon shot at the Hawaiian Open. The same season he became the first known golfer in history to reach Spyglass Hill's 600 yard first hole in two shots. When a computer expert constructed models of the swings of the PGA's leading pros and tried to arrive at the perfect golf swing, he said that Jack Nicklaus's swing best fit his model. But if the computer had been programmed for the best distance model, Love would have finished on top because he had the widest arc of any golfer tested.

"The human body isn't built to handle the kind of speed Davis generates," the expert said. "At impact the clubhead of Davis's driver traveled at 125 MPH, which was more than ten miles per hour faster than any other swing measured."

In 1992 Love proved that he had the skills to become a superstar. He went head-to-head with Couples in a duel that golf enthusiasts began to hope might replicate the Palmer-Nicklaus rivalry of years past. At the start of the season Couples defeated Love in a playoff at the Los Angeles Open. In the following weeks Davis recorded five top-10 finishes, then won the Players Championship at Sawgrass worth $324,000 and a ten-year exemption for Tour events. Davis played haphazardly in the Masters, which Freddy captured, but then Davis won at Harbour Town, finished first again the following week at Greensboro, and by April posted three victories, one second-place finish, and more than $1 million in prize money. His achievements were matched dollar-for-dollar by Couples, who teamed with Love to win the World Cup late in 1992. But then the next week Love triumphed at the Kapalua International, followed by another victory with partner Tom Kite in the Shark Shootout. That year Love banked $1,191,630 in official PGA Tour prize money, plus $645,000 from other unofficial

Hale Irwin (©PGA Tour).

events. Then he endured a string of lack-luster seasons and near misses in major championships, before rebounding in 1997 to win the PGA Championship, his first major victory.

Johnny Miller was quick to refute the notion that the 1990s boasted more exceptional players than his generation, despite the depth of talent that existed on the modern day tour.

"I honestly believe that the top guys I played against in my peak years in the 1970s were, as a group, better than today's best," Johnny argued. "I'm talking about players like Nicklaus, Lee Trevino, Watson, myself, Tom Weiskopf, Hale Irwin, Raymond Floyd, Ben Crenshaw, and Hubert Green. I think our best ten would have beaten the best ten Americans today."

Gene Sarazen claimed to be the only golfer alive who played with four generations of great pros, with Harry Vardon and Ted Ray, then with Hagen and Jones, next with Snead and Hogan and Nelson, and finally with Arnold Palmer and Jack Nicklaus. "The best I've ever seen?" recounted Sarazen.

It would have to be Ben Hogan! He was by far the best from tee to green that I've ever seen. You know he took a second rate swing and, by concentration and dedication, made it into a first rate swing. Even today he practices more than anyone else. I remember when I was first impressed with Hogan's toughness. It was in the World's Four Ball Championship at the Miami Biltmore Course in 1941. I was paired with Hogan. We won six of the first seven holes. Hogan came up to me on the eighth tee and said, "Wake up, Gene, we're loafing. Let's get to work!"

I said: "We won six of the last seven didn't we?"

"Yes," he said. "But we halved the other. We can't throw holes away like that!"

I thought he was kidding. He wasn't. His face was grim. He wanted to hurry up and win so he could go practice his putting. We won the tournament. Hogan was a brilliant golfer, like Jones. They were both wonderful strategists, great generals of the game. They were both brilliant thinkers even though Hogan never had much formal education and Jones got a law degree. Neither liked people very much. That was their drawback. People got on their nerves. Both would go quickly off the eighteenth green into the clubhouse. Times were different in the nineteen-twenties and thirties. Most of us spent a lot of time at parties. I don't think golfers then were the great athletes they are today. Now, after they putt out they go right home to their wife or mother or business. They're very smart and I'm a great admirer of them.

Because Chi Chi Rodriguez appeared younger than his years and remained successful on the Senior Tour, fans often were surprised to learn that he started his touring golf career as early as 1957, and so he had the opportunity to watch several generations of great players. "My opinion is that the only sports athletes that have gotten better are basketball and bowling," Chi Chi averred in a 1973 interview.

> Not golf. In the days when Hogan was winning we had twenty-five great names on the tour. I believe there were greater golfers then. Now there's maybe ten, if they're in a tournament, one will win it — Jack, Trevino, Arnold, Gary, Casper, Littler, Weiskopf, Dave Hill, Crampton. But when Hogan was great there was Hogan, Nelson, Snead, Mangrum, Demaret, Jackie Burke, Middlecoff, DeVincenzo, Peter Thompson, Stan Leonard, Bobby Locke, Skip Alexander, Pete Cooper, Claude Harmon, Paul Runyon, Doug Ford, Vic Ghezzi, Dutch Harrison, Jug McSpaden, the Turnesa brothers, Boros, Barber, George Fazio, Dick Mayer, the Furgols. They were skillful. Those guys could hit the ball two ways. They could hit a fade into the green when the flag was on the right, and they could hit a draw when the flag was on the left. Nowadays most of the young guys can hook the ball but they can't fade it. Jerry Heard is the only young golfer I've seen that can do both. I think John Mahaffey might learn someday, too. Most of the young guys just don't work as hard as the old timers did. In the days of Hogan, if they didn't make it on the tour, they had to go back to being a caddie master, or a starter, or an assistant pro. Now if you don't make it, you can still be an insurance salesman or a banker and make fifty thousand dollars a year because you got college. That's progress. I've played with Jack and Arnold, and I've played with Hogan and Snead. Hogan is like DaVinci, and Snead is like Picasso. If you put Jack and Arnold in a sand trap — now Jack and Arnold are great — but you always get the feeling that you might pick up a shot. But not with Hogan and Snead. Bobby Locke said once that "For them, being in a trap is like being on the green." Ben Hogan always shook my hand after we played. He would always say, "Chi Chi, I enjoyed playing with you. See you tomorrow. Good luck!" And he would look me straight in the eye, so I knew that he meant it. On the course, like Jimmy Demaret said once, the only thing Ben ever says is "You're away." But he always told me: "Good shot," or "Tough break." He always did. Hogan is the best shotmaker who ever lived. Snead and Nelson were very close. Hogan was the best with the driver and the fairway woods, Palmer with the one-iron, Hogan with the two-iron through the wedge, Snead with the sand wedge. For a putter, if my life depended on the putt going in, I'd take Arnold Palmer. Hogan knows more about golf than anybody. Gary Player is good but not as much as Hogan. Palmer knows the most about clubs, Jack and Trevino concentrate better than anybody else. Trevino is like a fox. He jokes with the gallery, but watch him sometime when he's near the ropes. He'll be cracking jokes, but if somebody says something back to him he won't be aware of it. He's not listening. He's thinking about his next shot. He doesn't trade lines with the fans, he thinking golf all the time.

The son of touring pro Jolly Jim Fraser recalled caddying for his father in an exhibition at Philadelphia in 1920 when Harry Vardon, Ted Ray, and Willie MacFarlane were competing. "The one thing I remember about that time," the young Fraser said, "was the four of them sitting in the locker room before the match and polishing off a whole fifth of Scotch whiskey. Then Vardon and Ray both made three's on the first hole, and one of them made another three on the second hole. From that point on no one could convince me of the evils of drink."

The first outstanding golfer of modern times, Walter Hagen, was very similar to Vardon and Ray in background and outlook. He was a consummate match-play competitor, who created a motto for the best players who followed him by believing that "the man who finishes second is soon forgotten. I like to win. I've always gone whole hog or nothing!" When Bobby Jones reached his prime, medal play was increasingly popular and Jones excelled at medal. Jones played only eight years of championship golf before retiring at age 28, the year after winning the Grand Slam. It is hard to project what Jones may have accomplished if given more time. Nicklaus at age 28 already

Chi Chi Rodriguez (author's collection).

had notched 33 victories, nine of them major championships, with more than a million dollars in prize money. Jones, however, at 28 recorded 13 major championships. In his last 11 British and U.S. Open Championships, Jones finished first or second ten times, winning seven of them.

The styles of the two golfers were very different. Jones, unlike Nicklaus, emphasized the power of hands and upper body. Jack subordinated hand action, concentrating a formidable swing with strong leg action. Those who watched Jones play or who have seen his films notice the lack of tension in his swing. He presented a casual, almost languid appearance on the tee, and could hit his shots a very long way with what seemed to be an almost effortless style.

Jones was succeeded by a generation of superstars whose longevity was much greater than that of professionals in the early part of the century. Sam Snead, for example, turned pro in 1934 and became the first man in the history of the Tour to shoot his age, a 67, in the 1979 Quad Cities Open. The next day he recorded a 66. A magnet for the galleries during his last years on the PGA Tour and then later on the Senior Tour, Snead was courted by sponsors but often resented by younger players who complained that uncompetitive older men were taking up too many tournament slots. This criticism, like so much else, bothered Snead not at all. Frank Beard, who played with Snead in the last years of his career, commented that,

> Snead is a terrific playing companion if you let him know early on that you appreciate who he is. You defer to him in little ways—asking him about the 1942 PGA Championship which he won, having him check your swing, never stepping on his story lines. You don't make it overt, but you let him know that you know he's Sam Snead, and he'll open up to you…. Sam's the only man I know who actually enjoys every round of golf he plays, whether it's in a tournament or just a casual game with friends at home. He keeps score in every practice round and treats it as if it's the only eighteen holes he's ever going to play. Afterward he reviews every single shot he hit, and he goes over his round again that night in bed.

Contemporaries were struck by Snead's powers of observation and retention. Despite his lack of formal education and backwoods personae, Snead's memory was prodigious. He could recite every shot played in a major championship from many decades earlier, noting which greens were missed and how many putts he and his rivals needed to sink. The real secret of his longevity was his emphasis on physical conditioning. Hours of stretching exercises every day enabled him to entertain men half his age by kicking the top of a seven-foot high doorway, or by retrieving balls from a hole without bending his knees. In the 1998 Masters Tournament, Snead — playing with Gene Sarazen and Byron Nelson — entertained the galleries with a drive off the first tee that carried more than two hundred yards, this after having been released the day before from a hospital. The constant exercise preserved the full turn and extremely wide arc of his swing, and he knew this was the key to his success.

When an elderly Snead was asked how the Tour differed from the year he started, he commented:

> I think what the modern swing does is stress power. I don't believe the guys today hit it any straighter, but they hit it further. So they're going in with shorter clubs, which makes them look as though they hit it straighter. Almost everyone out there on tour today has a closed clubface and a lot of body action. They're big strong kids. They have a big arc and they freeze the club at the top — very firm wrists — then they mash the ball with their bodies. Instead of having a five-iron left as the old timers would, they're coming in with a seven-iron. Longer courses are a factor too. Used to be, with the old three-quarters Scottish swing, a player would be happy to knock it 225 yards down the middle of the fairway. That was all he needed. Now he wouldn't get on the par-three holes. I had a good example of that the year I went to St. Andrews for the British Open — the year I got lucky and won. I was disappointed in the course, and a couple of the old boys over there asked me why. I told them because I wanted to play the same course as Vardon and Hagen and Jones and all those birds had played, but now they'd gotten new tees going back sixty or seventy yards, and it wasn't the same course. "Well," said one of the old timers, "that's because we heard there were some big knockers coming over from the States, and we didn't want them to eat up the Old Course."

Well, that's happened everywhere. Tournament courses now average 7100–7200 yards, where they used to be 6400–6500 yards. That's made everybody want to hit it farther. And that's changed attitudes toward the golf swing. Look who's winning. You don't see a lot of little fellas coming in first do you? Power — Distance — is clubhead speed. That's it, and there's no substitute for it. Strength alone doesn't get you clubhead speed. Joe Louis and Gene Tunney wouldn't hit the ball far.... To hit the ball far, you have to be able to make a fast arm swing and keep control of your body and the club.

Matched against other superstars Snead might win few popularity contests, but his 69.23 Tour scoring average set in 1950 is one of the all-time low scores. Snead's contemporary, Byron Nelson, agreed that power was a critical variable in comparing golfers of their generation against modern day players. Nelson commented about how he "tried to determine why the top players today don't shoot as consistently as the top players did in my time because they are absolutely wonderful players. It comes down to distance. My average drive was 254 yards. Tom Watson's average drive is about 277. If you added twenty-three yards to a lot of my drives they'd have been in the rough instead of the fairways."

Nelson was one of the most accurate shotmakers who ever lived, but like Bobby Jones he retired early and left the field to Snead and Hogan. Despite everything Snead accomplished, he was continually overshadowed by Hogan. No other player has had as much written about him by his contemporaries as Hogan. The recollections of Jackie Burke are representative.

"Remember, he'd been a caddie," Burke instructed:

Anybody who has been a caddie has been hustled by the greatest. See, if there are fifty golfers going out and there are one hundred caddies, the fifty caddies stuck in the pen hang around hustling on credit. And when the guys who got a bag get done, there are fifty guys just waiting for them. They've sharpened their swords. Dice, cards, chipping, you name it. Hogan knew about everything. He knew how to judge people and he knows to this day. He has been exposed to as much hustle as anybody on the planet. He has seen every conceivable kind of game employed around golf and all of the would-be guys who think they can play. He can look at you and tell in one second what you're made of. It helped him win a lot in tournaments. He'd look at a guy who was leading and could tell that the guy was going to lose shots coming in. So Hogan would just play conservative, par in, knowing the guy wasn't going to make it.... A person does whatever he can to cope with the "Struggle." People will pay big money to bear witness to the Struggle. They will build a big yacht to watch a fish struggle on a line. And there are people, I'm telling you, who would pay money to watch people being executed. Just to see how they handle it, you see. Hogan had a hell of a struggle in life, and he learned to deal with it the way he knew best, which was not talking to anybody. Trevino does it his way by talking. Chi Chi Rodriguez does his sword act. Hogan just said nothing. And he was a master at handling the Struggle. People are funny. They can be bloodthirsty. When there are 30,000 people waiting for you at 2 p.m. at Augusta National on Sunday in the Masters, a lot of them are there to see if you vomit all the way down the first fairway. The player is very much aware of this. You've got a four-shot lead and they want to see if you faint somewhere over the next five hours.

Hogan did not faint. The incomparable swing he honed on the practice tee held up as few others have done. The young Dave Marr played frequently with Hogan and watched him very carefully. After Hogan hit his shots and it was Marr's turn, Marr said he felt "completely inadequate. It was like I was playing another game called Fat Shot, or Oh No!" Players congregated near Hogan on the practice range to watch him. The balance and timing of his shotmaking impressed everyone, but even more startling was the power and accuracy he achieved. Hogan's swing has been immortalized in several spectacular photographs and in the books of instruction he authored.

One of the most vivid mementos of Hogan's fluidity and strength is the motion picture *Follow the Sun*. Actor Glenn Ford plays Ben in the film about his life, but interspersed throughout the footage are camera shots of Hogan hitting irons out of seemingly impossible lies. Situated behind the golfer, the camera follows the ball as it leaves Hogan's club on a low trajectory and bores silently through a narrow corridor of trees, then soars upward on an unerring path to the flag. Motion pictures of Bobby Jones and Sam Snead exist too, of course, but watching the films and comparing the styles of those men with Hogan is a revelation after which no golf fan need wonder about the traits that made Ben such a phenomenal player.

If Hogan's yips had been less severe it would have been possible to continue an entertaining rivalry with Snead. But his putting stroke became a torture, and he had too much pride to display it in public. Fellow Texan Lee Trevino was invited by Hogan to visit his factory one day. At the conclusion of a tour Hogan asked Trevino if there was anything he could do for him. Trevino said, "Ben, I'm putting terrible. Do you have any putters?"

Trevino hoped that Hogan would take him to a back room somewhere, and from a private bin he might select something special. But instead Hogan abruptly said: "We don't make putters." There was no elaboration, and a gloomy silence descended on the room. Hogan's assistant was sitting next to Trevino, and he intruded to explain, "What Ben's trying to tell you is he doesn't make them because he doesn't like any of them. They look bad, and Ben feels no one would buy a putter with his name on it anyway."

With that even Hogan joined in the laughter.

In 1990 Ben Hogan founded a new tournament structure for younger players to test their talent and to climb onto the PGA Tour if merited. Sponsored by his manufacturing company, the Hogan Tour started with 30 events, each carrying about $100,000 in prize money. The top five money winners received one-year exemptions on the PGA Tour the following year, and many future standouts, including Tom Lehman, got their start here. The Hogan Tour raised over a million dollars for charity, and the Hogan Scholarship Fund awarded hundreds of thousands to needy students. Ben also saw to it that his company donated thousands of free clubs through the PGA's "Clubs for Kids" program. Eventually, the Nike Corporation took over the Hogan Tour, and it continued to serve as a springboard for young players.

As long as golf is played, enthusiasts will narrate memories of Ben Hogan. Some of the most telling anecdotes were supplied by protégé Ken Venturi. At one Dallas tournament the CBS broadcast team on assignment included Venturi and Gary McCord. McCord had played the tour off and on for many years, and was the man who proposed that the number of exempt players to be eligible for any tournament should be raised to 125, which eventually was accepted by the PGA. McCord become familiar to millions as Ben Wright's sidekick, and he was banned from the Masters telecast in 1995 because he announced on the air that "They don't cut the greens at Augusta, they use bikini wax." But that came later. When Ken Venturi invited McCord to meet Hogan, McCord was relatively unknown despite his broadcasting assignments. When the twosome walked up to Hogan's table at the Colonial Country Club grill, Venturi introduced McCord and they sat down. After a few minutes of exchanging pleasantries with Venturi, Hogan turned to look at McCord and asked, "What did you say your name was?"

Gary repeated his name and added, "I work for CBS and I'm a pro and I'm on the Tour."

Hogan changed the conversation to a different topic and a few minutes passed before Hogan asked McCord, "How long have you been on tour?"

"I have been on tour sixteen years," McCord said.

"What have you won?" Hogan asked.

"I haven't won anything," McCord answered.

Hogan went back to talking with Venturi, then stopped abruptly and stared at McCord before blurting, "What the hell are you doing on tour?"

"I don't know," McCord admitted.

Hogan's final years of tournament golf paralleled the rise of a charismatic new star. The records compiled by Arnold Palmer did not quite measure up to Hogan's achievements. Palmer won three Masters, one U.S. Open, and two British Opens, plus 60 victories on the regular PGA Tour. Hogan, on the other hand, won two Masters, four U.S. Opens, one British Open, two PGA Championships, and 63 regular PGA Tour events. Palmer exhibited the same unquenchable drive to succeed as Hogan, but few fans would contend that he commanded overall skills that equaled Hogan's, or even Snead's. Yet Palmer achieved a mass popularity that far overshadowed the older men, and he was the catalyst for the greatest boom in golf of any era. His participation in the Senior Tour ensured a prosperous future for that circuit, which his peers freely acknowledged, just as they agreed he had been responsible for the fantastic increases in prize money on the PGA Tour during the '50s and '60s. Seldom in American sport did fans come to idolize an athlete the way they revered

Arnold Palmer. The adulation galleries had for Palmer was exceeded only by the passion he had for golf, and that undoubtedly was a large measure of his success. When he was 59, Palmer was asked by a friend: "If you didn't know how old you were, how old would you think you were?"

"About 29," Arnold replied.

If stature in a sport were measured only by victories, then Jack Nicklaus would have to be ranked even above Hogan and Palmer as the non-pareil golfer of the 1900s. Tom Weiskopf, who jousted unsuccessfully with Nicklaus as much as anyone, summed up the superstar quality of Nicklaus.

"It's not that Nicklaus is smarter than anyone else," Tom contended. "And I don't think he's greater in any part of his game than anybody else. But the guy has the patience and the guts to make himself do what he has to do. That is what makes him far and away superior to anyone else. Sure, if I had Jack's mind, with my swing you might never have heard of Nicklaus. But that's him. God made him that way."

Weiskopf acknowledged in Nicklaus what so many critics complained the younger Ohio State alum lacked. Unlike Weiskopf, Nicklaus had the determination and intensity to concentrate on winning above all else. Unstinting preparation and planning presaged frequent victories, especially in major championships. Yet, at the same time he seemed to have a more rounded life than many of his fellow superstars. Early in his career he took frequent skiing excursions, far flung fishing trips, and spent many hours beating tennis balls. Then there were his businesses.

"I'd have to say my biggest goal outside of golf is to be successful at business," Nicklaus said in the early 1970s.

> I'm not a guy who when he quits playing golf is going to spend his life fishing or sitting in the sun. I mean, there's nothing I'd love more than a week's fishing, but if I thought that's all there was to do, if that was my only way of achieving, catching the next fish, I'd go straight up the wall. I make my living out of golf, but it's still a game. If I were ever to make it totally a business, it would lose a lot of its appeal. Maybe all its appeal. Golf is a sport. I believe one of the reasons Arnold Palmer is so popular is that he plays it that way; he near loses sight of that fact. A lot of people there on Tour who are quite good players are never going to attain much public following because they look at the game mainly from a money standpoint. The fan, the average golfer, doesn't look at the game that way, so he doesn't like that approach.

Despite the rivalry that persisted between Palmer and Nicklaus, Nicklaus always went out of his way to publicly praise the older star. "I like Palmer very much," he commented.

> Obviously we have our differences. Any two people who have enjoyed such intense competition with each other for so long are going to have their differences. When we stand up there on the first tee and pat each other on the backs

and kid around, I think we both are saying in our hearts, "I'm going to beat you!" And that's fine. Neither of us would want it any other way.... You have to be envious of what Arnold has accomplished as a man, and as a personality — his way with people. But that doesn't mean I want to take anything away from him. I might want to be a little more like him in some ways, but I would not like to live Arnold's life. Nor do I think he would want to live mine.

When it came time to judge the premier talents of all time, David Feherty spoke for a majority. "Jack Nicklaus is the greatest player of all time," Feherty stated. "With a record like that, I don't think it will ever be beaten. He was an inspiration to me, a role model, if you like, and I'm sure for hundreds of thousands, maybe millions.... He's a God."

Although Nicklaus at times could be insensitive with criticisms of other players, few touring pros responded with negative views of him. Feherty also had a theory about that: "It's dangerous to criticize a god. You might get struck by lightning or something. His status has put him in an environment where maybe he feels he can do no wrong."

Nicklaus angered many of the PGA Tour regulars with comments about the all-exempt tour and what he seemed to perceive as lack of backbone in many young players. Remarks he expressed at the 1987 International Tournament in Castle Rock were typical. After questioning the heart and desire to win of some young pros following the defeat of the Nicklaus-captained Ryder Cup Team at his home course, Muirfield Village, Nicklaus was asked why American players could not regularly beat foreigners like Seve Ballesteros and Greg Norman.

"We need people to go after it," Jack answered. "You take Seve. Whether you like the man or not has nothing to do with it. The man has heart!... I'd like to see American guys who want to win. My desire when I turned pro was to be the best in the game. Second place didn't mean anything."

"There is a welfare feeling out here," Nicklaus continued his excoriation of the Tour. "Mediocrity excels. Fred Couples— here's a guy with tremendous talent, but you never see him doing much. Bruce Lietzke — he plays golf so he can go fishing."

In a sport where derogatory comments about another pro's performance were as rare as public criticism among heart surgeons, Nicklaus's published comments caused a sensation. The named players were not amused, and when the next Ryder Cup team was selected Nicklaus was ignored. Despite David Feherty's opinion that Nicklaus had received few critical notices from his fellow pros, Dave Hill and Arnold Palmer occasionally voiced opinions. In Palmer's 1973 book *Go for Broke*, he wrote:

> Nicklaus can drive some golfers nuts, not only by playing with them but by simply showing up in the same round with them; he's been the target of complaints by pros who feel that four or five or six holes back they're being held up while Jack stands over a putt for one or two eternities.

And irrepressible Dave Hill responded with vitriol when Nicklaus disparaged the competitive level of the Senior Tour.

For a time it appeared that Lee Trevino or Tom Watson would inherit Nicklaus's mantle. Both men compiled imposing rosters of victories while reigning as top drawing cards for tournament sponsors, but their popularity never approached that of Palmer or Nicklaus. Trevino was respected but not revered by many fans who were amused by his idiosyncrasies, while Watson's unpredictability found outlet in contretemps with Gary Player and others. Byron Nelson served for a time as a part-time teacher and mentor for Watson, and he was very generous with his appraisals, going so far as to include Tom in the exalted grouping of superstars.

"The quality that set Hogan, Nicklaus, and Watson apart from their contemporaries," Byron commented,

> is an immeasurable mental toughness. Their dispositions are in some ways very similar. They're highly motivated.... Even one of Hogan's closest friends wouldn't dare go up to him during a round. It'd break Ben's concentration, and Hogan would bite his head off. In the end it may have shortened his career, concentrating so hard. There is a difference in the type of concentration that Ben had and that Jack and Tom have. They're all very good concentrators, but when Hogan concentrated it was almost as if he went into a trance. If something happened on the course to break this curtain of concentration Ben had a difficult time collecting himself again. Whereas if something happens to break Nicklaus's concentration, he has the ability to pull his thought patterns quickly together again. And Tom has it to some degree also ... I would say Hogan practiced the most and Jack Nicklaus practices the least of the three. Jack really isn't as hard working at his game except on the occasions when he is bearing down in preparation for a major; then he works really hard. However, I don't think he ever — even before a major — stood on the practice tee and beat balls as much as Hogan did or as Tom does now. It takes a lot of physical strength to hit balls for extended periods of time. I must say Watson is the only player I have ever seen physically strong enough to hit as many practice balls as Hogan did in his prime.

Watson was the quintessential individualist in a solitary sport, and the oversized ego that Tom Weiskopf believed was essential to superstardom created resentment of Watson from time to time among other pros. Watson was not as caustic about the all-exempt tour as Nicklaus, but the views of the younger man closely paralleled Hogan, Palmer, and Nicklaus.

"It bothers me to think that a young player or even a journeyman doesn't have to perform very well and can still make a good deal of money," Tom said in the mid–1980s.

> Look at tennis for a moment. The 125 players on that list make about one quarter as much as a golfer of the same caliber, while the top tennis players make three to four times the money earned by the best golfers. Tennis has become a game of the stars while golf has turned into a sport for the masses. From a strictly business point of view I think the PGA Tour should be more concerned with

the happiness of the top players in the game rather than worry about the 150th player on the list. Matching the top player in a TV package guarantees that the fans would see a Trevino or a Nicklaus or a Palmer going head to head and would stimulate interest in the pro game. If you need evidence just look at the success of the Skins Game.

Tom Weiskopf was in substantial agreement with Watson concerning the all-exempt tour. "Great players want to play other great players," Weiskopf contended. "The mediocre players like things just the way they are. The problem is that mediocrity breeds mediocrity. The guy who is 150th on the money list has the same vote as Jack Nicklaus. Is that fair?... I'd question the assumption that everyone who makes the cut deserves to win."

Watson's and Weiskopf's opinions had no more effect on Tour policy than those of earlier critics Palmer and Nicklaus. Too many men were making a comfortable living with the system to allow for radical redesigns. By the mid–1990s there were no superstars dominating the PGA Tour. Jack Nicklaus, Arnold Palmer, Lee Trevino, Raymond Floyd, and Gary Player were playing before huge, appreciative galleries on the Senior Tour, which was growing richer by the day. The number of tournaments had grown to 42 a year, with over $40 million in prize money. Golf fans increasingly looked backward to a glorious past, as aging superstars reminded them of the importance of enduring rivalries—Jones vs. Hagen, Hogan vs. Snead, Palmer vs. Nicklaus—and what that meant to the popularity of the sport. Comparing the talents of one generation with another was an entertaining pastime, but as inevitably fruitless as comparing the present state of baseball with the teams of the 1950s. Yet fans could not be deterred from wondering what made men like Hogan and Nicklaus tick, what marvels of talent or courage did they possess, and what seemed to have disappeared with them?

David Feherty believed that in order to become a superstar it was necessary to be extremely egotistical and competitive. "In business you'll find the same thing," Feherty argued.

> People who get to the top aren't generally popular, certainly not with their peers. You have to have a high opinion of yourself, and that's quite often confused with arrogance. The top tier is very self-opinionated; very self-motivated people who have devoted their lives to golf. You make a choice of what sort of quality of life you want and how much you're prepared to sacrifice. It takes up all of your time if you're going to be number one.

Tom Weiskopf agreed with Feherty, and was not hesitant to go out on a limb to rank the greatest stars:

> The four greatest players I ever saw were Hogan and Snead, numbers one and two. Hogan is first because he was better with his woods, both driver and fairway. There was no area where I felt Sam was better. Hogan was the best player

I ever saw. Driving, iron play, chipping, pitching, sand play, everything. I'll add that people have told me that Byron was every bit as good, but I never saw him so I can't honestly rate him. Jack Nicklaus was third, and Lee Trevino was fourth. Jack's weakness was his short irons; Lee's was his long irons—compared to the other guys. Of course, when I say weak it's all relative.... Jack was the best pressure putter I've ever seen. Name one missed putt that cost him a championship. How many times have you seen the guy come to the eighteenth green and hole a putt just to make the cut? Unbelievable pride. I think all of us who played against Jack or even saw Jack play have been incredibly privileged. He's a great sportsman. I mean, look at all the times I finished second or third to him, but it was a thrill to be out there because if I beat him, there was no better feeling in the world. I loved to play Jack head-to-head on the last day. I was a better player because of Jack. So were Tom Watson, Trevino, Johnny Miller and all the other guys who challenged him. Hogan was a better player because of Nelson and Snead.

Down through the generations no one could rival Nicklaus's combination of huge natural talent and capacity to hold up under extreme pressure. Stress hounded Bobby Jones and Byron Nelson out of competitive golf, and it left Ben Hogan with an ugly case of yips. Nicklaus appeared impervious to stress.

"I don't think a lot of the guys who play for a living actually enjoy the pressure," David Feherty commented.

When things are going well and you're cruising along in the second round, you enjoy that. But when it gets down to the end and you're asked the question: "Can you do this?"—That's exam time. I don't think anyone enjoys that. Nicklaus said he did. That's just so much macho bull. Players create auras to protect themselves. I bet he enjoyed having done it, not doing it. Any sign of weakness might be construed as vulnerability, so they are afraid to show any human tendencies. Everyone chokes. Everyone gets to stages in his career where he can look back and say: "Oh God, I choked like a pig there." Absolutely everyone has done it, but there are very few people who admit it. It's refreshing to find someone who tells the truth.

As far as overall talent is concerned, few pros would concede a rival to Jack Nicklaus. Raymond Floyd, who turned pro the same year as Nicklaus and watched him play through four decades, summed up the argument.

"I have to give the young players their due," Raymond said. "The really good ones can beat us now. But that's the way it has always been. You think a young Nicklaus wouldn't have beaten Bobby Jones and Gene Sarazen? You can kiss this steel shafted wooden driver if you think he couldn't!"

Raymond Floyd's comments were delivered prior to the astonishing advent of Tiger Woods, but the description seemed to fit the young sensation perfectly. After an interval of more than a decade, dating from the 1986 Masters victory of Jack Nicklaus, no new superstar had emerged to dominate the PGA Tour. After Woods's performance in the 1997 Masters Tournament, where his winning score was 12 strokes better than the nearest competitor, it appeared that golf finally had found a worthy successor to the champions of previous decades. Here was the charismatic young star who evoked comparisons of Bobby Jones and Arnold Palmer, one whom sports fans flocked to see for his electrifying style. The 21-year-old Woods was the Tour's leading money winner in 1997, his first full year as a professional. Nicklaus predicted that Woods's talent would result in more Masters victories than he and Palmer had gained in tandem, ten in all. The 1997 season performance by Woods attracted millions of new television viewers and players of all ages to the sport.

In subsequent seasons Woods demolished other records. In the first four years of his professional career, Woods won 29 tournaments, including the 1999 PGA Championship, and the 2000 U.S. Open, British Open, and PGA Championships. He matched the record of Ben Hogan in winning three major championships in the same year, and became the youngest golfer to complete the career Grand Slam of professional major championships. At the close of the 2000 season, Woods boasted five professional major championships and three U.S. Amateur titles, bringing his total to eight major championships at age 24. At that age Jack Nicklaus had recorded three professional major victories and two U.S. Amateur titles. No one else in golf history approached the extraordinary success of Tiger Woods's first years on the PGA Tour.

As the final years of the 20th century drew to a close, professional golf prospered as never before. Corporate sponsorship of tournaments had started in 1933 when the Hershey Chocolate Corporation hosted the Hershey Open. This modest beginning expanded to a present day slate of 45 official PGA Tour events sponsored by Mercedes, Buick, AT&T, and other major companies, with total prize money of $96 million. In addition, the Senior PGA Tour added 38 official tournaments with prize money of $45 million, the LPGA hosted 37 tournaments with $20 million in prize money, and the Nike Tour organized another 30 events with $7 million in prizes. Professional golf had avoided the labor strife, financial concerns, and litigation besetting several other major sports, and the PGA Tour entered the 21st century with expectations of continued success in all its enterprises.

Notes

1 — Early History

On golf in Scotland: Tom Scott. *The Story of Golf, from Its Origins to the Present Day*. London: Barker, 1972.

On president golfers: H. B. Martin. *Fifty Years of American Golf*. New York: Dodd Mead, 1936.

On the life of Walter Hagen: Walter Hagen. *The Walter Hagen Story*. New York: Simon and Schuster, 1956.

On the memories of Hagen's chauffeur: "Walter Hagen for Real." *Golf Digest*, January 1994, p. 53.

2 — The 1920s

On the life of Bobby Jones. Grantland Rice. *The Bobby Jones Story*. Atlanta: Tupper and Love, 1953.

On Clifford Roberts: Charles Price. *A Golf Story: Bobby Jones, Augusta National, and the Masters Tournament*. New York: Atheneum, 1986.

On Jones and Woodruff in Scotland: Charles Elliot. "Bobby the Angler." *Golf*, January 1980, p. 76–81.

On Jones at St. Andrews: Ross Goodner. "A Long Courtship." *Golf*, February 1967, p. 63; Pat Ward-Thomas. "Fascinating Friends I've Made in Golf." *Golf Digest*, April 1982, p. 115.

On Orv White's memories of Jones: Charles Price. "How Good Was Bobby Jones Really?" *Golf Digest*, May 1986, p. 46.

On films of Bobby Jones: Charles Price. "Bobby Jones on Videotape." *Golf Digest*, January 1988, p. 20.

On Alister Mackenzie and Augusta National: Ken Bowden. "Alister Mackenzie: He Laid Out Augusta National and Changed American Course Design Forever." *Golf Digest*, April 1977, p. 60–65.

On Bobby Jones's illness: Clifford Roberts. "Bob Jones: The Heart and Spirit of Augusta National." *Golf Digest*, April 1976, p. 102–116.

On Gene Sarazen's memories of Jones: "A Conversation with Gene Sarazen." *Golf Digest*, August 1972, p. 68–73.

On anxiety and the stress of competition: Al Laney. "The Inner Struggle." *Golf Digest*, February 1980, p. 225–227.

189

3 — The 1930s

On the early days of the PGA tour: Al Barkow. *The History of the PGA Tour.* New York: Doubleday, 1989.

On the life of Fred Corcoran: Chris Smith. "Fred Corcoran." *Golf,* March 1994, p. 136; Charles Price. "The Man Who Invented the Tour." *Golf Digest,* August 1991, p. 108.

On the life of Tommy Armour: Charles Price. "The Silver Scot." *Golf,* November 1981, p. 42–48; Robert Rickey. "Enter the Silver Scot." *Golf,* August 1976, p. 51–52; John Husar. "Back to Medinah." *Golf,* June 1975, p. 47–49; Dave Anderson. "The Lore of Winged Foot." *Golf Digest,* June 1974, p. 52–55.

On Jimmy Demaret: Dwayne Netland. "Living Legends Turn Back the Clock." *Golf Digest,* May 1978, p. 90–101; Jimmy Demaret. "It Isn't the Same." *Golf,* September 1983, p. 52–55; Mike Purkey. "Jimmy Demaret." *Golf,* November 1993, p. 104–105.

On Bing Crosby: Dwayne Netland. "Bing Made the Crosby a January Tradition." *Golf Digest,* January 1978, p. 102–107; Bob Hope. "Bob Remembers Bing." *Golf,* February 1979, p. 221–235.

On Ky Laffoon: Al Barkow. "Ky Laffoon, Dustbowl Dandy." *Golf,* February 1978. P. 88–93; Al Barkow. *Getting' to the Dance Floor: An Oral History of American Golf.* New York: Atheneum, 1988, p. 277; Larry Guest. "The Greatest Name in Golf." *Golf,* February 1993, p. 82.

On "Wild Bill" Mehlhorn: Larry Dennis. "The Not So Wild Theories of Wild Bill Mehlhorn." *Golf Digest,* June 1977, p. 114–121.

On Gene Sarazen: Gene Sarazen. "You Have to Love That Putter." *Golf,* April 1969, p. 43–47.

4 — The 1940s

On Ben Hogan's early life and career: Gene Gregston. *Hogan: The Man Who Played for Glory.* Englewood Cliffs, N.J.: Prentice Hall, 1978.

On Hogan's comments about hitting a golf shot straight: "Ben Hogan." *Golf,* September 1987, p. 65–67.

On Hogan as a teacher: Tom Vogt. "My Lesson from Hogan." *Golf Digest,* March 1969, p. 26–27.

On Paul Runyan's comments about Hogan: *Golf Digest,* March 1982, p. 40.

On Sam Snead's remarks about Hogan: Sam Snead. *Slammin' Sam.* New York: Donald I. Fine, 1986.

On Hogan's revolutionary swing change: Nick Seitz. "Hogan — Some Things Never Change." *Golf Digest,* June 1985, p. 36–40.

On Hogan's trip to Scotland: Nick Seitz. "Hogan Relives His Unparalleled 1953 Season." *Golf Digest,* March 1978, p. 64–93.

On Hogan's court case: Al Barkow. "Ben Hogan's Day in Court." *Golf,* January 1971, p. 46.

On Jackie Burke's memories of Hogan at the Masters: Al Barkow. *Gettin' to the Dance Floor: An Oral History of American Golf.* New York: Atheneum, 1988, p. 262.

On reporter Ward-Thomas's memories of Hogan: Pat Ward-Thomas. "Friends I've Made in Golf." *Golf Digest,* April 1982, p. 9.

On fellow pros' comments about Hogan: Dave Anderson. "The Hogan Legend." *Golf Digest,* February 1986, p. 132–138.

On Byron Nelson and comparisons of Hogan Nicklaus, Watson: Jerry Tarde. "Hogan vs. Nicklaus vs. Watson." *Golf Digest,* March 1982, p. 38–57.

5 — The 1950s

On Arnold Palmer's career: Arnold Palmer. *Go For Broke: My Philosophy of Winning Golf.* New York: Simon and Schuster, 1973.

On the growth of golf: Nick Seitz. "The Changing State of the Game." *Golf Digest,* June 1979, p. 109–118.

On Eisenhower's golf: "A Love for the Game." *Golf,* June 1969, p. 23; Robert Caleo. "The Hidden Scorecards of Pennsylvania Avenue." *Golf,* September 1969, p. 46–48.

On Kennedy's golf: "Pro to the Presidents." *Golf,* February 1967, p. 73.

On the touring pros vs. PGA: Al Wright. "Revolt of the Golf Pros." *Sports Illustrated,* August 9, 1965, p. 14–17.

On Dave Marr and Glenna Vare: Richard Miller. "The Fifty Snobbiest Clubs in America." *Golf,* June 1985, p. 58–62.

On Sarazen's comments about Palmer: Gene Sarazen. "A Conversation with Gene Sarazen." *Golf Digest,* August 1972, p. 68.

On Winnie Palmer: Jeanne Parr. "Life with Arnie." *Golf,* October 1976, p. 45–47.

On survival on the Tour: Peter Dobereiner. "Survival: Name of the Game on Tour." *Golf Digest,* July 1979, p. 50–53.

On Palmer and television: John Garrity. "Through Arnie's Eyes." *Golf Digest,* May 1987, p. 109.

On Howard Hughes: Mac Hunter. "I Taught Hollywood to Play." *Golf Digest,* December 1982, p. 102–110.

On Tommy Bolt at the 1960 Open: "The 1960 Open." *Golf,* January 1969, p. 63.

On Mark McCormack's comments about Palmer: Mark McCormack. "The Game's Royalty. *Golf,* August 1969, p. 38.

On Palmer and individuality: "Arnie Sounds Off." *Golf Digest,* February 1982, p. 152–167.

On Tommy Bolt's career: "The Man Called Thunder." *Golf Digest,* June 1993, p. 220–234.

On Bolt's views about Casper, Weiskopf, & Hogan: "Tommy Bolt." *Golf,* May 1989, p. 70–82.

On Weiskopf's memories of Bolt: Jolee Edmondson. "Thunder, They Name Is Still Bolt." *Golf,* April 1979, p. 66–67.

On Cary Middlecoff's career: "Cary Middlecoff." *Golf,* June 1968, p. 92.

On Sarazen's comments about Middlecoff: Dwayne Netland. "Living Legends Turn Back the Clock." *Golf Digest,* May 1978, p. 90–101.

On Orville Moody's career: Max Brown. "The Soothsayer's Choice." *Golf,* September 1969, p. 38.

On Orville Moody's yips: Ross Goodner. "Who Said There's No Time for Sergeants?" *Golf Digest,* December 1984, p. 119–124.

On Moody and Doug Sanders: Dwayne Netland. "Orville Moody Struggles Back from Oblivion." *Golf Digest,* August 1978, p. 50–53.

On Tony Lema's career: Tony Lema. *Golfer's Gold.* Boston: Little Brown, 1964.

On Lema's British Open win: Robin McMillan. "Champagne Tony." *Golf,* July 1984, p. 34–35.

On Lema's death: Ross Goodner. "Triumphs and Tragedy of Champagne Tony." *Golf Digest,* August 1986, p. 86–88.

On Doug Sanders: Vincent Pastena. "Peacock of the Fairways." *Golf,* February 1969, p. 68–70.

On Sarazen's opinion of Billy Casper: "Casper Marches to His Own Drummer." *Golf,* April 1970, p. 62–65.

On letters to Casper: Wallace Dill. "Strange Letters from Billy Casper's Fans." *Golf Digest*, August 1968, p. 40–42.

On Frank Beard and caddies: Frank Beard. "Caddies: Partners or Bag Toters?" *Golf Digest*, May 1974, p. 166–168.

On Dave Hill's opinion of Beard: Dave Hill. *Teed Off*. Englewood Cliffs, N.J.: Prentice-Hall, 1977, p. 135.

On Gary Player's career: Michael McDonnell. "The Man in Black." *Golf*, November 1985, p. 58–59.

On Gary Player and Hogan: *Golf Digest*, February 1975, p. 52–56.

6 — The 1960s

On Nicklaus and Palmer: Gretchen Travis. "The Woman Behind the Man." *Golf*, January 1981, p. 126–131.

On Nicklaus's life style: Ken Bowden. "Why Nicklaus is Back On Top." *Golf Digest*, July 1971, p. 47–49.

On Nicklaus's diet: Will Grimsley. "How Jack Nicklaus Became Beautiful and Loved." *Golf*, December 1970, p. 52–54.

On Nicklaus's hobbies: Davis Pearson. "How Nicklaus Recharges His Batteries." *Golf Digest*, July 1968, p. 34–36.

On Nicklaus's drive: "What Makes Jack Run?" *Golf Digest*, April 1976, p. 46.

Dave Hill's comments on Nicklaus: Dave Hill. *Teed Off*, p. 79.

On Cary Middlecoff's statements: *Golf*, June 1968, p. 97.

On Nicklaus's course design: Jerry Tarde. "As Designers Jack Nicklaus and Pete Dye Have Fired Up Controversy." *Golf Digest*, October 1983, p. 56–63.

On Nicklaus's marketing company: Glen Waggoner. *Divots, Shanks, Gimmes, Mulligans: A Life in 18 Holes*. New York: Villard, 1993.

On Nicklaus's criticism of young players: Dwayne Netland. "Tour Feud." *Golf Digest*, December 1987, p. 42–45.

On Frank Beard's opinion of Nicklaus: Frank Beard. "Golfers Who Win Most Make Fewest Mental Errors." *Golf Digest*, June 1973, p. 160.

On Nicklaus's assessment of himself: Jack Nicklaus. "Nicklaus Psychoanalyzes the Superstars." *Golf Digest*, March 1977, p. 38–41.

On Nicklaus compared to other pros: Nick Seitz. "Why Nicklaus Is Still the Man to Beat." *Golf Digest*, July 1978, p. 78–86.

7 — The 1970s

On Tom Watson's rivalry with Nicklaus: Dwayne Netland. "A Great Rivalry is Born." *Golf Digest*, February 1978, p. 48–52.

On Watson's comments about choking: "Watson and Lopez Talk Golf." *Golf Digest*, February 1980, p. 46–58.

On Twitty's comments about Watson: Nick Seitz. "The Two Worlds of Tom Watson." *Golf Digest*, July 1984, p. 44–51.

On Watson's comments about qualifying: "Watson on Watson." *Golf*, August 1985, p. 66.

On Watson and Gary Player controversy: "Watson and Player." *Golf Digest*, February 1984, p. 35–36.

On Watson's views of the LPGA: "Tom Watson." *Golf Digest*, May 1993, p. 176–198.

On Watson's biggest regret: James Dodson. "Lion in Winter." *Golf*, October 1993, p. 62–66.

On Johnny Miller's training: Art Spander. "Johnny Miller: A Pre-Destined Pro." *Golf*, August 1971, p. 38–41.

On Miller and choking: *Golf Digest*, February 1975, p. 53.

On Miller's life style: Nick Seitz. "The Enigma of Johnny Miller." *Golf Digest*, January 1978, p. 30–35.

On Miller's caddies: "Mac O'Grady." *Sports Illustrated*, April 16, 1984, p. 77.

On Miller's television debut: "Johnny Miller." *Golf Digest*, July 1990, p. 99.

On Lee Trevino's early career: Lee Trevino. *They Call Me Super Mex*. New York: Random House, 1982.

On Trevino and Jacklin: *Golf Digest*, May 1993, p. 194.

On Trevino's personality and swing: Thomas Boswell. *Strokes of Genius*. New York: Doubleday, 1987.

On Trevino's opinion of socializing: Al Barkow. "Hot Summer of 1971." *Golf*, January 1972, p. 54–57.

On Trevino's accident with lightning: Micky Herskowitz. "Last Time Up for Lee." *Golf Digest*, January 1983, p. 40–45.

On Trevino and pro-ams: "Lee Trevino." *Golf*, October 1987, p. 49–51.

On Trevino and Senior Tour: Chris Smith. "Lee Trevino." *Golf*, July 1991, p. 48–50.

8 — The 1980s

On the all-exempt tour: Dan Jenkins. "1985: A Wonderful Year to Forget." *Golf Digest*, February 1986, p. 54–59.

On Sam Snead and Lee Trevino's views of younger generation: Shaw Glick. "Out of the Sticks." *Golf*, July 1984. p. 72–75.

On Ray Floyd: Tom Callahan. "Stare Master." *Golf Digest*, September 1992, p. 54.

On Jack Nicklaus and Hale Irwin: Dwayne Netland. "Tour Feud." *Golf Digest*, December 1987, p. 42–45.

On rabbits: Desmond Tolhurst. "Rabbits No More." *Golf*, January 1984, p. 59–68.

On Gary Player: Don Wade. "Foreign Exchange." *Golf Digest*, November 1986, p. 50–55.

On Mark McCormack: Mark McCormack. "Too Fat." *Golf*, January 1987, p. 34–35.

On Byron Nelson: Byron Nelson. *How I Played the Game*. Dallas: Taylor, 1993.

On Arnold Palmer and Mark McCormack: "Deane Beman: Spreading the Wealth." *Forbes*, August 10, 1987, p. 74–81.

On Johnny Miller: "Johnny Miller." *Golf Digest*, May 1991, p. 102–117.

On televised golf: Al Barkow. "The Shot That Turned on the Tube." *Golf*, August 1978, p. 64–65.

On the USGA and NBC: Peter McCleery. "The USGA and NBC: Big Money, Big Questions." *Golf Digest*, August 1994, p. 141–142.

On Beman and Jackie Burke, Jr., and Jim Colbert: Mickey Herskowitz. "Deane Beman — Short Hitter with a Long Reach." *Golf Digest*, April 1986, p. 42.

On financial sponsors: Greg Larson. "Sugar Daddies." *Golf*, September 1985, p. 52–55.

On Nicklaus and Mark McCormack: Larry Guest. *Arnie: Inside the Legend*. Orlando: Tribune Publishing, 1993.

On Seve Ballesteros's early career: Mick McDonnell. "Ballesteros." *Golf*, October 1978, p. 46–49.

On Ballesteros's disagreement with PGA Tour: Peter Dobereinger. "The Enigma of Seve Ballesteros." *Golf Digest*, October 1980, p. 94–98; "Ballesteros Grounded." *Golf Digest*, January 1986, p. 15.

On Feherty's comments about Ballesteros: "David Feherty." *Golf Digest*, November 1992, p. 118.

On Greg Norman's early career: Ross Goodner. "The Australian Way." *Golf Digest*, May 1978, p. 58; Larry Guest. "Norman Conquest." *Golf*, October 1983, p. 42–45.

On Norman and Nicklaus: Jerry Tarde. "What's Behind the Norman-Nicklaus Connection." *Golf Digest*, May 1988, p. 74–77.

On Norman and Azinger: Rick Reilly. "High Noon at Troon." *Sports Illustrated*, July 31, 1989, p. 20–27.

On Ian Woosnam: Dai Davies. "Europe's Longest, Shortest, Tough Guy." *Golf Digest*, October 1987, p. 46–49.

On Bernhard Langer: "Bernhard Langer." *Golf Digest*, April 1994, p. 136–152; Larry Dorman. "Langer Is Well-Suited for Second Green Coat." *New York Times*, April 7, 1994, p. B13.

On Nick Faldo: "The Iceman Melteth." *People Weekly*, August 17, 1992, p. 97–98; "Nick Faldo." *Sports Illustrated*, April 8, 1991, p. 78.

9 — The 1990s

On the Senior Tour: "The Senior Tour Journal." *Golf Digest*, February 1990, p. 144–150.

On pro-ams: Frank Beard. *Making the Turn: A Year Inside the PGA Senior Tour.* New York: Macmillan, 1992, p. 138–139.

On Don January: Robert Lyons. "Golf's Sensational Seniors." *Saturday Evening Post*, May 1991, p. 46–49.

On Walt Zembriski: Nick Seitz. "From Hard Hat to Endorsement Logo." *Golf Digest*, October 1988, p. 112.

On purse splitting: Al Wright. "The Big Golf Secret." *Sports Illustrated*, September 24, 1962, p. 20–23; Jerry Tarde. "Playing the Game in Secret." *Golf Digest*, July 1994, p. 20–22.

On John Daly: John Garrity. "Rookie John Daly Was the Big Winner at Skins Game." *Sports Illustrated*, December 9, 1991, p. 46–49; Jim Moriarity. "The King of Over-Torque." *Golf Digest*, November 1993, p. 50–53; "David Feherty." *Golf Digest*, November 1992, p. 120; "Reckless Driving." *Golf*, December 1993, p. 32; Mike Kiley. "Daly Claims PGA Should Test for Drugs." *Chicago Tribune*, July 9, 1994, p. C1; "More Troubles for Daly." *Chicago Sun Times*, August 29, 1994, p. 96.

On Tommy Bolt: Dave Hill. *Teed Off*, p. 78–79.

On Lee Elder: Dwayne Netland. "Lee Elder's Long Road to Augusta." *Golf Digest*, April 1975, p. 60–64.

On Charlie Sifford: William Johnson. "Call Back the Years." *Sports Illustrated*, March 31, 1969.

On Jim Thorpe: Don Wade. "I'm No Fluke, Man." *Golf Digest*, March 1986, p. 28; Thomas Boswell. *Strokes of Genius*, p. 164; Larry Dorman. "Surprising Thorpe Rides the Breeze." *New York Times*, March 4, 1994.

On Calvin Peete: Ira Berkow. "Lonely at the Top." *Golf Digest*, July 1986, p. 55; Thomas Boswell. *Strokes of Genius*, p. 154; Chris Smith. "Re-Peete." *Golf*, July 1993, p. 58–59.

On purse splitting: Al Wright. "The Big Golf Secret." *Sports Illustrated*, September 24, 1962, p. 20–23; Jerry Tarde. "Playing the Game in Secret." *Golf Digest*, July 1994, p. 20–22.

10— *History of Golf Course Architecture in America*

On Clifford Roberts: Nick Seitz. "Inside the Masters War Room." *Golf Digest*, April 1971, p. 58–61; Clifford Roberts. "The Inside Story of Augusta National." *Golf Digest*, March 1976, p. 64–82; Ross Goodner. "The Man Who Would Walk on Water." *Golf Digest*, April 1986, p. 60; Jolee Edmondson. "It's Not All Peachy for CBS in Georgia." *Golf Digest*, April 1984, p. 66.

On Augusta's greens: Jerry Tarde. "Digging Into the Greens Controversy Again." *Golf Digest*, April 1982, p. 68–69.

On Hogan at the Masters: David Barrett. "The First Time." *Golf*, April 1987, p. 62–65.

On Hord Hardin: Arnold Palmer. "A Masters Suggestion." *Golf*, April 1990. P. 32; "Talking Golf, A Conversation with Hord Hardin." *Golf*, April 1989, p. 34–43.

On Arnold Palmer: Arnold Palmer. "A Masters Suggestion." *Golf*, April 1990, p. 32.

On Lee Trevino: "Lee Trevino." *Golf*, October 1987, p. 51.

On Augusta pin placements: "Were Pins at the Masters Fiendishly Placed?" *New York Times*. April 12, 1994, B3.

On Robert Trent Jones: "The Jones." *Sports Illustrated*, May 31, 1993, p. 84–98; "Robert Trent Jones." *Golf*, November 1987, p. 61; Hugh Delehanty. "Trent Jones, Too." *Golf Digest*, November 1986, p. 32–35; "Chip Off the Old Block." *Golf Digest*, March 1993, p. 141.

On Pete Dye: Herbert Wind. "Pete Dye: Improving on Mother Nature." *Golf Digest*, May and June 1978, p. 66–86 and 128–149; Jerry Tarde. "As Designers, Jack Nicklaus and Pete Dye Have Fired Up Controversy." *Golf Digest*, October 1983, p. 56–63; Peter Andrews. "Playing the Monster with Dr. Frankenstein." *Golf Digest*, June 1987, p. 76–80; "The Game According to Pete Dye." *Golf Digest*, April 1987, p. 176; Peter Thomson. "Looking for Golf Courses Grandma Would Love." *Golf Digest*, February 1987, p. 26; Gary Nuhn. "Made for TV Courses." *Golf Digest*, May 1987, p. 124–128.

On Deane Beman: John Garrity. "Mea Culpa." *Sports Illustrated*, July 16, 1990, p. 70–74.

On Bill Rogers: "Tim Rosaforte. "Grand Designs." *Golf*, January 1986, p. 90–96.

On Jack Nicklaus: George Peper. "Jack's Other Career." *Golf*, March 1981, p. 34–39.

On David Feherty: "David Feherty." *Golf Digest*, November 1992, p. 106–118.

On Jimmy Demaret: "It Isn't the Same." *Golf*, September 1983, p. 52–55.

On top architects: Ron Whitten. "Master of All He Surveys." *Golf Digest*, November 1991, p. 96–97.

11— *Advances in Technology and Equipment*

On golf equipment: "Tom Weiskopf." *Golf Digest*, March 1991, p. 98–105; "Ray Floyd." *Golf Digest*, February 1994, p. 94–109; Dwayne Netland. "Tour Feud." *Golf Digest*, December 1987, p. 42–45.

On Greg Norman: "Perception vs. Reality." *Golf Digest*, May 1989, p. 33–34.

On Lanny Wadkins: "Lanny Wadkins, Fast on the Draw." *Golf Digest*, April 1993, p. 206–221.

On Jim Flick: E.M. Swift. "Golf Technology." *Sports Illustrated*, July 9, 1990, p. 40–48.

On Mark McCumber: Ed Weathers. "The Tests of Time." *Golf Digest*, June 1994, p. 158.

On Superstars' opinions of equipment change: Jaime Diaz. "Has Golf Gotten Too Groovy?" *Sports Illustrated*, August 3, 1987, p. 52–59.

On Lee Trevino: Don Wade. "The Foreign Exchange." *Golf Digest*, November 1986, p. 50–55.

On Solheim's lawsuit: "Square Deal." *Golf*, June 1993, p. 142–144; Marcia Chambers. "Groove Settlement Leaves Golf Better Off." *Golf Digest*, July 1993, p. 48–56; *Golf Digest*, August 1987, p. 115.

On knock-offs: John Garrity. "Bad Business." *Sports Illustrated*, July 9, 1990, p. 47–53.

12 — Great American Golfers and Golf Rivalries

On Johnny Miller: Johnny Miller. "Golf's Broad Canvas Is Ready for a Master Stroke." *New York Times*, March 7, 1993, L9.

On Gary Nicklaus: *New York Times*, April 20, 1994, B3.

On Jackie Burke, Jr.: Al Barkow. *Gettin' to the Dance Floor: An Oral History of American Golf.* Springfield, N.J.: Burford, 1986.

On Dave Stockton: Kathy Jonah. "Tour Wives Find Golf Comes First, Family Second." *Golf Digest*, March 1974, p. 80.

On Davis Love: Jaime Diaz. "Power of Love." *Sports Illustrated*, March 23, 1987, p. 44–55.

On Gene Sarazen: "A Conversation with Gene Sarazen." *Golf Digest*, August 1972, p. 68–73.

On Chi Chi Rodriguez: Dave Anderson. "The Change in Chi Chi." *Golf Digest*, June 1973, p. 60–62.

On Jolly Jim Fraser: Al Barkow. *Gettin' to the Dance Floor*, p. 144.

On Sam Snead: Nick Seitz. "Sam Snead. How He Just Keeps Rolling Along." *Golf Digest*, February 1 980, p. 62–67; "Sam Snead Talks About His Golf Game and Yours." *Golf Digest*, February 1973, p. 70.

On Ben Hogan: Lee Trevino. *They Call Me Super Mex.* P. 179; Ken Venturi. "Interview." *Golf Digest*, May 1994, p. 204.

On Jack Nicklaus: Al Barkow. "Tom Terrific Tells All About Terrible Tom." *Golf*, July 1977, p. 39; Ken Bowden. "Why Nicklaus Is Back on Top." *Golf Digest*, July 1971, p. 47–49; "David Feherty." *Golf Digest*, November 1992, p. 120; Dwayne Netland. "Tour Feud." *Golf Digest*, December 1987, p. 42–45; Dave Anderson. "Pairings the Pros Do and Don't Like." *Golf Digest*, November 1976, p. 43–47; "Tom Weiskopf Interview." *Golf Digest*, March 1991, p. 98–111.

On Tom Watson: Byron Nelson. *How I Played the Game.* Dallas: Taylor, 1993, p. 54; Lew Fishman. "Watson on Watson." *Golf*, August, 1985, p. 66.

Index